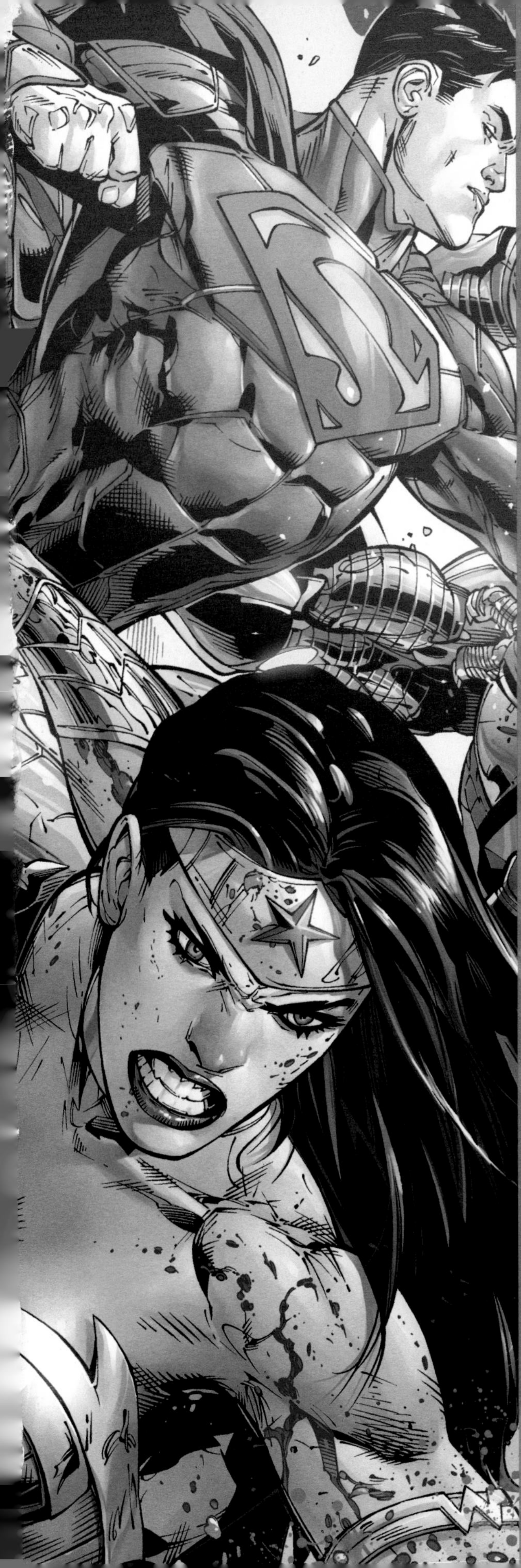

VOLUME 3

CASUALTIES OF WAR

SUPERMAN/WONDER WOMAN

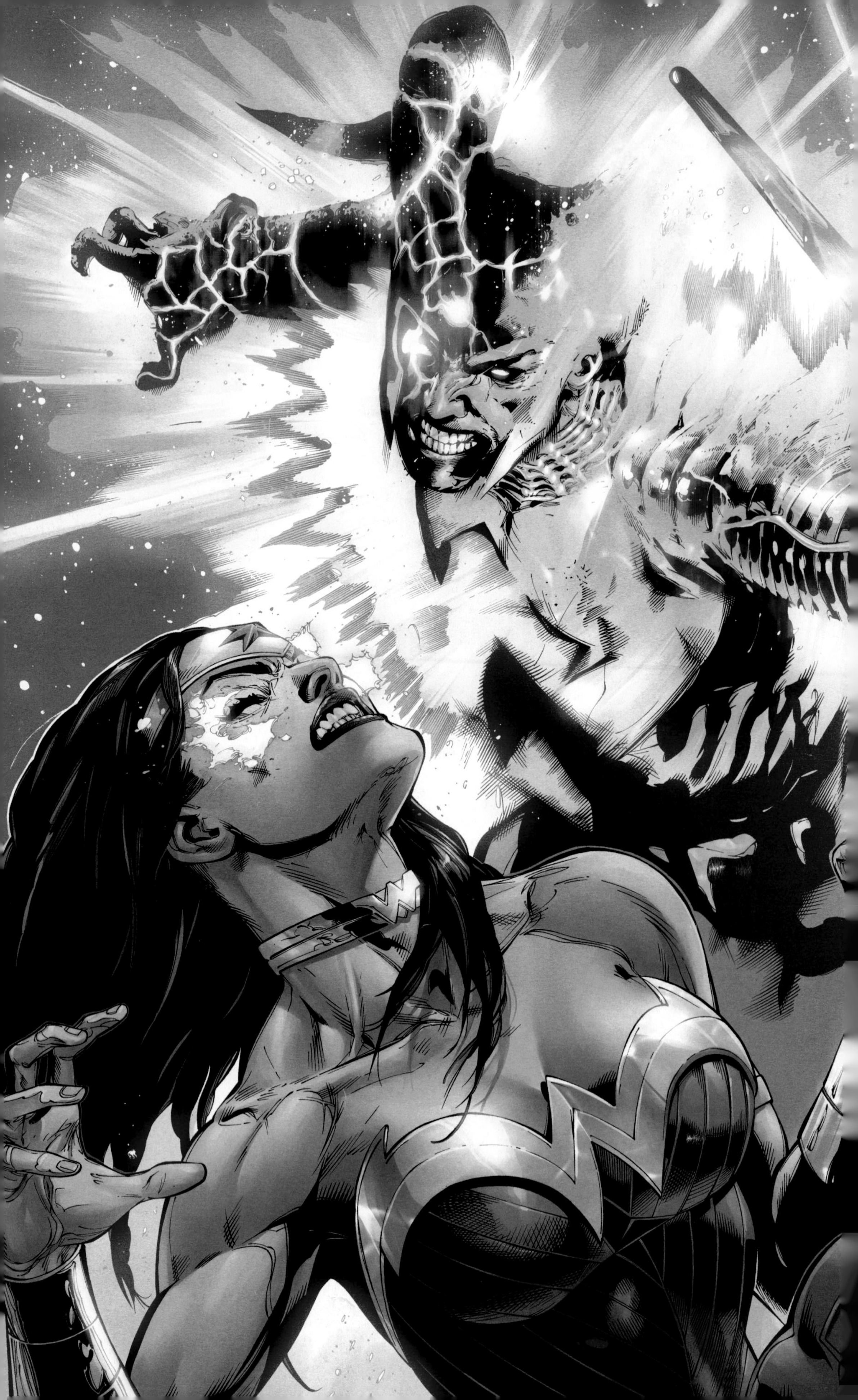

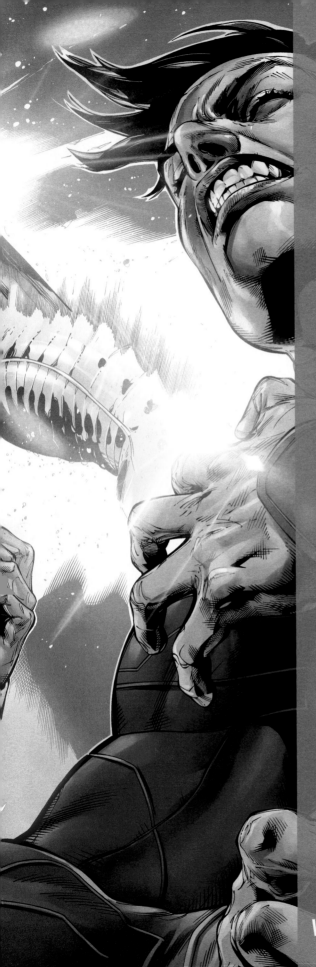

SUPERMAN/WONDER WOMAN

VOLUME 3
CASUALTIES
OF WAR

WRITTEN BY
PETER J. TOMASI

PENCILS BY
DOUG MAHNKE
ED BENES

INKS BY
JAIME MENDOZA
DON HO
NORM RAPMUND
CHRISTIAN ALAMY
MARK IRWIN
ED BENES
DOUG MAHNKE
KEITH CHAMPAGNE

COLOR BY
TOMEU MOREY
HI-FI
MARCELO MAIOLO
PETE PANTAZIS
WIL QUINTANA

LETTERS BY
ROB LEIGH
CARLOS M. MANGUAL
TAYLOR ESPOSITO

COLLECTION COVER ART BY
DOUG MAHNKE
& TOMEU MOREY

SUPERMAN CREATED BY
JERRY SIEGEL &
JOE SHUSTER
BY SPECIAL ARRANGEMENT
WITH THE JERRY SIEGEL FAMILY

WONDER WOMAN CREATED BY
WILLIAM MOULTON MARSTON

EDDIE BERGANZA Editor – Original Series
JEREMY BENT Assistant Editor – Original Series
JEB WOODARD Group Editor – Collected Editions
LIZ ERICKSON Editor – Collected Edition
DAMIAN RYLAND Publication Design

BOB HARRAS Senior VP – Editor-in-Chief, DC Comics

DIANE NELSON President
DAN DIDIO and JIM LEE Co-Publishers
GEOFF JOHNS Chief Creative Officer
AMIT DESAI Senior VP – Marketing & Global Franchise Management
NAIRI GARDINER Senior VP – Finance
SAM ADES VP – Digital Marketing
BOBBIE CHASE VP –Talent Development
MARK CHIARELLO Senior VP – Art, Design & Collected Editions
JOHN CUNNINGHAM VP – Content Strategy
ANNE DEPIES VP – Strategy Planning & Reporting
DON FALLETTI VP – Manufacturing Operations
LAWRENCE GANEM VP – Editorial Administration & Talent Relations
ALISON GILL Senior VP – Manufacturing & Operations
HANK KANALZ Senior VP – Editorial Strategy & Administration
JAY KOGAN VP – Legal Affairs
DEREK MADDALENA Senior VP – Sales & Business Development
JACK MAHAN VP – Business Affairs
DAN MIRON VP – Sales Planning & Trade Development
NICK NAPOLITANO VP – Manufacturing Administration
CAROL ROEDER VP – Marketing
EDDIE SCANNELL VP – Mass Account & Digital Sales
COURTNEY SIMMONS Senior VP – Publicity & Communications
JIM (SKI) SOKOLOWSKI VP – Comic Book Specialty & Newsstand Sales
SANDY YI Senior VP – Global Franchise Management

SUPERMAN/WONDER WOMAN VOLUME 3: CASUALTIES OF WAR

Published by DC Comics. Compilation Copyright © 2015 DC Comics. All Rights Reserved.

Originally published in single magazine form in SUPERMAN/WONDER WOMAN 13-17 © 2015 DC Comics. All Rights Reserved.
All characters, their distinctive likenesses and related elements featured in this publication are trademarks of DC Comics.
The stories, characters and incidents featured in this publication are entirely fictional. DC Comics does not read or accept
unsolicited ideas, stories or artwork.

DC Comics, 4000 Warner Blvd., Burbank, CA 91522
A Warner Bros. Entertainment Company.
Printed by RR Donnelley, Salem, VA, USA. 10/16/15. First Printing.
ISBN: 978-1-4012-5768-2

Library of Congress Cataloging-in-Publication Data

Tomasi, Peter.
Superman/Wonder Woman. Volume 3, Casualties of war / Peter Tomasi, writer ; Doug Mahnke, penciller ; Jaime Mendoza, inker.
pages cm
ISBN 978-1-4012-5768-2 (hardback)
1. Graphic novels. I. Mahnke, Doug, illustrator. II. Mendoza, Jaime, illustrator. III. Title. IV. Title: Casualties of war.
PN6728.S9T66 2015
741.5'973—dc23
2015028076

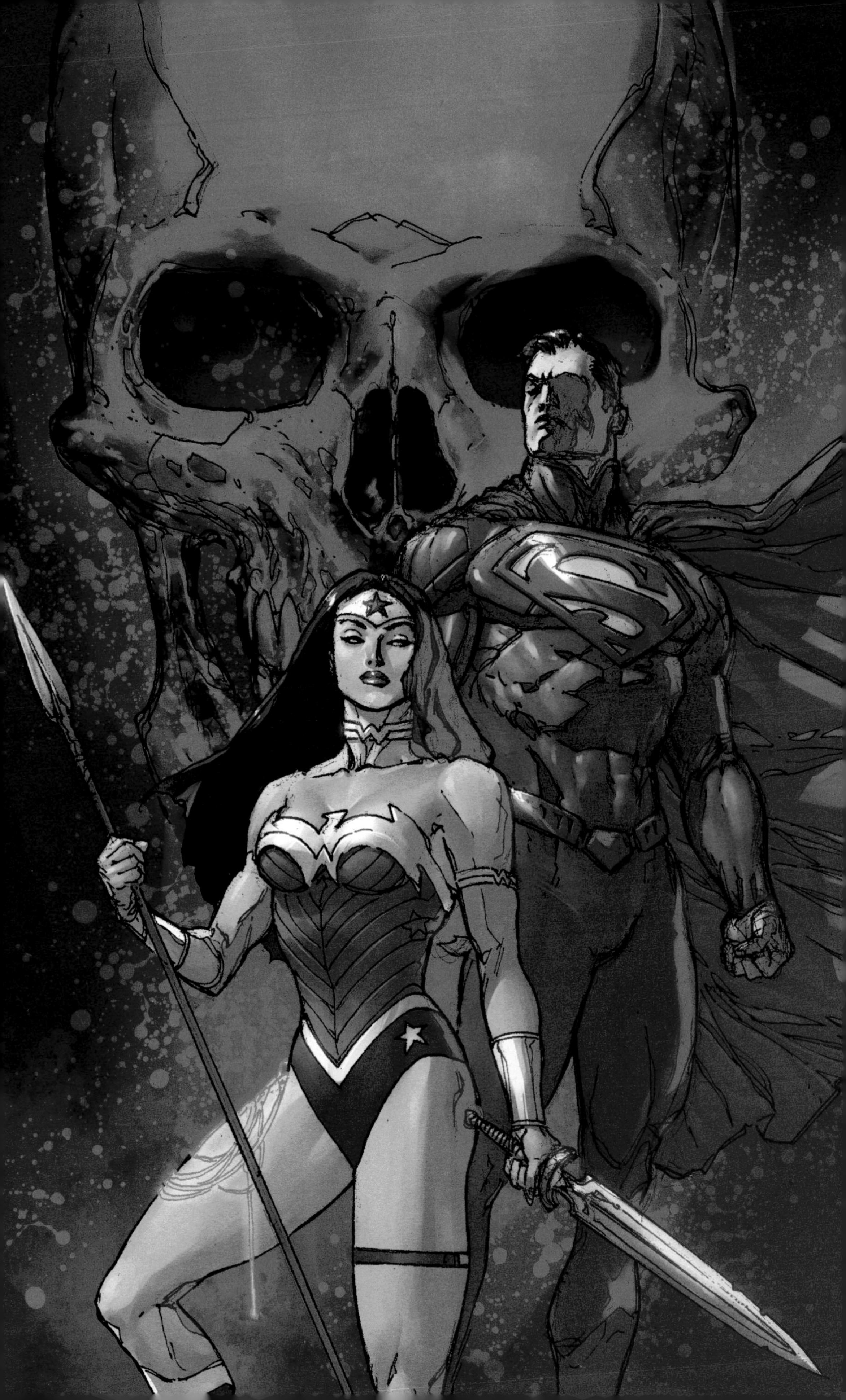

BATTLEFIELD OF LOVE

PETER J. TOMASI writer DOUG MAHNKE penciller JAIME MENDOZA DON HO inkers TOMEU MOREY colorist CARLOS M. MANGUAL letterer cover by MAHNKE & MOREY

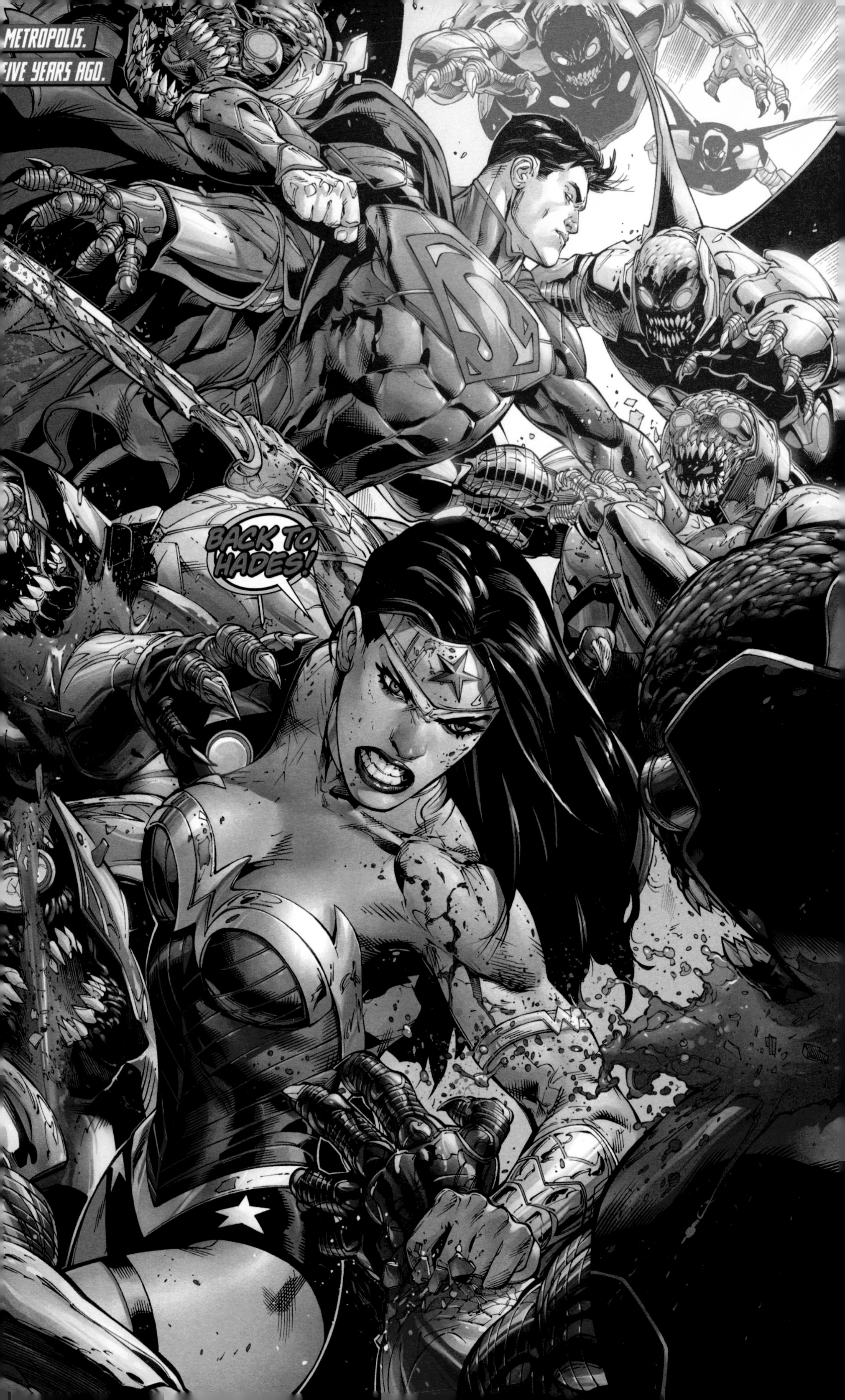
METROPOLIS.
FIVE YEARS AGO.
BACK TO HADES!

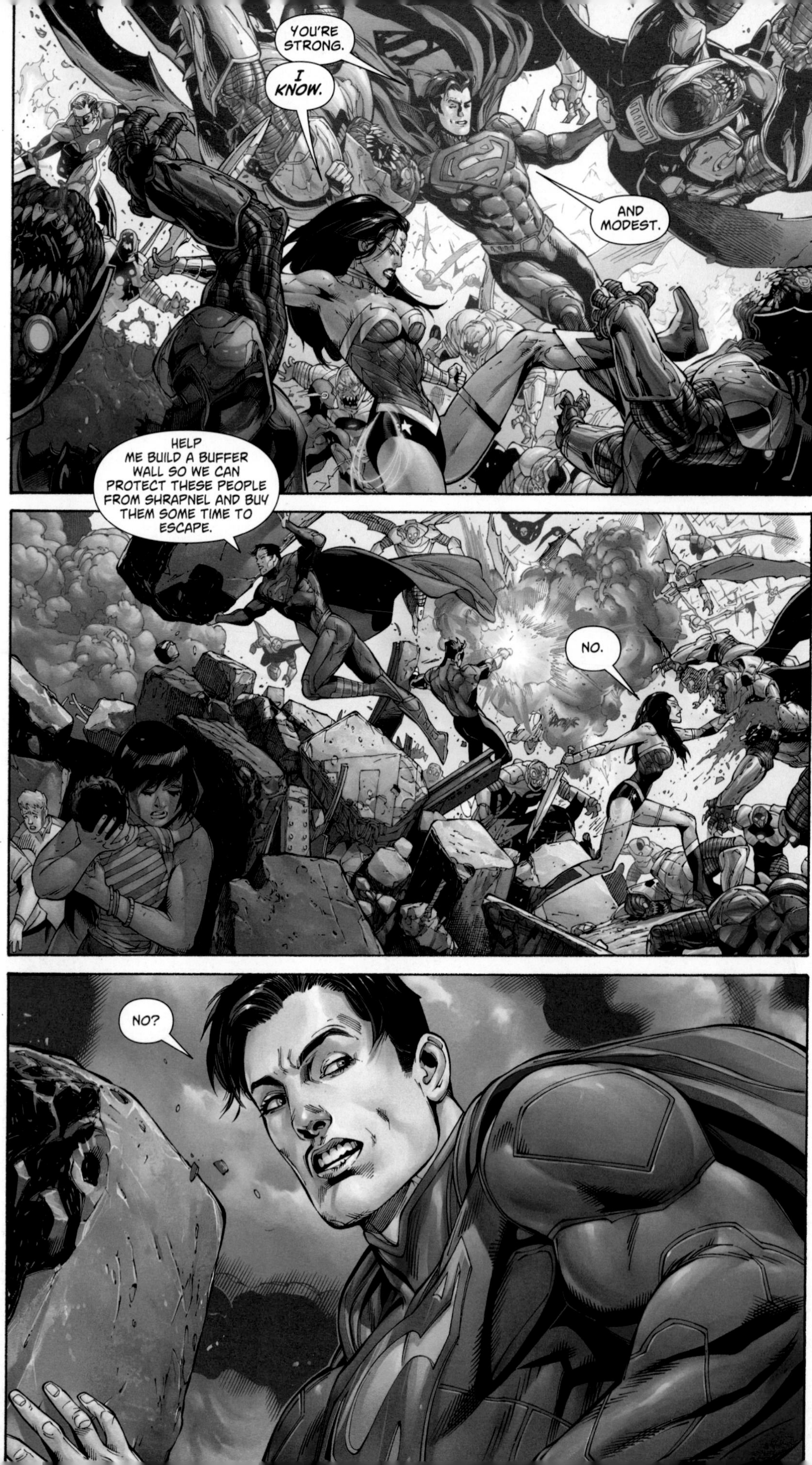
YOU'RE STRONG.
I KNOW.
AND MODEST.
HELP ME BUILD A BUFFER WALL SO WE CAN PROTECT THESE PEOPLE FROM SHRAPNEL AND BUY THEM SOME TIME TO ESCAPE.
NO.
NO?

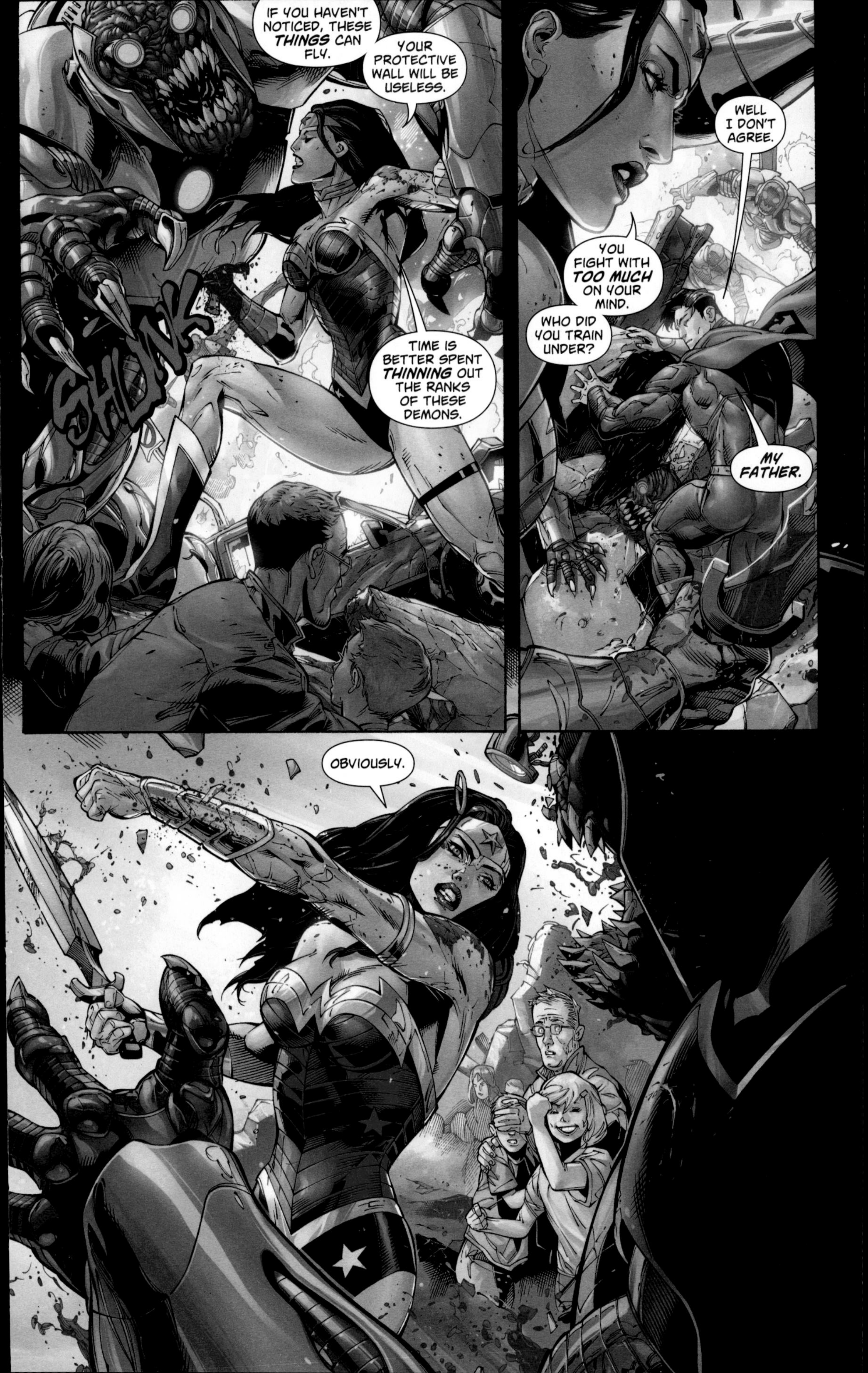
IF YOU HAVEN'T NOTICED, THESE THINGS CAN FLY.
YOUR PROTECTIVE WALL WILL BE USELESS.
TIME IS BETTER SPENT THINNING OUT THE RANKS OF THESE DEMONS.
SHUNK
WELL I DON'T AGREE.
YOU FIGHT WITH TOO MUCH ON YOUR MIND.
WHO DID YOU TRAIN UNDER?
MY FATHER.
OBVIOUSLY.

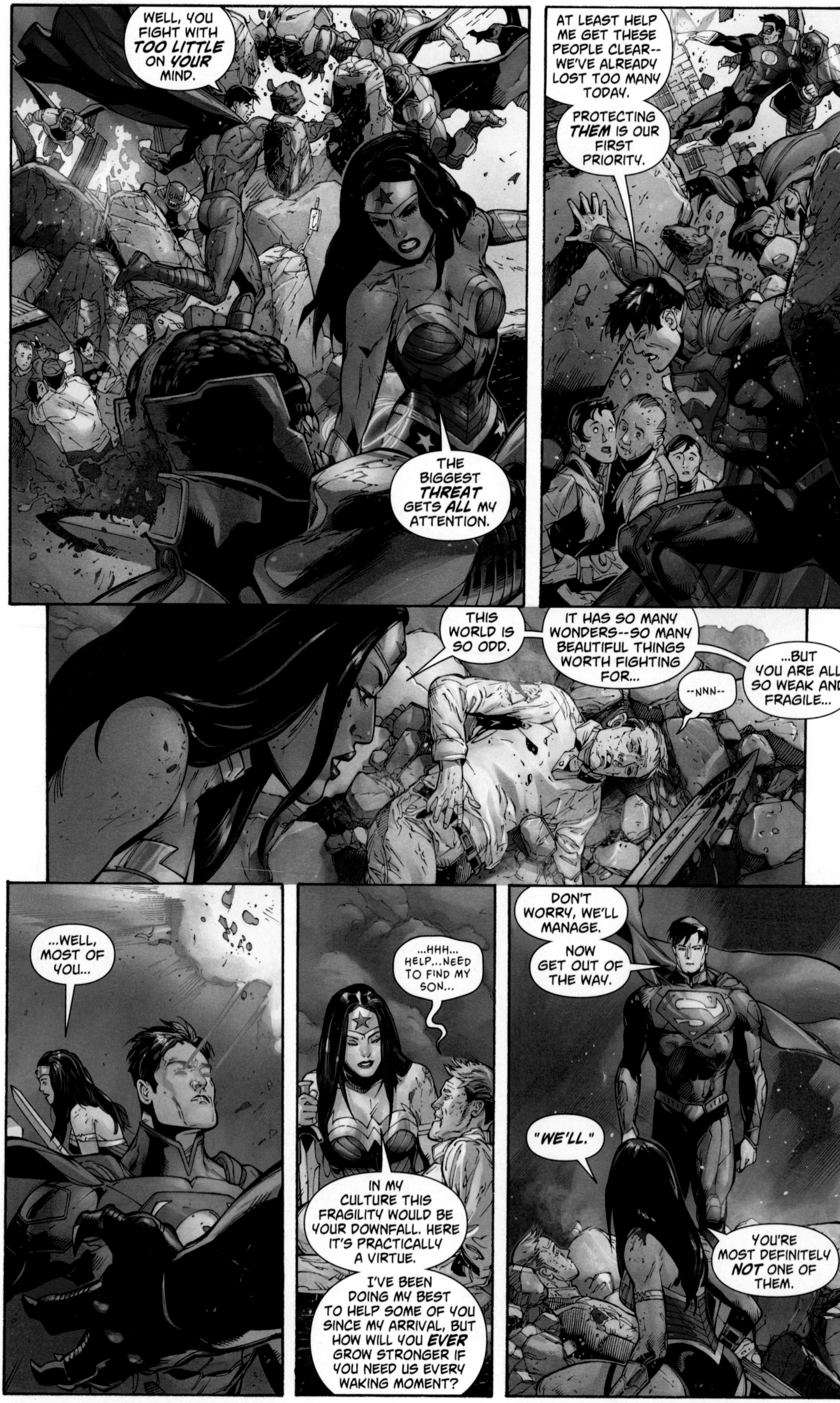
WELL, YOU FIGHT WITH TOO LITTLE ON YOUR MIND.
THE BIGGEST THREAT GETS ALL MY ATTENTION.
AT LEAST HELP ME GET THESE PEOPLE CLEAR--WE'VE ALREADY LOST TOO MANY TODAY.
PROTECTING THEM IS OUR FIRST PRIORITY.
THIS WORLD IS SO ODD.
IT HAS SO MANY WONDERS--SO MANY BEAUTIFUL THINGS WORTH FIGHTING FOR...
--NNN--
...BUT YOU ARE ALL SO WEAK AND FRAGILE...
...WELL, MOST OF YOU...
...HHH... HELP...NEED TO FIND MY SON...
IN MY CULTURE THIS FRAGILITY WOULD BE YOUR DOWNFALL. HERE IT'S PRACTICALLY A VIRTUE.
I'VE BEEN DOING MY BEST TO HELP SOME OF YOU SINCE MY ARRIVAL, BUT HOW WILL YOU EVER GROW STRONGER IF YOU NEED US EVERY WAKING MOMENT?
DON'T WORRY, WE'LL MANAGE.
NOW GET OUT OF THE WAY.
"WE'LL."
YOU'RE MOST DEFINITELY NOT ONE OF THEM.

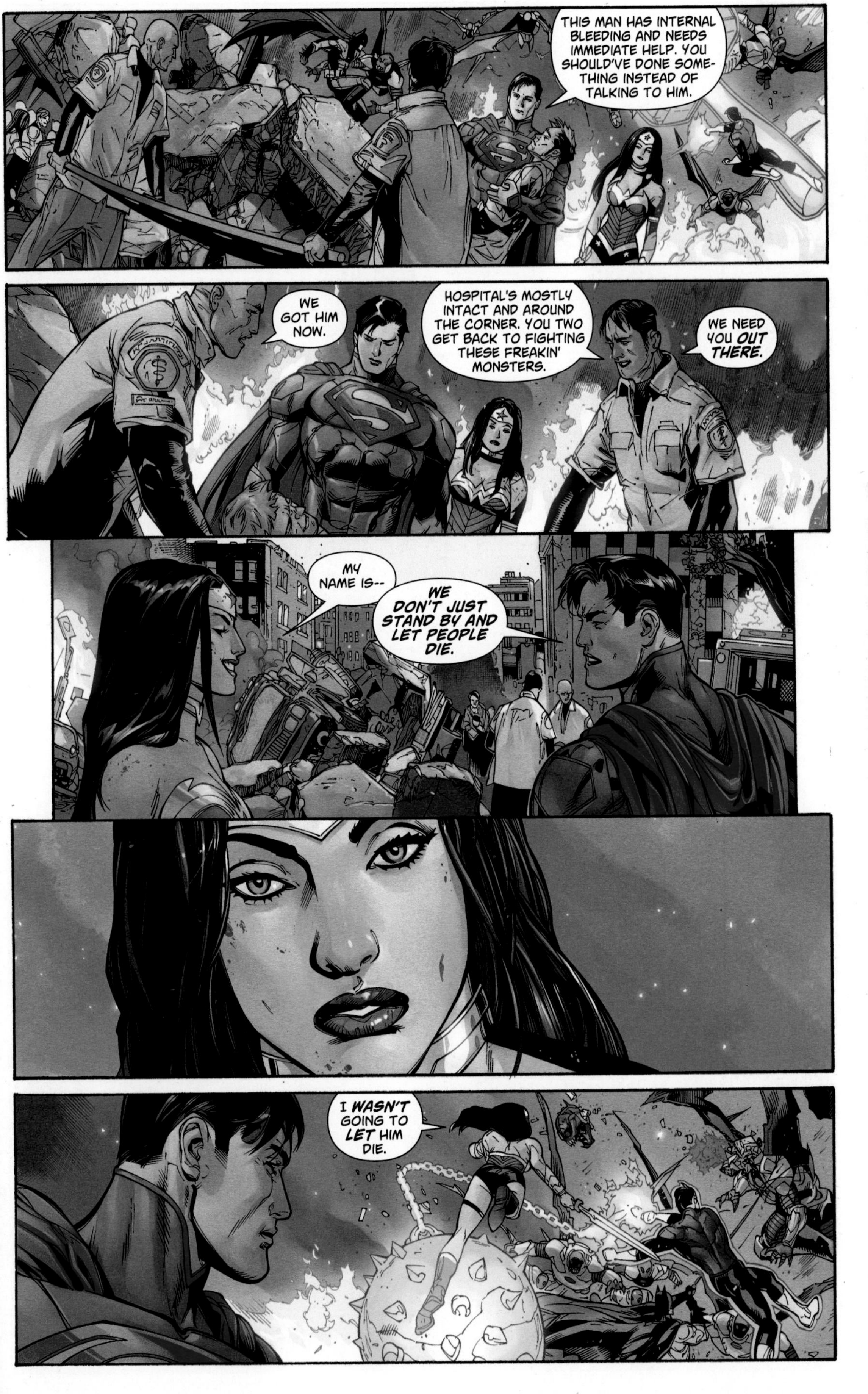
THIS MAN HAS INTERNAL BLEEDING AND NEEDS IMMEDIATE HELP. YOU SHOULD'VE DONE SOME-THING INSTEAD OF TALKING TO HIM.
WE GOT HIM NOW.
HOSPITAL'S MOSTLY INTACT AND AROUND THE CORNER. YOU TWO GET BACK TO FIGHTING THESE FREAKIN' MONSTERS.
WE NEED YOU OUT THERE.
MY NAME IS--
WE DON'T JUST STAND BY AND LET PEOPLE DIE.
I WASN'T GOING TO LET HIM DIE.

...UM...

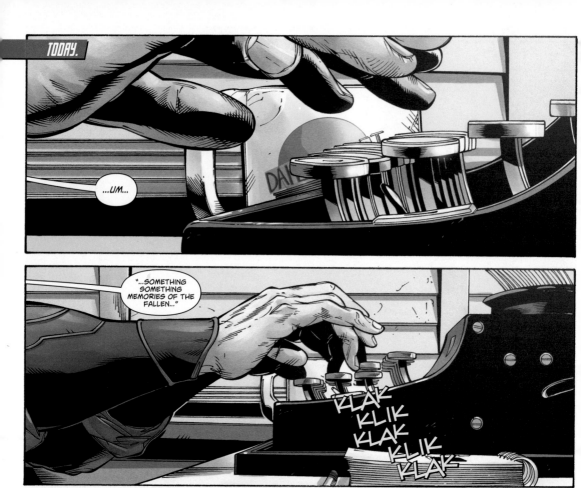

"...SOMETHING SOMETHING MEMORIES OF THE FALLEN..."

KLAK
KLIK
KLAK
KLIK
KLAK

...NO...THAT STINKS...WHAT'S WRONG WITH YOU, PINHEAD?...

...PUT SOME WORDS TOGETHER THAT ACTUALLY *SAY* WHAT YOU'RE THINKING...

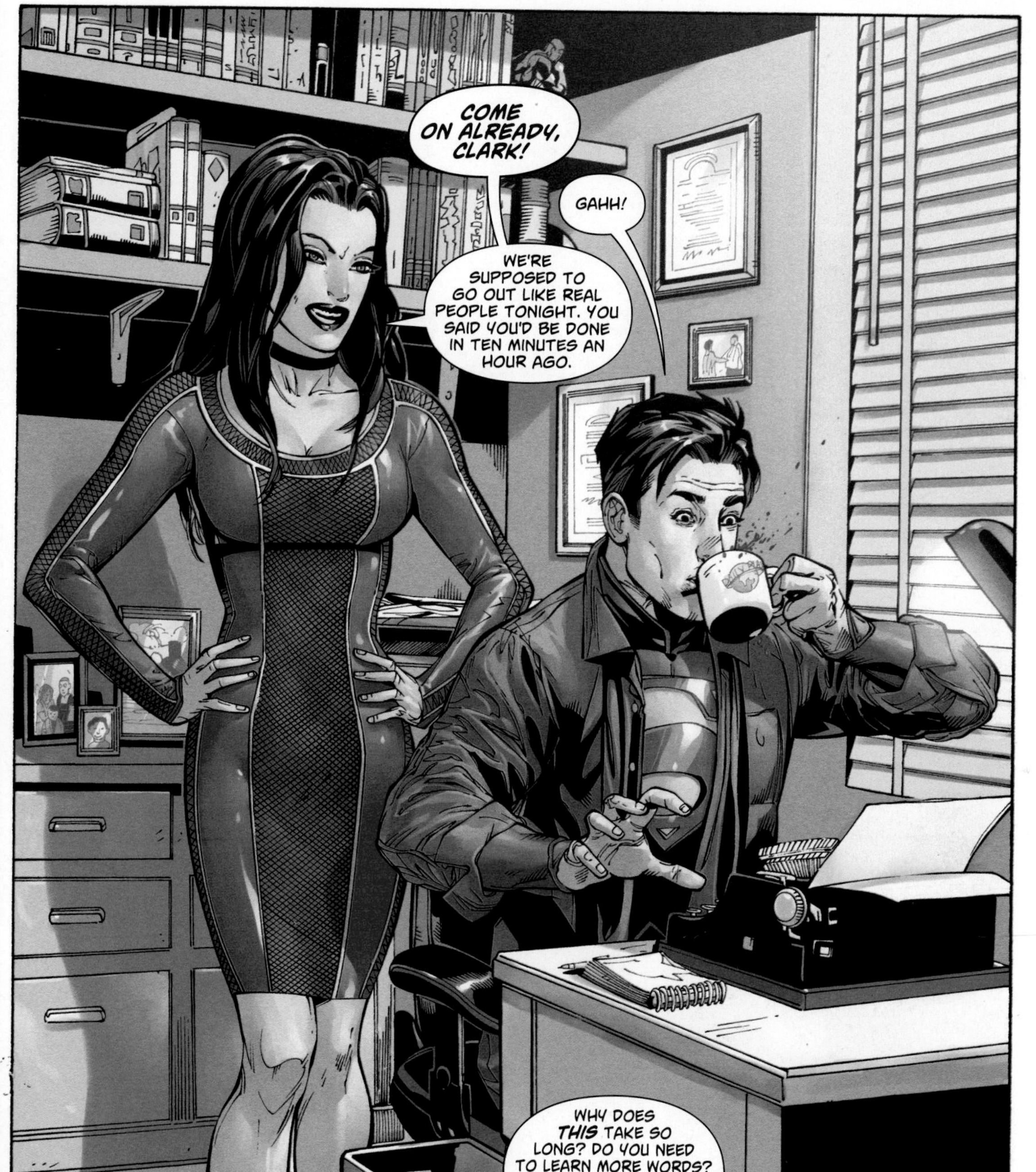
COME ON ALREADY, CLARK!
WE'RE SUPPOSED TO GO OUT LIKE REAL PEOPLE TONIGHT. YOU SAID YOU'D BE DONE IN TEN MINUTES AN HOUR AGO.
GAHH!
WHY DOES THIS TAKE SO LONG? DO YOU NEED TO LEARN MORE WORDS? AND WHY ARE YOU USING THIS ANCIENT RELIC INSTEAD OF YOUR LAPTOP?

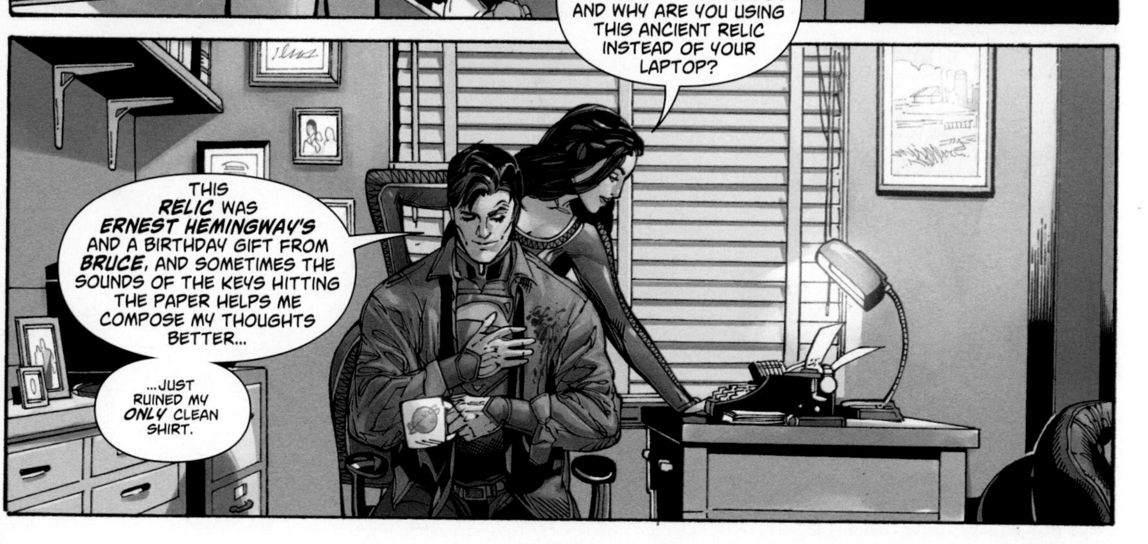
THIS RELIC WAS ERNEST HEMINGWAY'S AND A BIRTHDAY GIFT FROM BRUCE, AND SOMETIMES THE SOUNDS OF THE KEYS HITTING THE PAPER HELPS ME COMPOSE MY THOUGHTS BETTER...
...JUST RUINED MY ONLY CLEAN SHIRT.

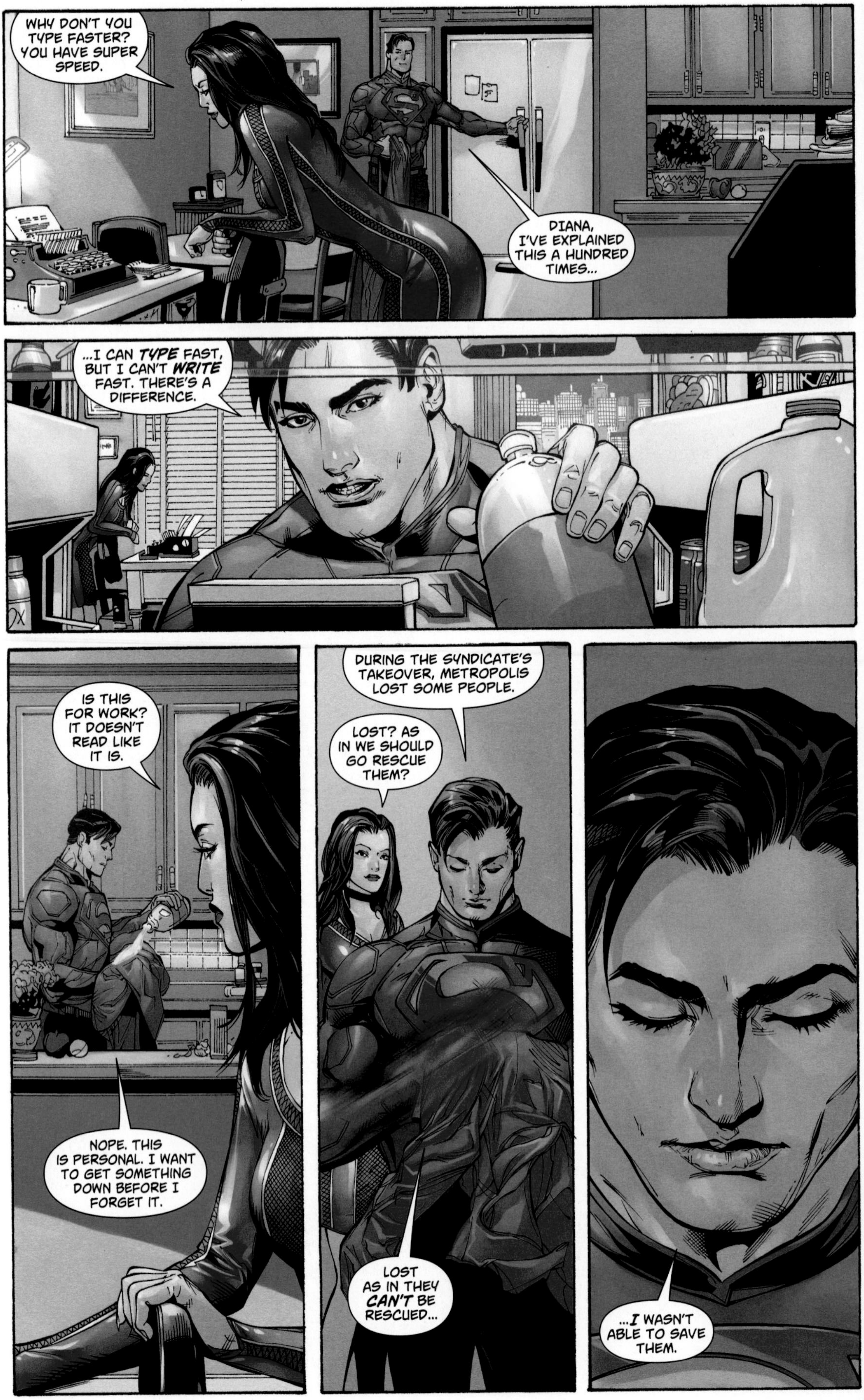
WHY DON'T YOU TYPE FASTER? YOU HAVE SUPER SPEED.
DIANA, I'VE EXPLAINED THIS A HUNDRED TIMES...
...I CAN *TYPE* FAST, BUT I CAN'T *WRITE* FAST. THERE'S A DIFFERENCE.
IS THIS FOR WORK? IT DOESN'T READ LIKE IT IS.
NOPE. THIS IS PERSONAL. I WANT TO GET SOMETHING DOWN BEFORE I FORGET IT.
DURING THE SYNDICATE'S TAKEOVER, METROPOLIS LOST SOME PEOPLE.
LOST? AS IN WE SHOULD GO RESCUE THEM?
LOST AS IN THEY *CAN'T* BE RESCUED...
...*I* WASN'T ABLE TO SAVE THEM.

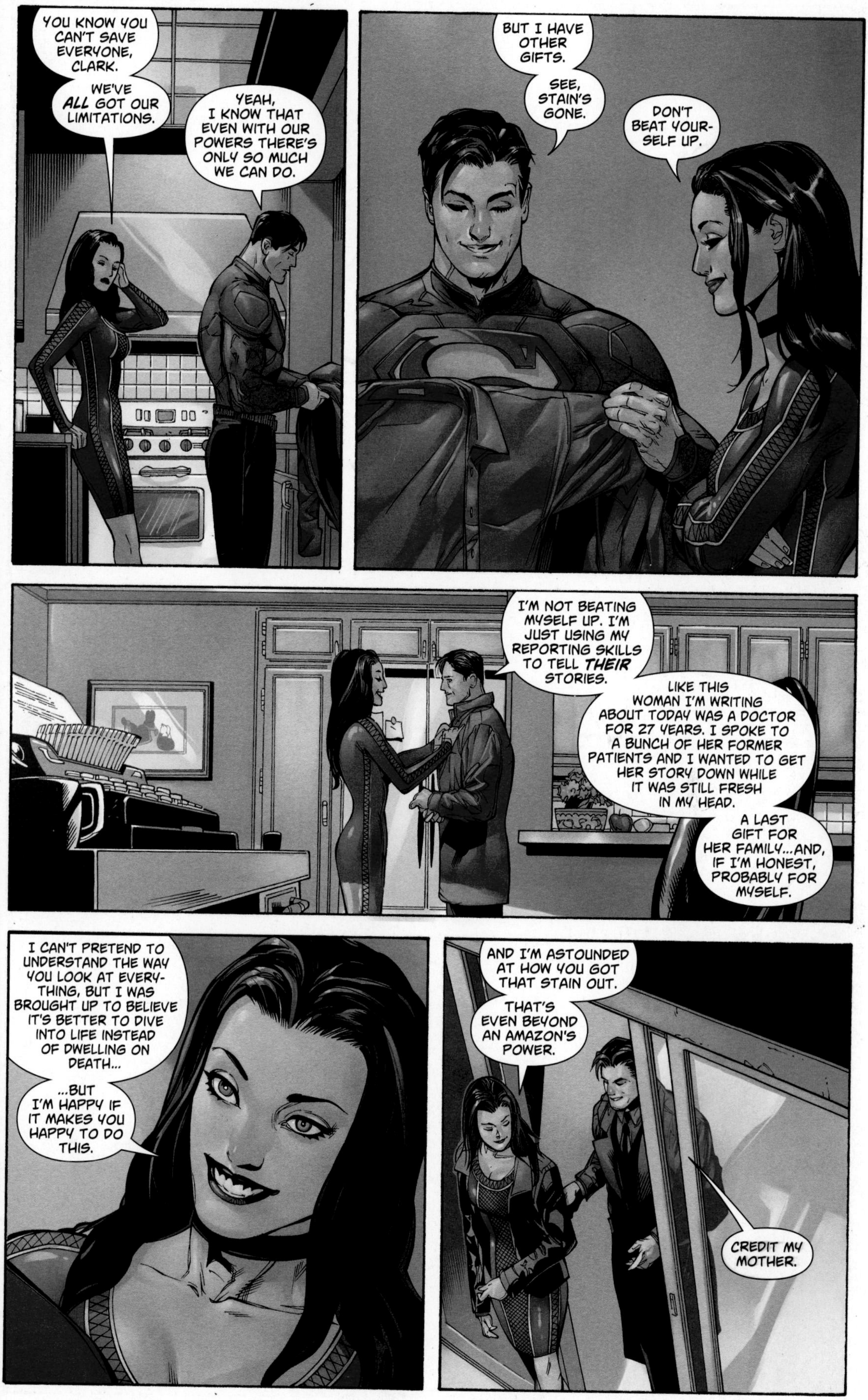
YOU KNOW YOU CAN'T SAVE EVERYONE, CLARK.
WE'VE ALL GOT OUR LIMITATIONS.
YEAH, I KNOW THAT EVEN WITH OUR POWERS THERE'S ONLY SO MUCH WE CAN DO.
BUT I HAVE OTHER GIFTS.
SEE, STAIN'S GONE.
DON'T BEAT YOURSELF UP.
I'M NOT BEATING MYSELF UP. I'M JUST USING MY REPORTING SKILLS TO TELL THEIR STORIES.
LIKE THIS WOMAN I'M WRITING ABOUT TODAY WAS A DOCTOR FOR 27 YEARS. I SPOKE TO A BUNCH OF HER FORMER PATIENTS AND I WANTED TO GET HER STORY DOWN WHILE IT WAS STILL FRESH IN MY HEAD.
A LAST GIFT FOR HER FAMILY...AND, IF I'M HONEST, PROBABLY FOR MYSELF.
I CAN'T PRETEND TO UNDERSTAND THE WAY YOU LOOK AT EVERYTHING, BUT I WAS BROUGHT UP TO BELIEVE IT'S BETTER TO DIVE INTO LIFE INSTEAD OF DWELLING ON DEATH...
...BUT I'M HAPPY IF IT MAKES YOU HAPPY TO DO THIS.
AND I'M ASTOUNDED AT HOW YOU GOT THAT STAIN OUT.
THAT'S EVEN BEYOND AN AMAZON'S POWER.
CREDIT MY MOTHER.

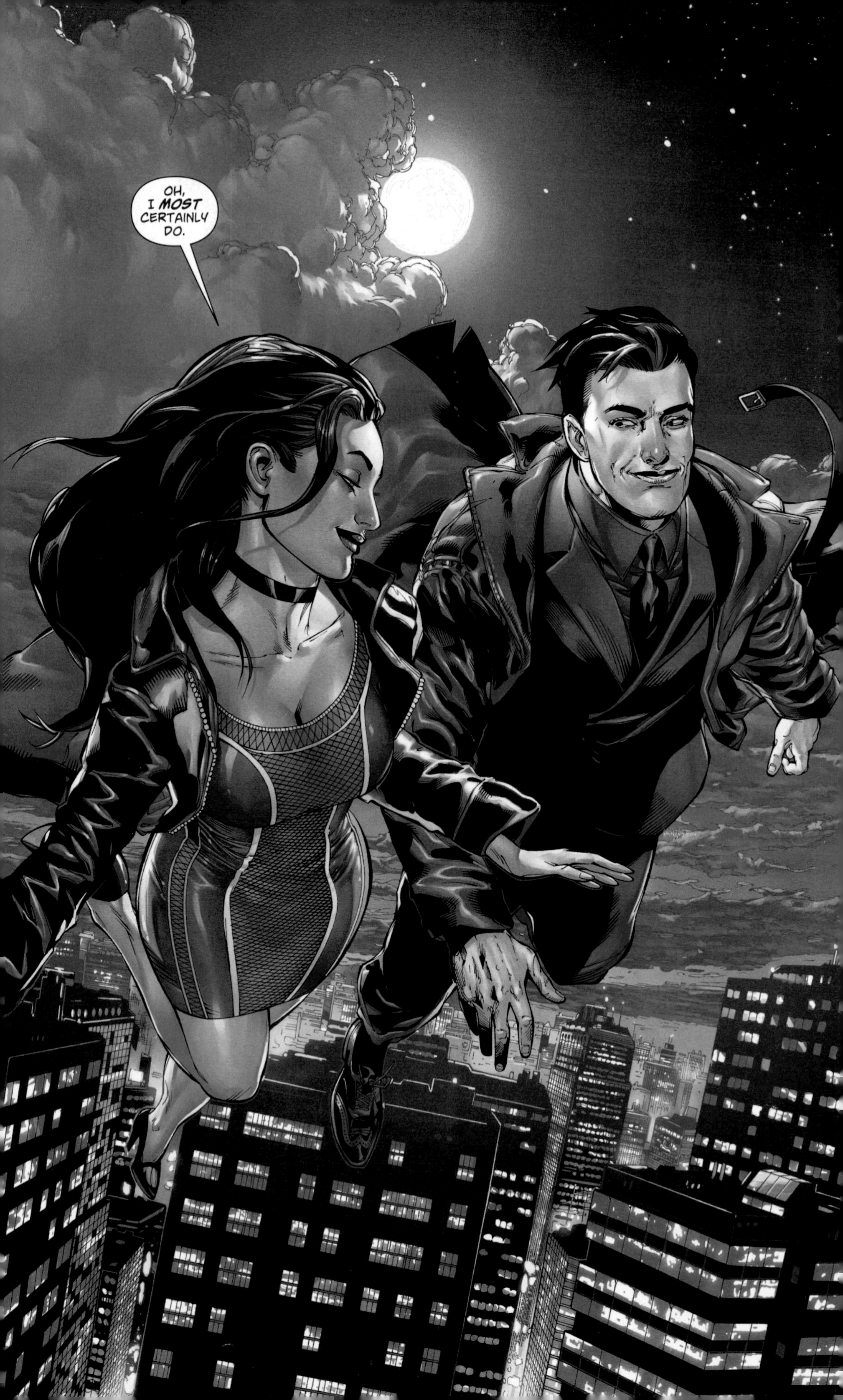
OH, I MOST CERTAINLY DO.

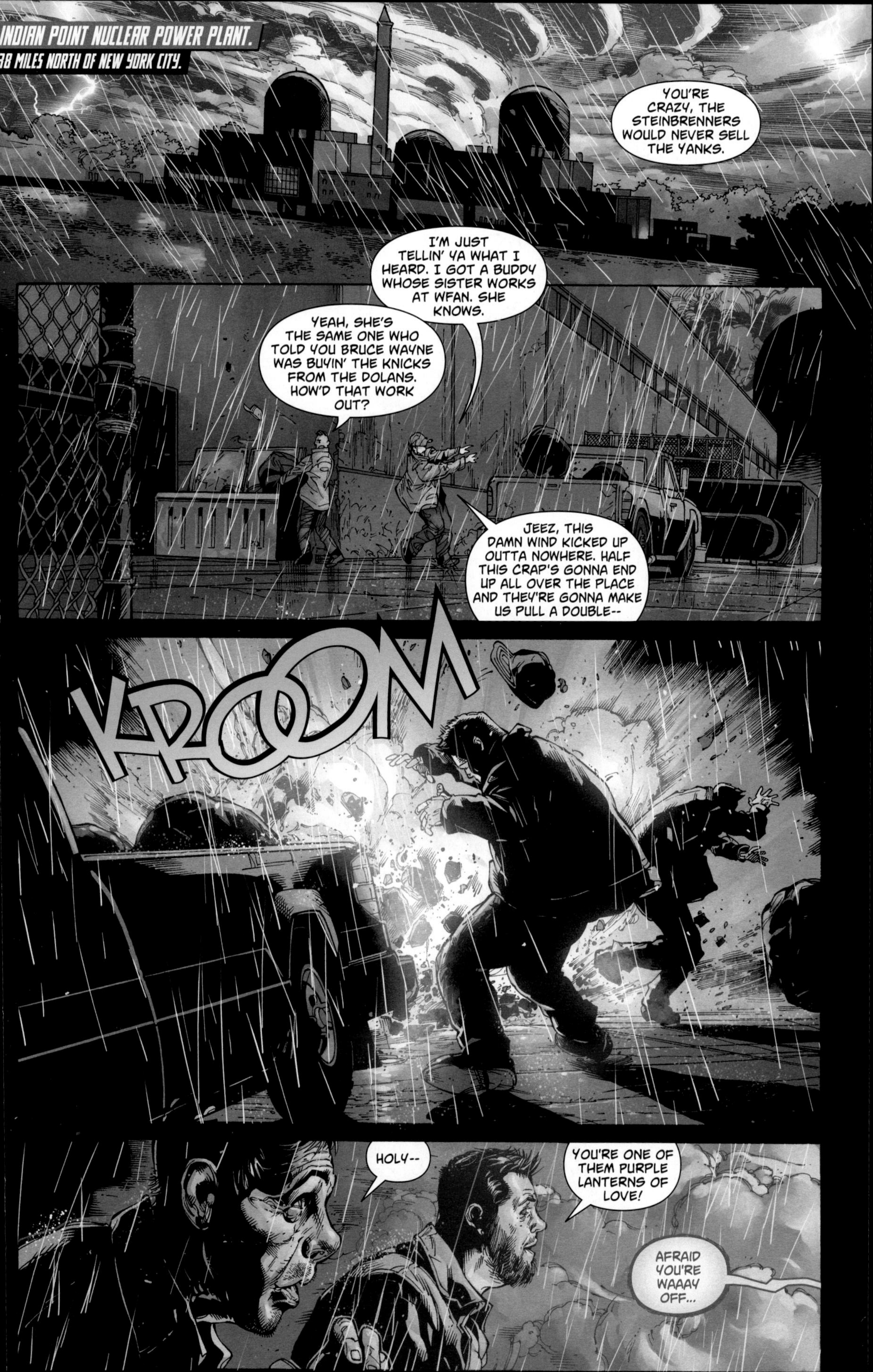
INDIAN POINT NUCLEAR POWER PLANT.
38 MILES NORTH OF NEW YORK CITY.
YOU'RE CRAZY, THE STEINBRENNERS WOULD NEVER SELL THE YANKS.
I'M JUST TELLIN' YA WHAT I HEARD. I GOT A BUDDY WHOSE SISTER WORKS AT WFAN. SHE KNOWS.
YEAH, SHE'S THE SAME ONE WHO TOLD YOU BRUCE WAYNE WAS BUYIN' THE KNICKS FROM THE DOLANS. HOW'D THAT WORK OUT?
JEEZ, THIS DAMN WIND KICKED UP OUTTA NOWHERE. HALF THIS CRAP'S GONNA END UP ALL OVER THE PLACE AND THEY'RE GONNA MAKE US PULL A DOUBLE--
KROOM
HOLY--
YOU'RE ONE OF THEM PURPLE LANTERNS OF LOVE!
AFRAID YOU'RE WAAAY OFF...

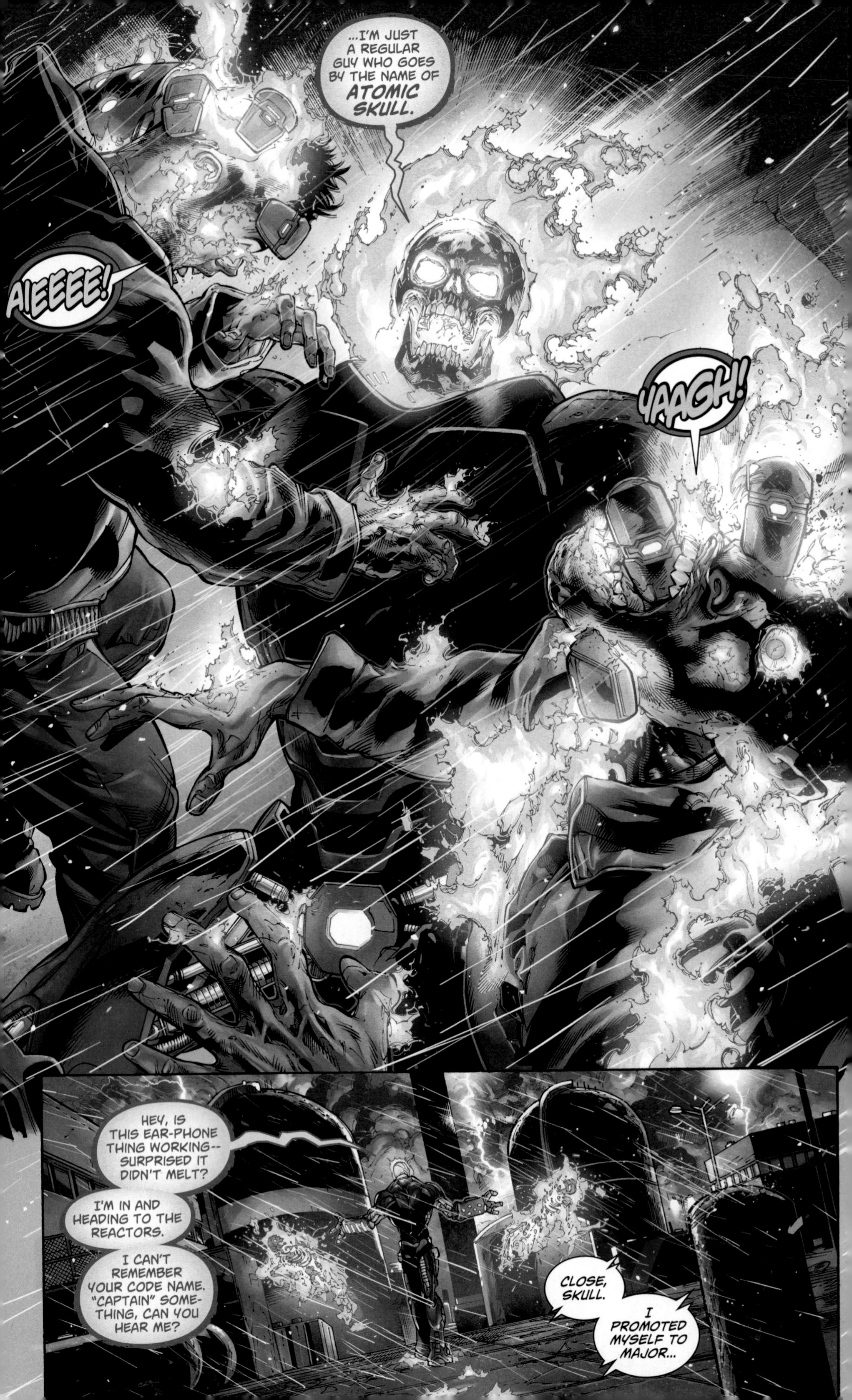
...I'M JUST A REGULAR GUY WHO GOES BY THE NAME OF ATOMIC SKULL.
AIEEEE!
YAAGH!
HEY, IS THIS EAR-PHONE THING WORKING-- SURPRISED IT DIDN'T MELT?
I'M IN AND HEADING TO THE REACTORS.
I CAN'T REMEMBER YOUR CODE NAME. "CAPTAIN" SOME-THING, CAN YOU HEAR ME?
CLOSE, SKULL.
I PROMOTED MYSELF TO MAJOR...

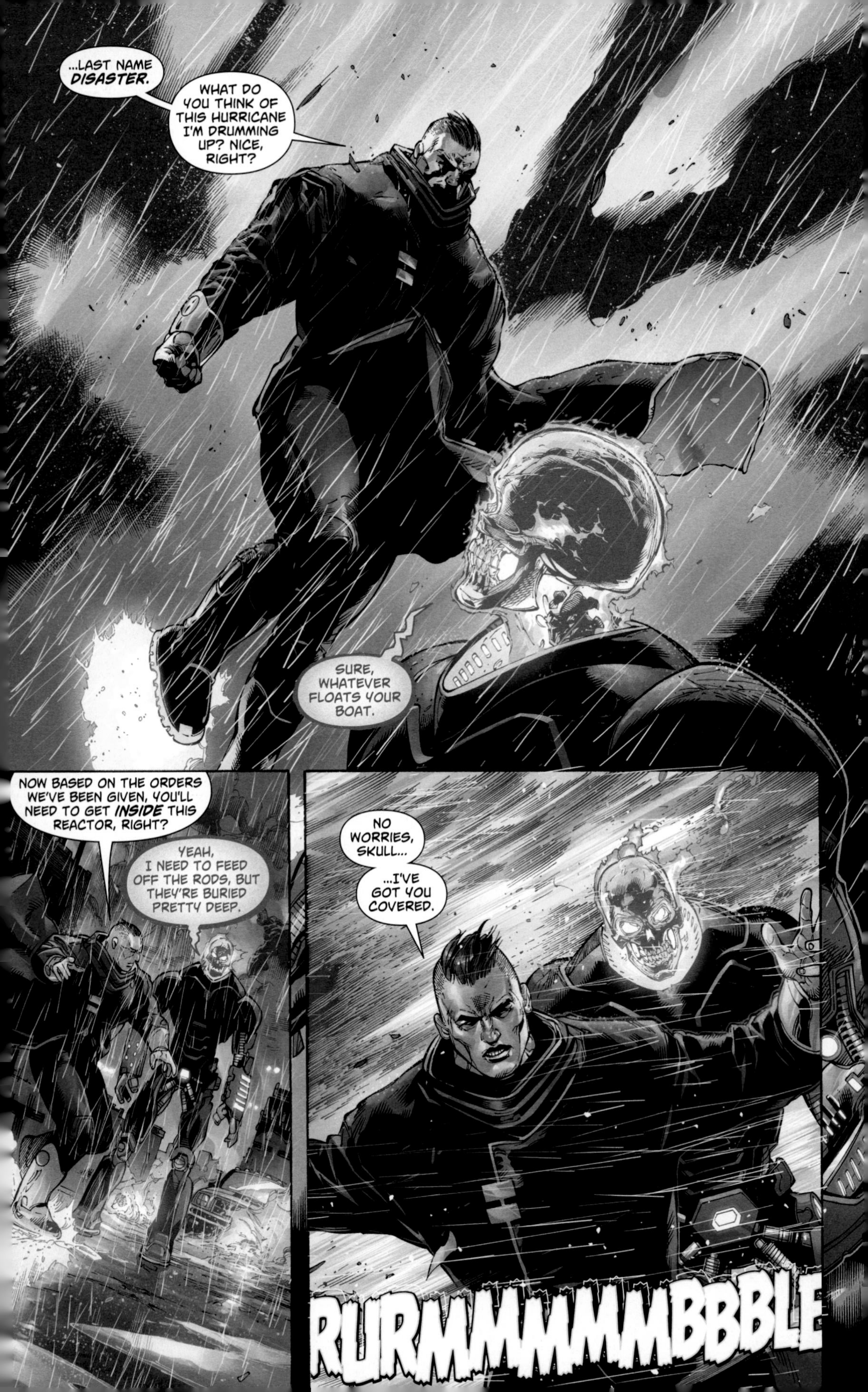
...LAST NAME DISASTER.
WHAT DO YOU THINK OF THIS HURRICANE I'M DRUMMING UP? NICE, RIGHT?
SURE, WHATEVER FLOATS YOUR BOAT.
NOW BASED ON THE ORDERS WE'VE BEEN GIVEN, YOU'LL NEED TO GET INSIDE THIS REACTOR, RIGHT?
YEAH, I NEED TO FEED OFF THE RODS, BUT THEY'RE BURIED PRETTY DEEP.
NO WORRIES, SKULL...
...I'VE GOT YOU COVERED.
RURMMMMMMBBBLE

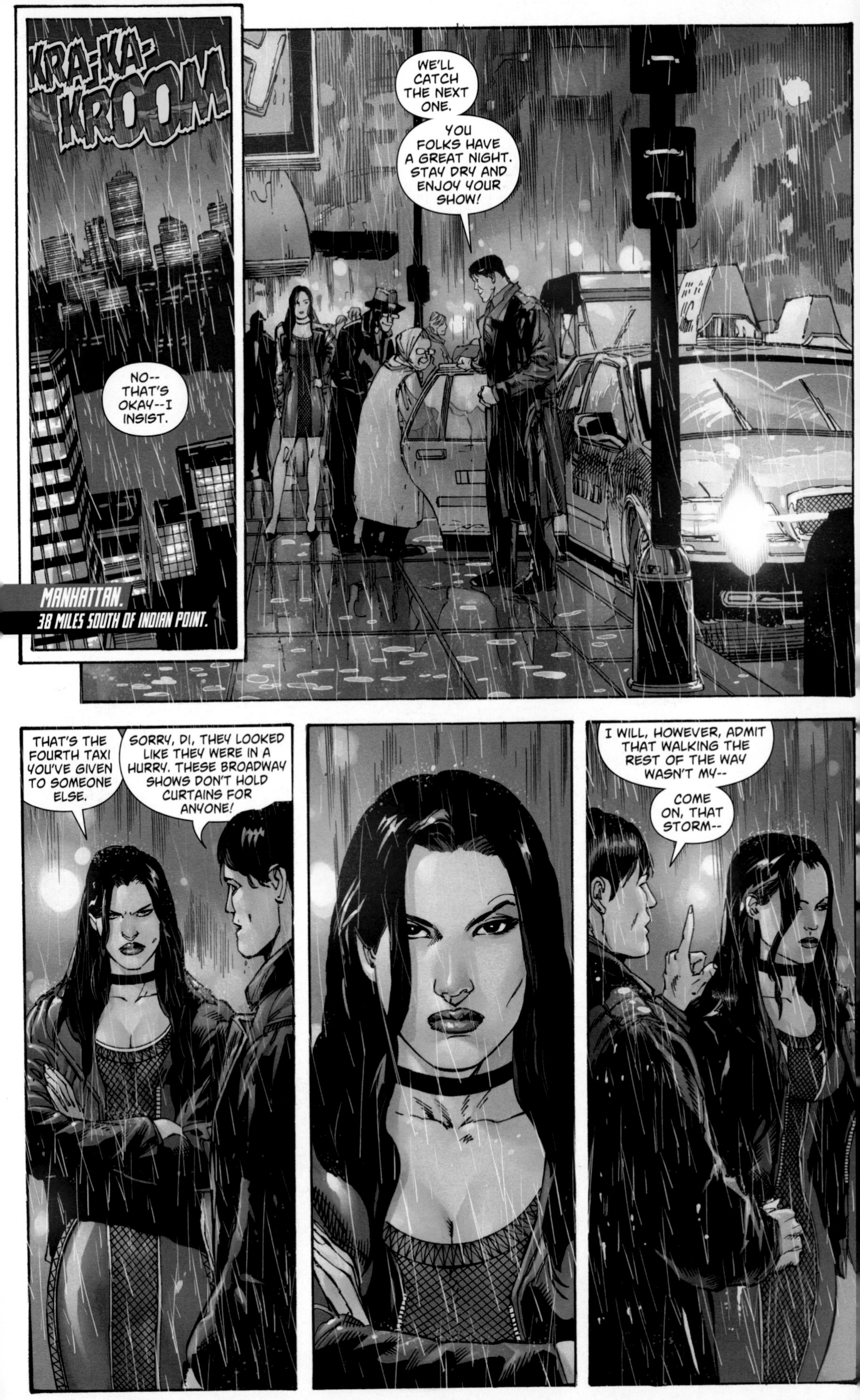
KRA-KA-KROOM
MANHATTAN.
38 MILES SOUTH OF INDIAN POINT.
NO--THAT'S OKAY--I INSIST.
WE'LL CATCH THE NEXT ONE.
YOU FOLKS HAVE A GREAT NIGHT. STAY DRY AND ENJOY YOUR SHOW!
THAT'S THE FOURTH TAXI YOU'VE GIVEN TO SOMEONE ELSE.
SORRY, DI, THEY LOOKED LIKE THEY WERE IN A HURRY. THESE BROADWAY SHOWS DON'T HOLD CURTAINS FOR ANYONE!
I WILL, HOWEVER, ADMIT THAT WALKING THE REST OF THE WAY WASN'T MY--
COME ON, THAT STORM--

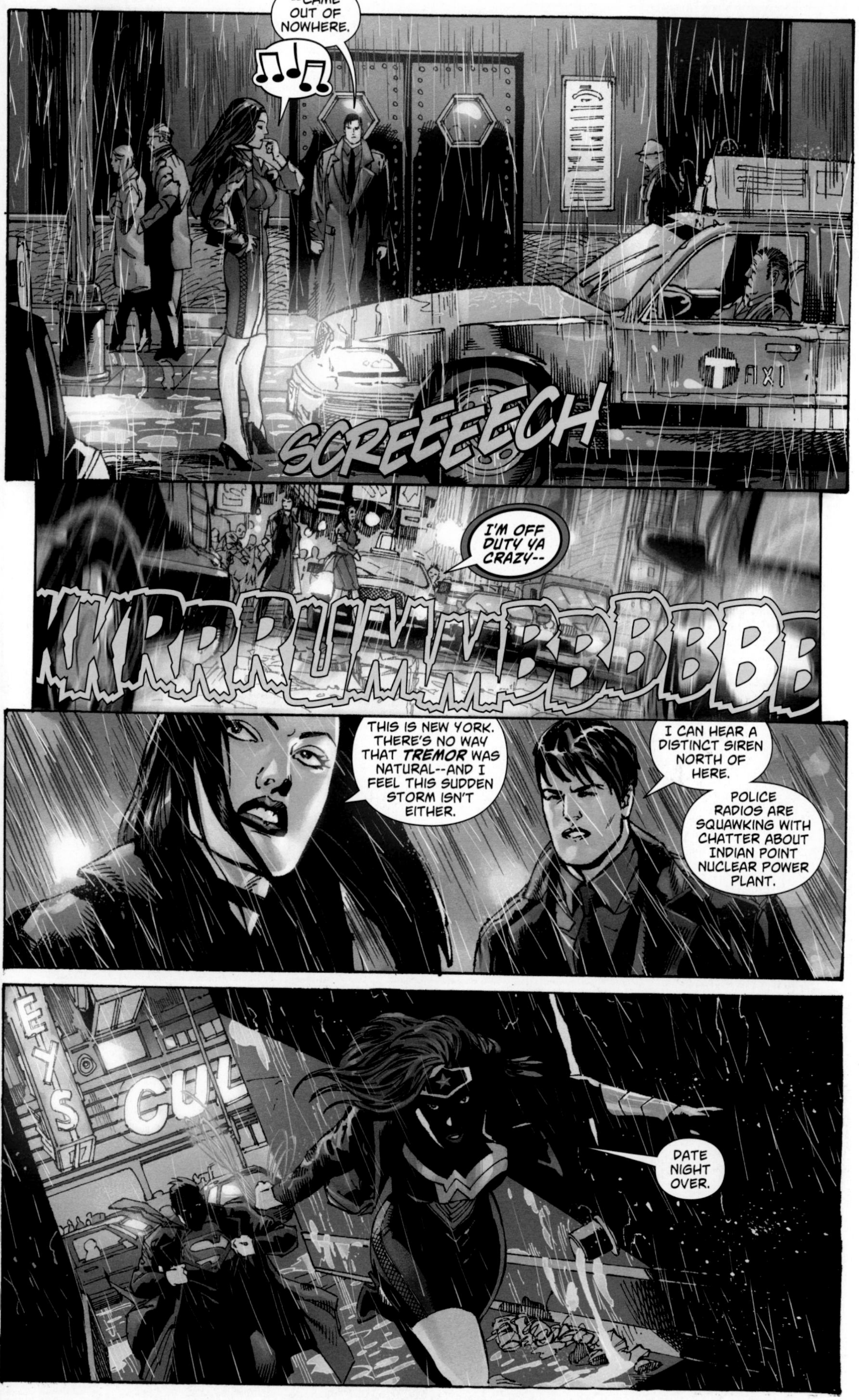
--CAME OUT OF NOWHERE.
SCREEEEECH
TAXI
I'M OFF DUTY YA CRAZY--
KRRRUMMBBBBB
THIS IS NEW YORK. THERE'S NO WAY THAT *TREMOR* WAS NATURAL--AND I FEEL THIS SUDDEN STORM ISN'T EITHER.
I CAN HEAR A DISTINCT SIREN NORTH OF HERE.
POLICE RADIOS ARE SQUAWKING WITH CHATTER ABOUT INDIAN POINT NUCLEAR POWER PLANT.
DATE NIGHT OVER.

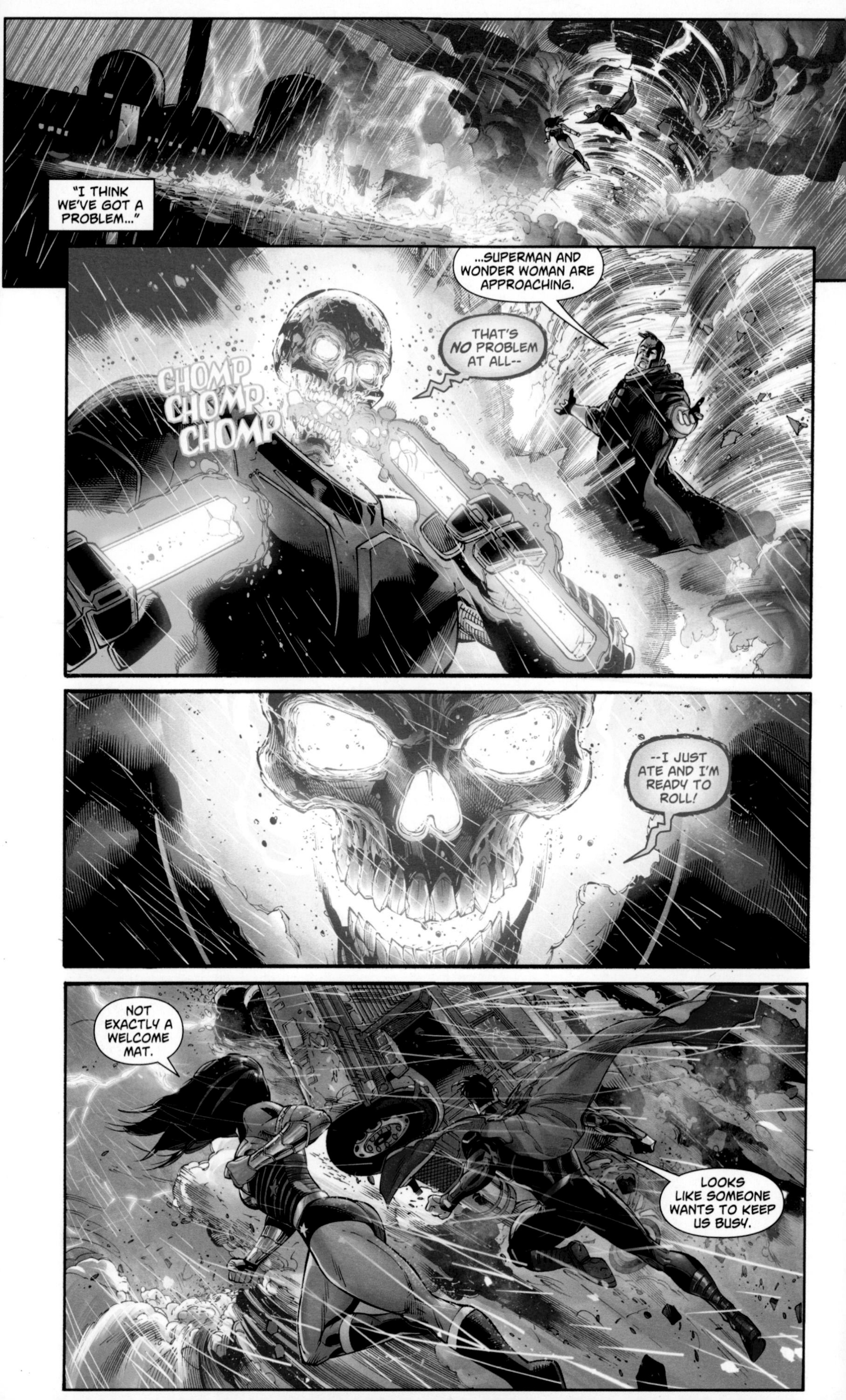
"I THINK WE'VE GOT A PROBLEM..."
...SUPERMAN AND WONDER WOMAN ARE APPROACHING.
THAT'S NO PROBLEM AT ALL--
CHOMP CHOMP CHOMP
--I JUST ATE AND I'M READY TO ROLL!
NOT EXACTLY A WELCOME MAT.
LOOKS LIKE SOMEONE WANTS TO KEEP US BUSY.

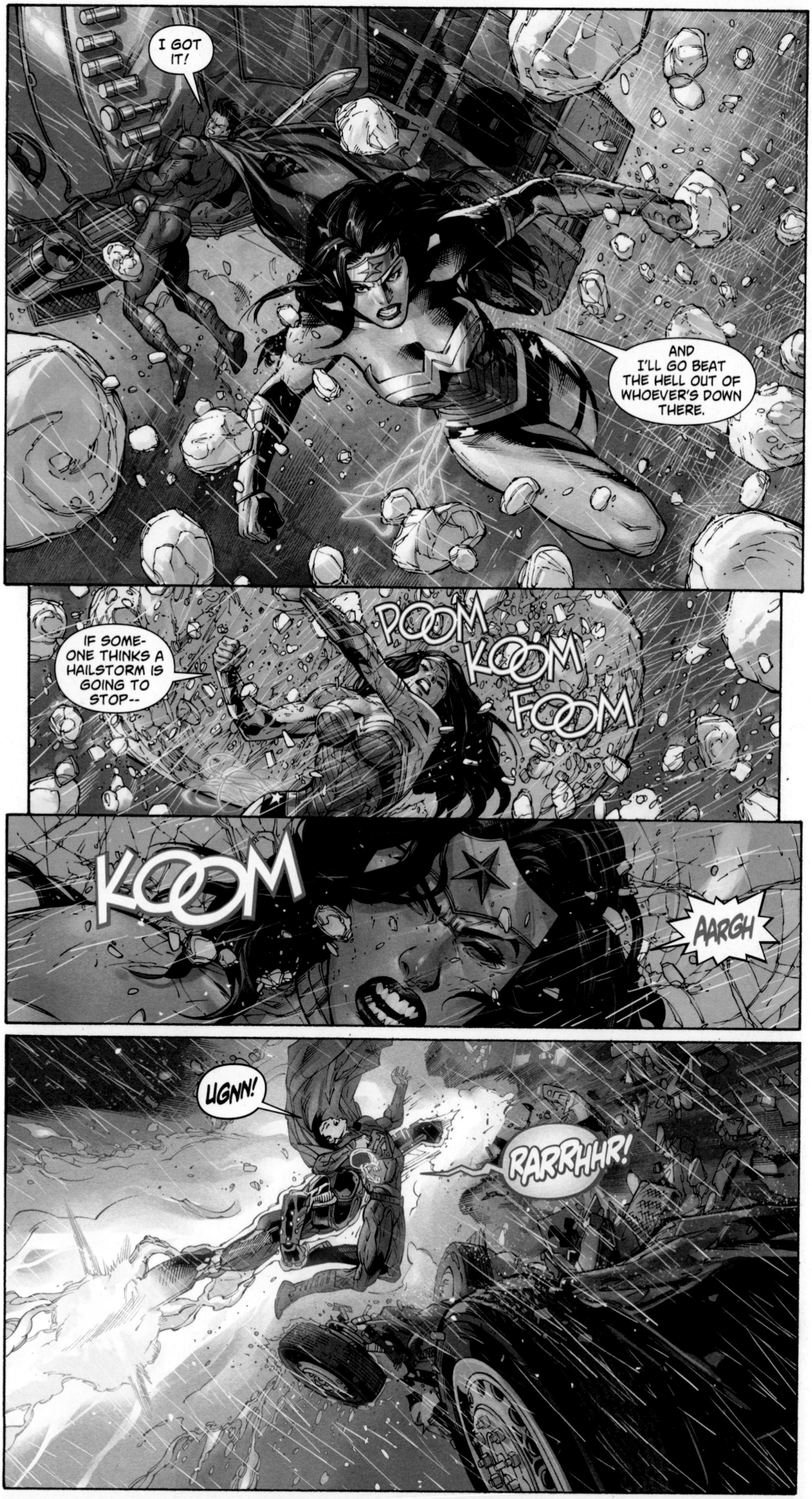
I GOT IT!
AND I'LL GO BEAT THE HELL OUT OF WHOEVER'S DOWN THERE.
IF SOME-ONE THINKS A HAILSTORM IS GOING TO STOP--
POOM
KOOM
FOOM
KOOM
AARGH
UGNN!
RARRHHR!

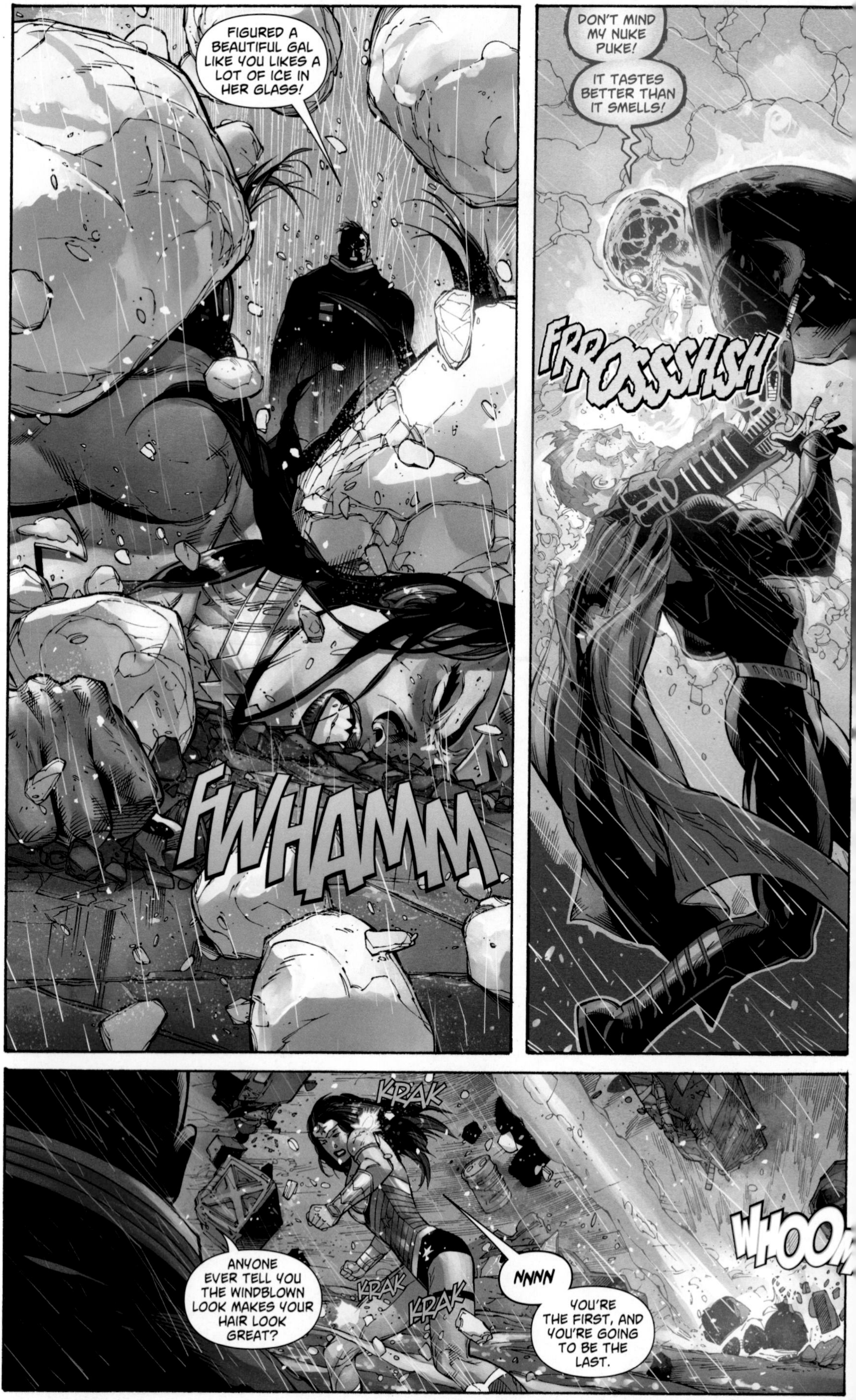
FIGURED A BEAUTIFUL GAL LIKE YOU LIKES A LOT OF ICE IN HER GLASS!
FWHAMM
DON'T MIND MY NUKE PUKE!
IT TASTES BETTER THAN IT SMELLS!
FRROSSSHSH
KRAK
ANYONE EVER TELL YOU THE WINDBLOWN LOOK MAKES YOUR HAIR LOOK GREAT?
KRAK
KRAK
NNNN
YOU'RE THE FIRST, AND YOU'RE GOING TO BE THE LAST.
WHOOM

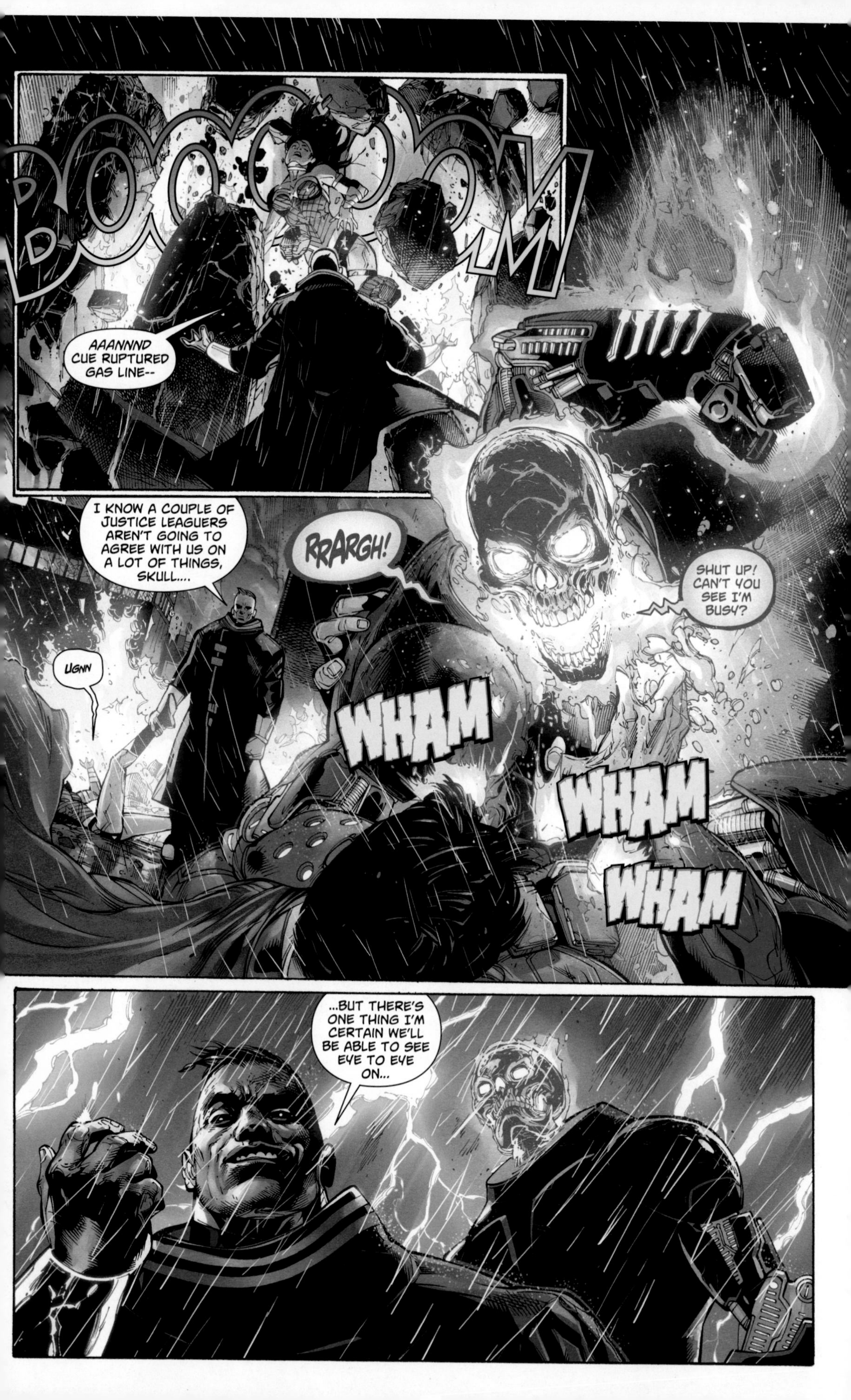
BOOOOOOM
AAANNND CUE RUPTURED GAS LINE--
I KNOW A COUPLE OF JUSTICE LEAGUERS AREN'T GOING TO AGREE WITH US ON A LOT OF THINGS, SKULL....
RRARGH!
SHUT UP! CAN'T YOU SEE I'M BUSY?
UGNN
WHAM
WHAM
WHAM
...BUT THERE'S ONE THING I'M CERTAIN WE'LL BE ABLE TO SEE EYE TO EYE ON...

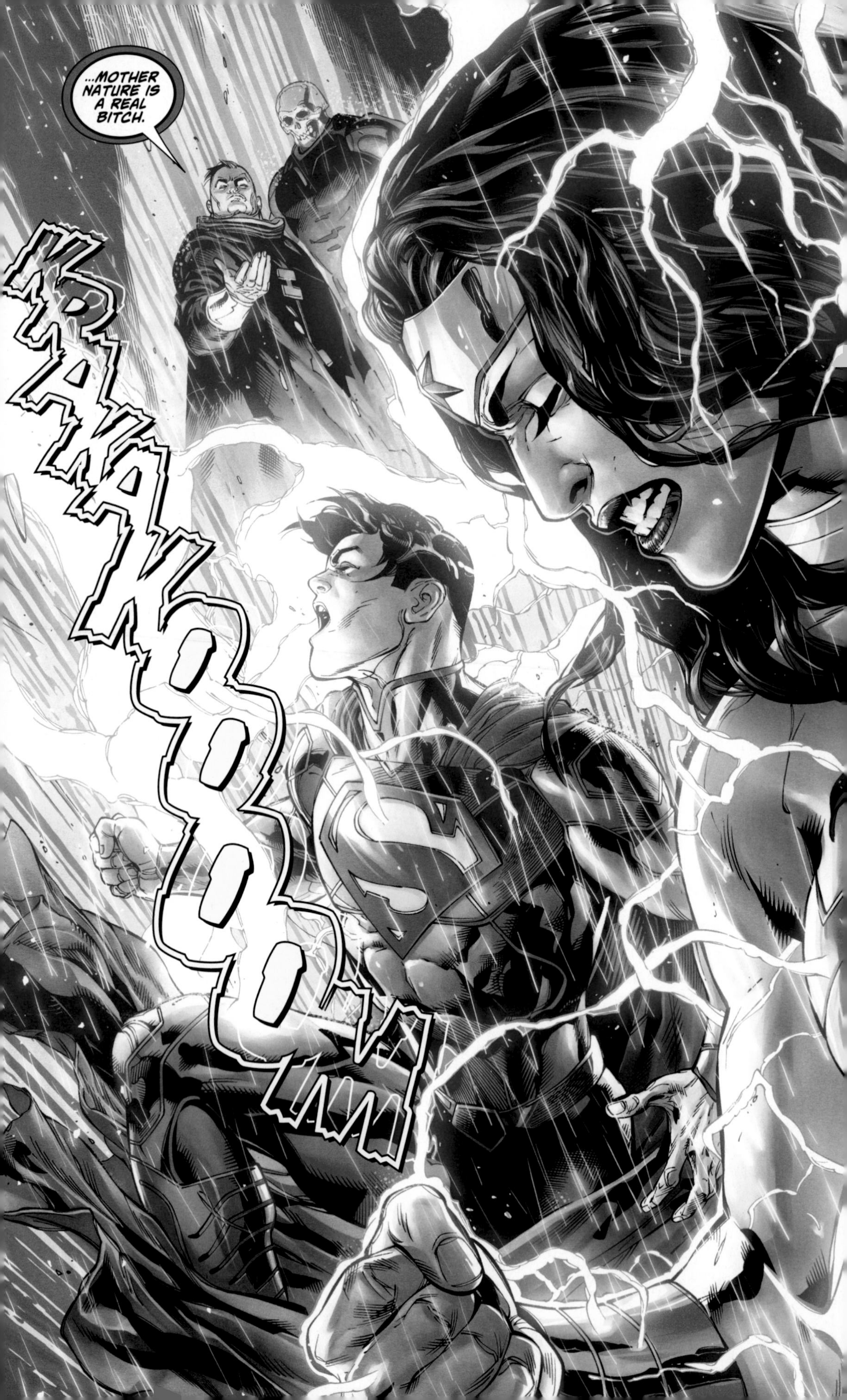
...MOTHER NATURE IS A REAL BITCH.
KRAKAKOOOOM

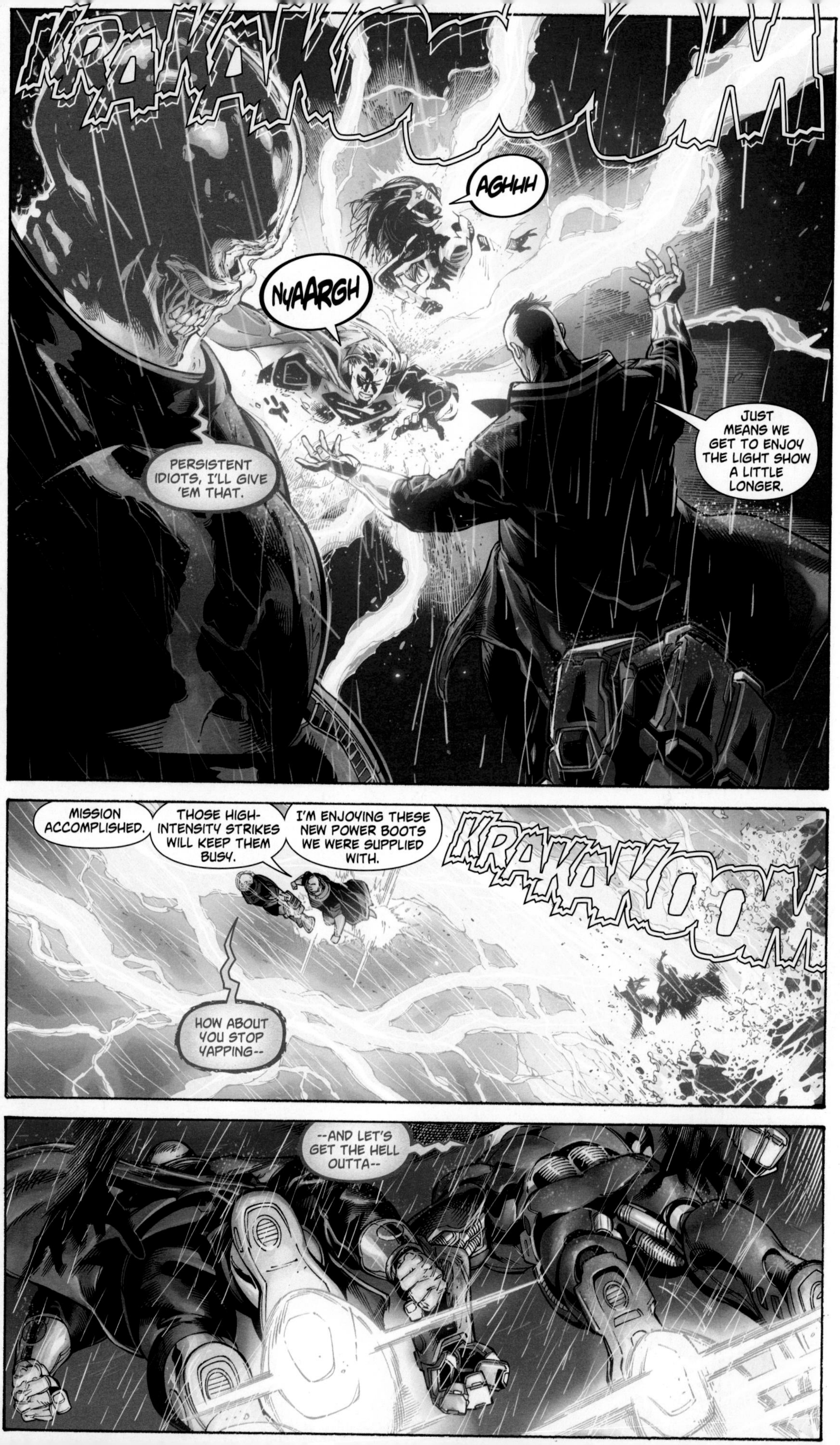
KRAKAKOOOM
AGHHH
NYAARGH
JUST MEANS WE GET TO ENJOY THE LIGHT SHOW A LITTLE LONGER.
PERSISTENT IDIOTS, I'LL GIVE 'EM THAT.
MISSION ACCOMPLISHED.
THOSE HIGH-INTENSITY STRIKES WILL KEEP THEM BUSY.
I'M ENJOYING THESE NEW POWER BOOTS WE WERE SUPPLIED WITH.
KRAKAKOOOM
HOW ABOUT YOU STOP YAPPING--
--AND LET'S GET THE HELL OUTTA--

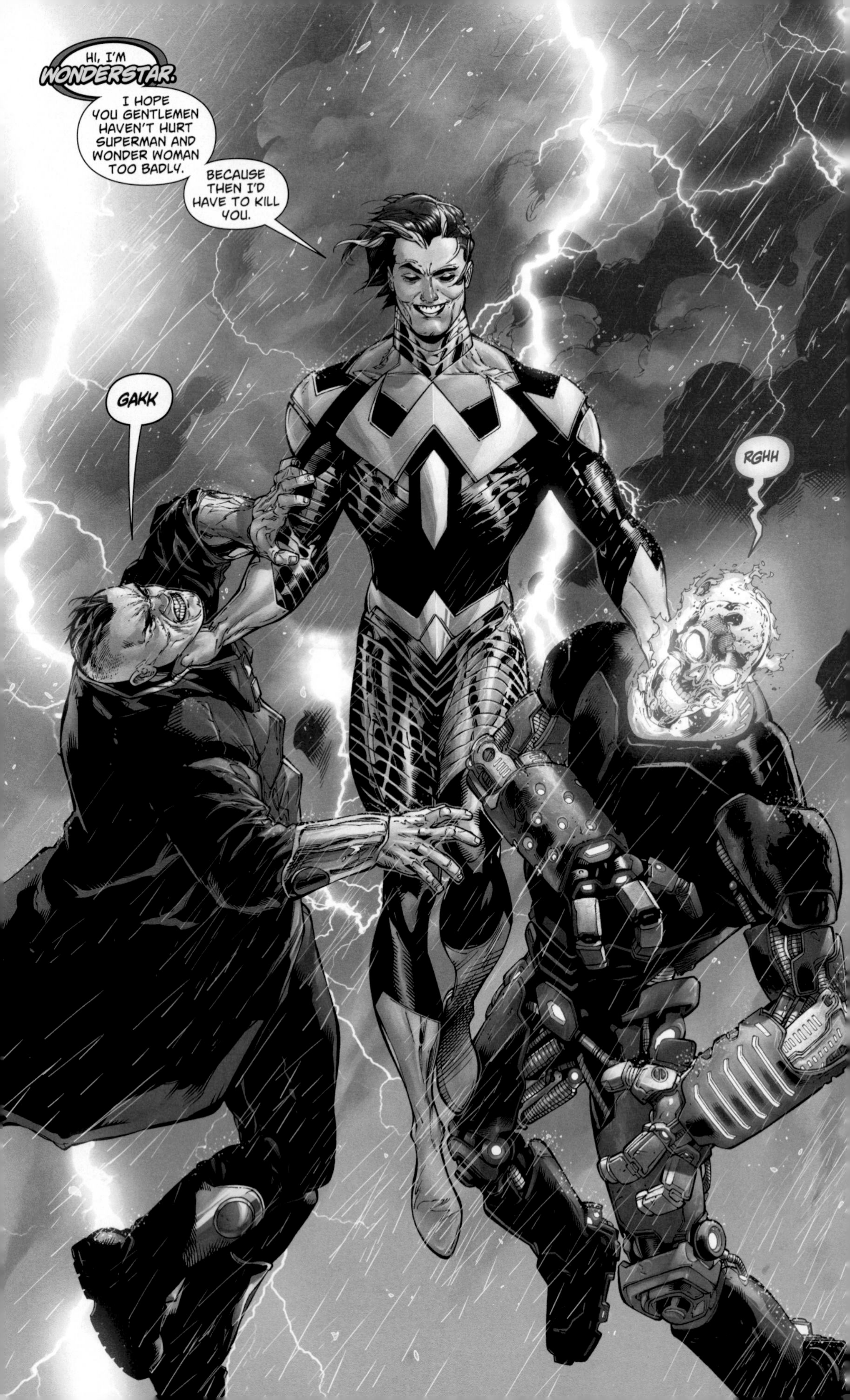
HI, I'M WONDERSTAR.
I HOPE YOU GENTLEMEN HAVEN'T HURT SUPERMAN AND WONDER WOMAN TOO BADLY.
BECAUSE THEN I'D HAVE TO KILL YOU.
GAKK
RGHH

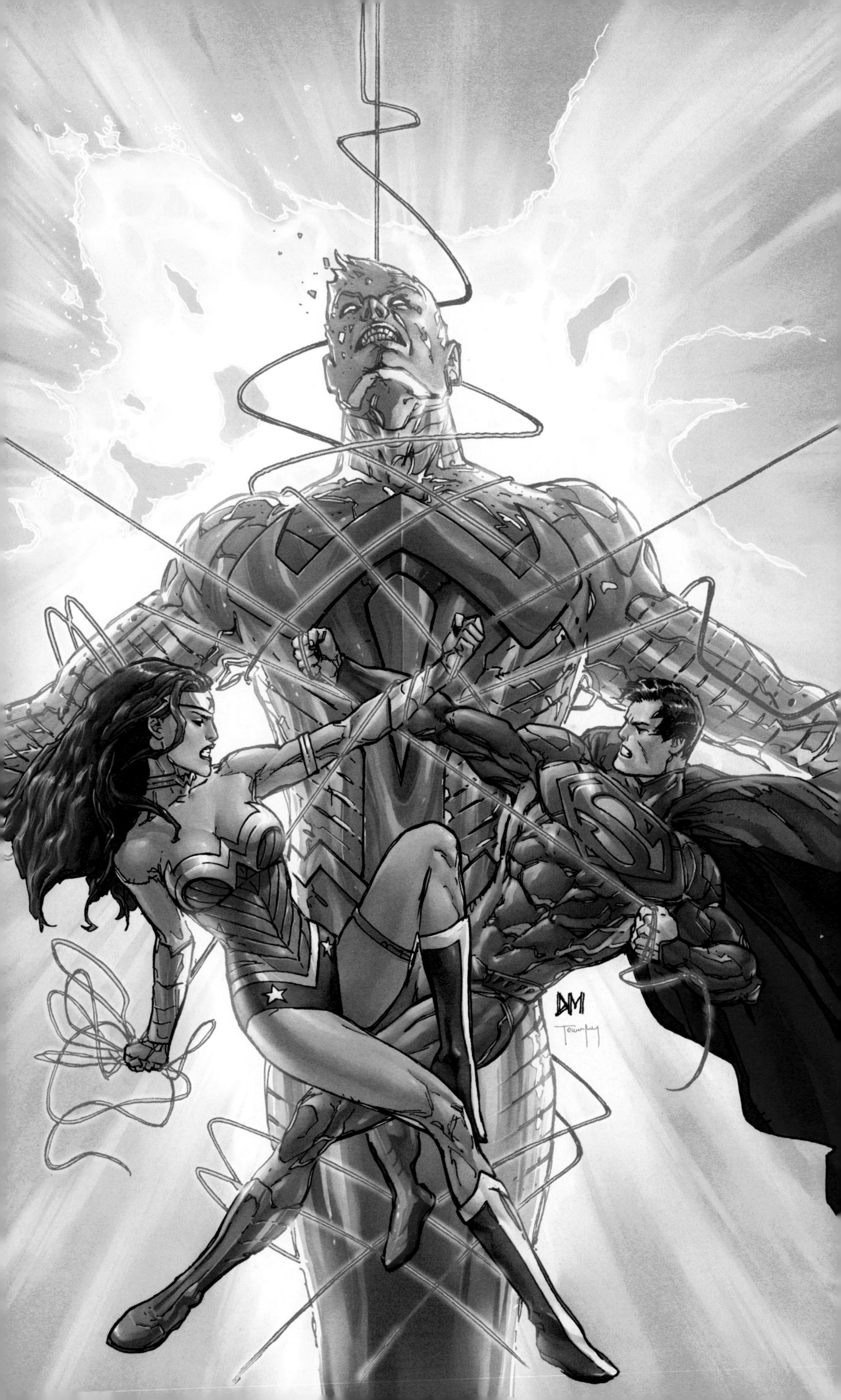

ALL THAT BURNS

PETER J. TOMASI writer DOUG MAHNKE penciller JAIME MENDOZA NORM RAPMUND CHRISTIAN ALAMY DON HO inkers TOMEU MOREY HI-FI colorists
ROB LEIGH letterer cover by MAHNKE & MOREY

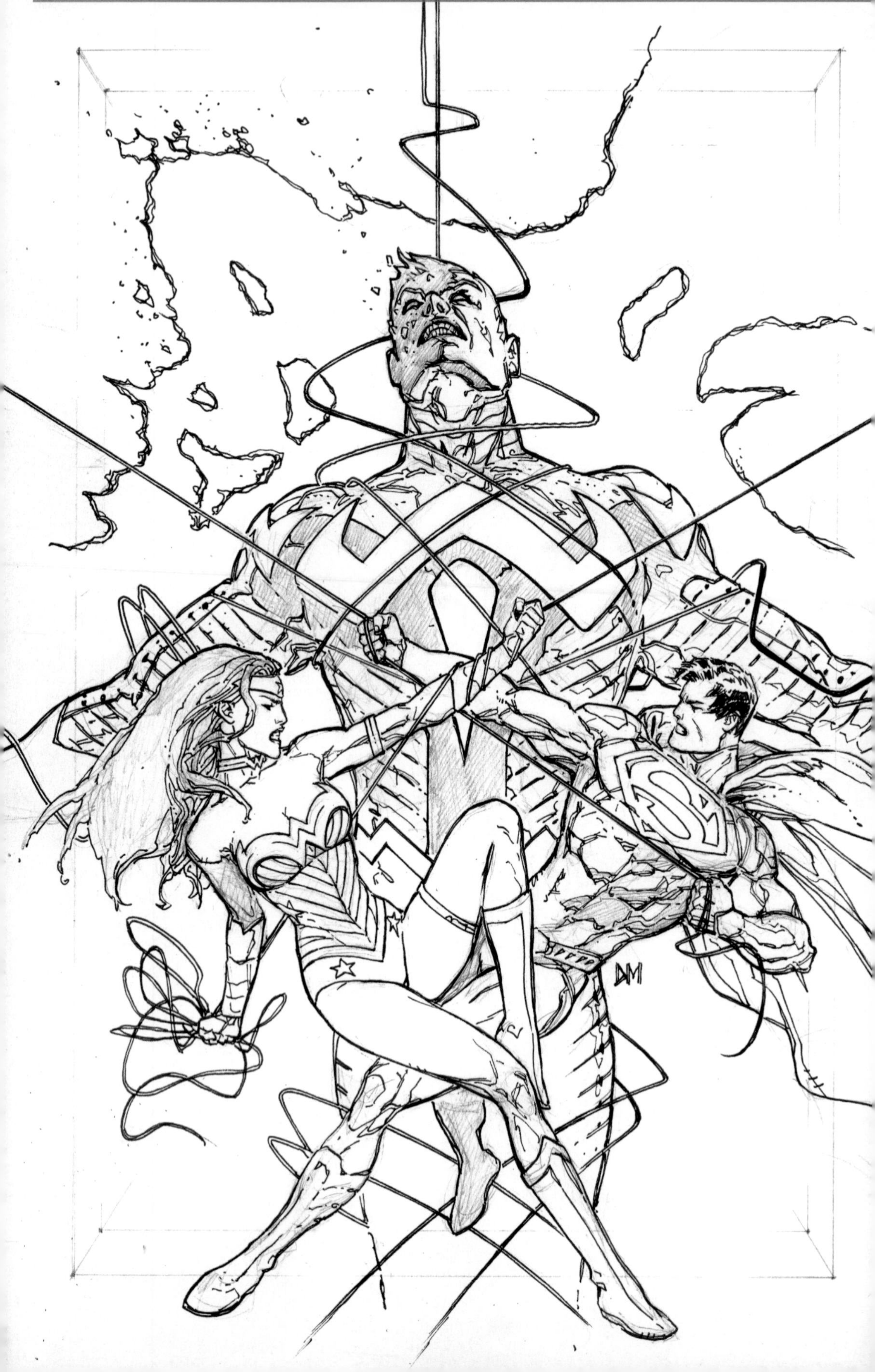

DM

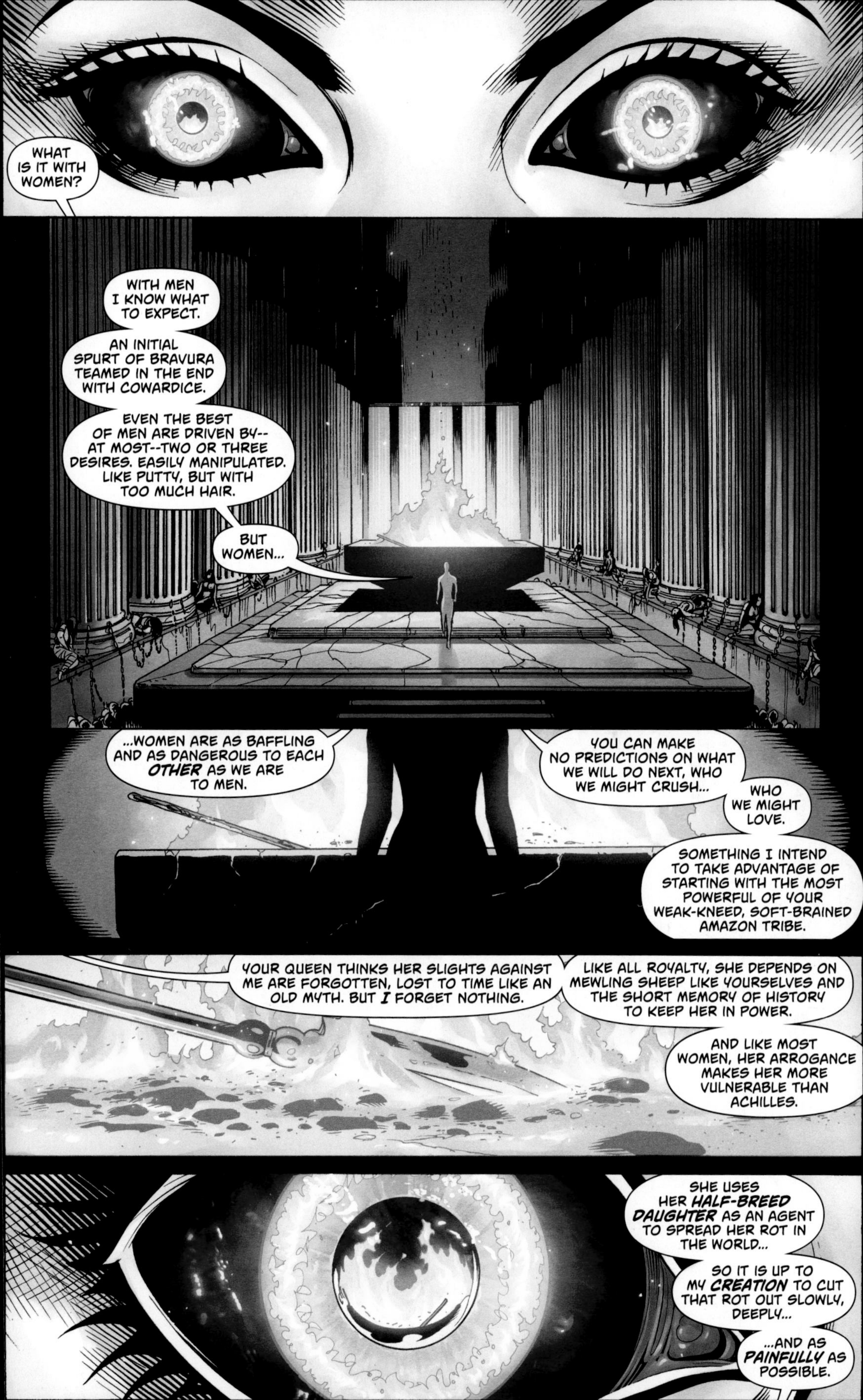
WHAT IS IT WITH WOMEN?
WITH MEN I KNOW WHAT TO EXPECT.
AN INITIAL SPURT OF BRAVURA TEAMED IN THE END WITH COWARDICE.
EVEN THE BEST OF MEN ARE DRIVEN BY--AT MOST--TWO OR THREE DESIRES. EASILY MANIPULATED. LIKE PUTTY, BUT WITH TOO MUCH HAIR.
BUT WOMEN...
...WOMEN ARE AS BAFFLING AND AS DANGEROUS TO EACH OTHER AS WE ARE TO MEN.
YOU CAN MAKE NO PREDICTIONS ON WHAT WE WILL DO NEXT, WHO WE MIGHT CRUSH...
WHO WE MIGHT LOVE.
SOMETHING I INTEND TO TAKE ADVANTAGE OF STARTING WITH THE MOST POWERFUL OF YOUR WEAK-KNEED, SOFT-BRAINED AMAZON TRIBE.
YOUR QUEEN THINKS HER SLIGHTS AGAINST ME ARE FORGOTTEN, LOST TO TIME LIKE AN OLD MYTH. BUT I FORGET NOTHING.
LIKE ALL ROYALTY, SHE DEPENDS ON MEWLING SHEEP LIKE YOURSELVES AND THE SHORT MEMORY OF HISTORY TO KEEP HER IN POWER.
AND LIKE MOST WOMEN, HER ARROGANCE MAKES HER MORE VULNERABLE THAN ACHILLES.
SHE USES HER HALF-BREED DAUGHTER AS AN AGENT TO SPREAD HER ROT IN THE WORLD...
SO IT IS UP TO MY CREATION TO CUT THAT ROT OUT SLOWLY, DEEPLY...
...AND AS PAINFULLY AS POSSIBLE.

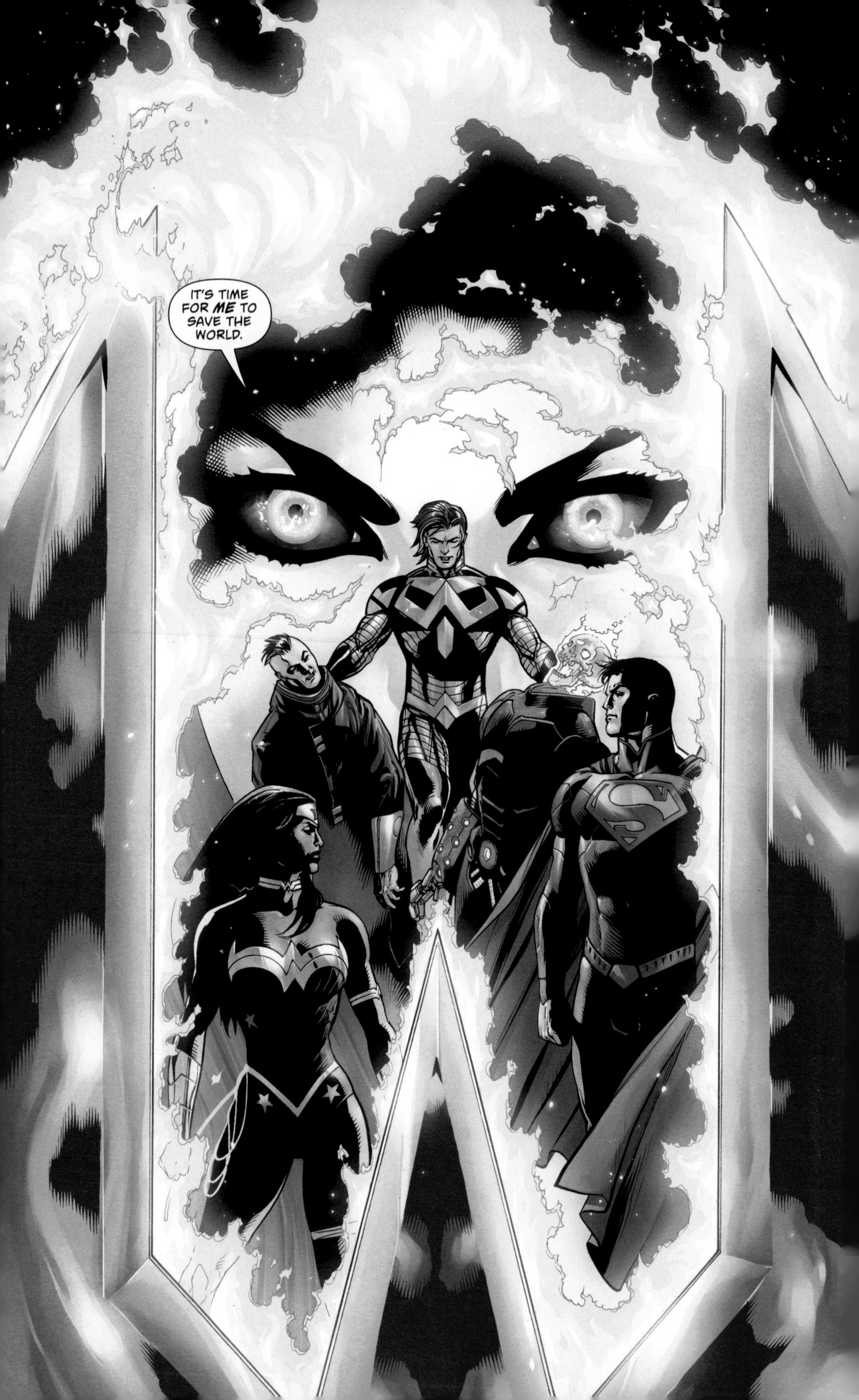
IT'S TIME FOR ME TO SAVE THE WORLD.

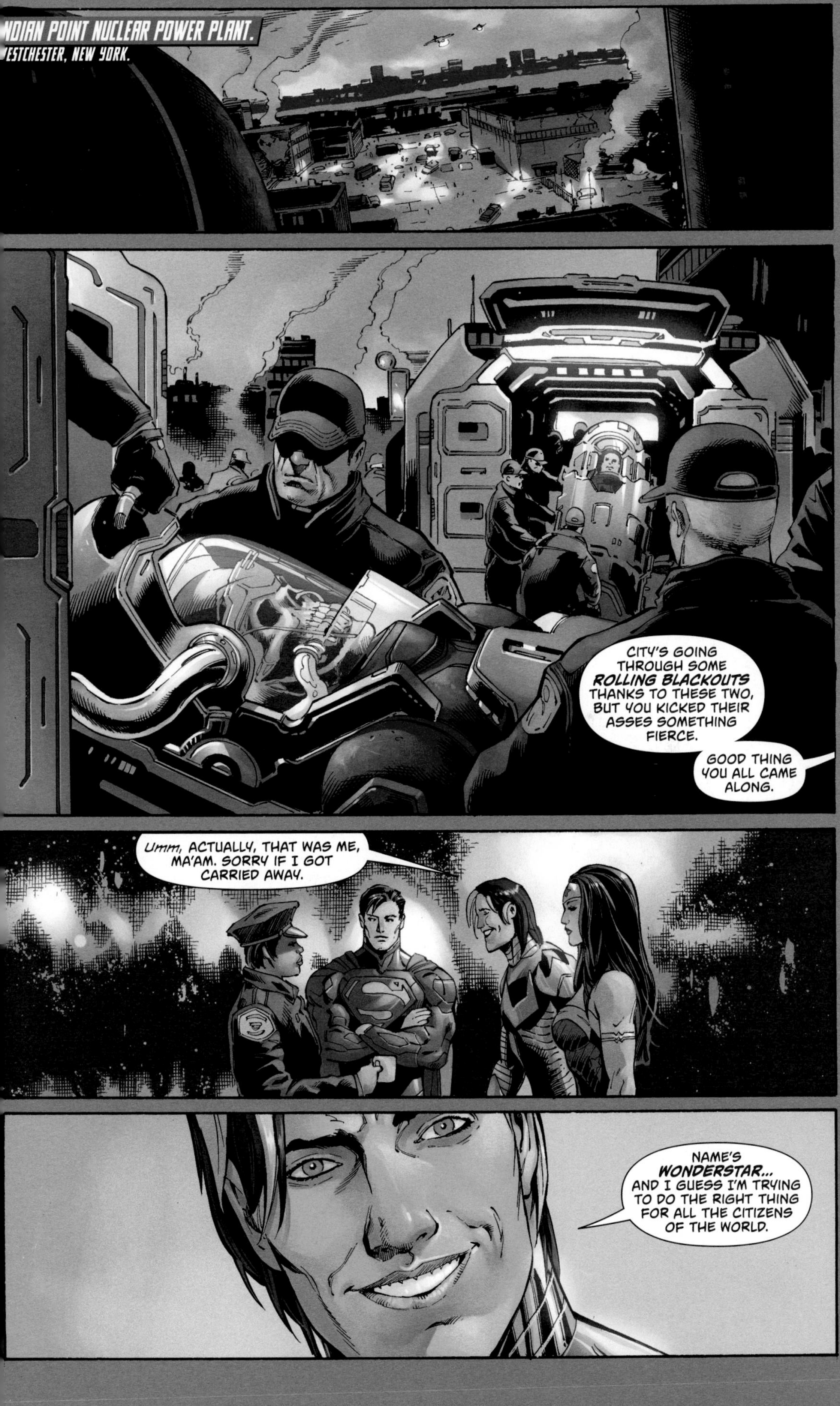
NDIAN POINT NUCLEAR POWER PLANT.
ESTCHESTER, NEW YORK.
CITY'S GOING THROUGH SOME ROLLING BLACKOUTS THANKS TO THESE TWO, BUT YOU KICKED THEIR ASSES SOMETHING FIERCE.
GOOD THING YOU ALL CAME ALONG.
Umm, ACTUALLY, THAT WAS ME, MA'AM. SORRY IF I GOT CARRIED AWAY.
NAME'S WONDERSTAR... AND I GUESS I'M TRYING TO DO THE RIGHT THING FOR ALL THE CITIZENS OF THE WORLD.

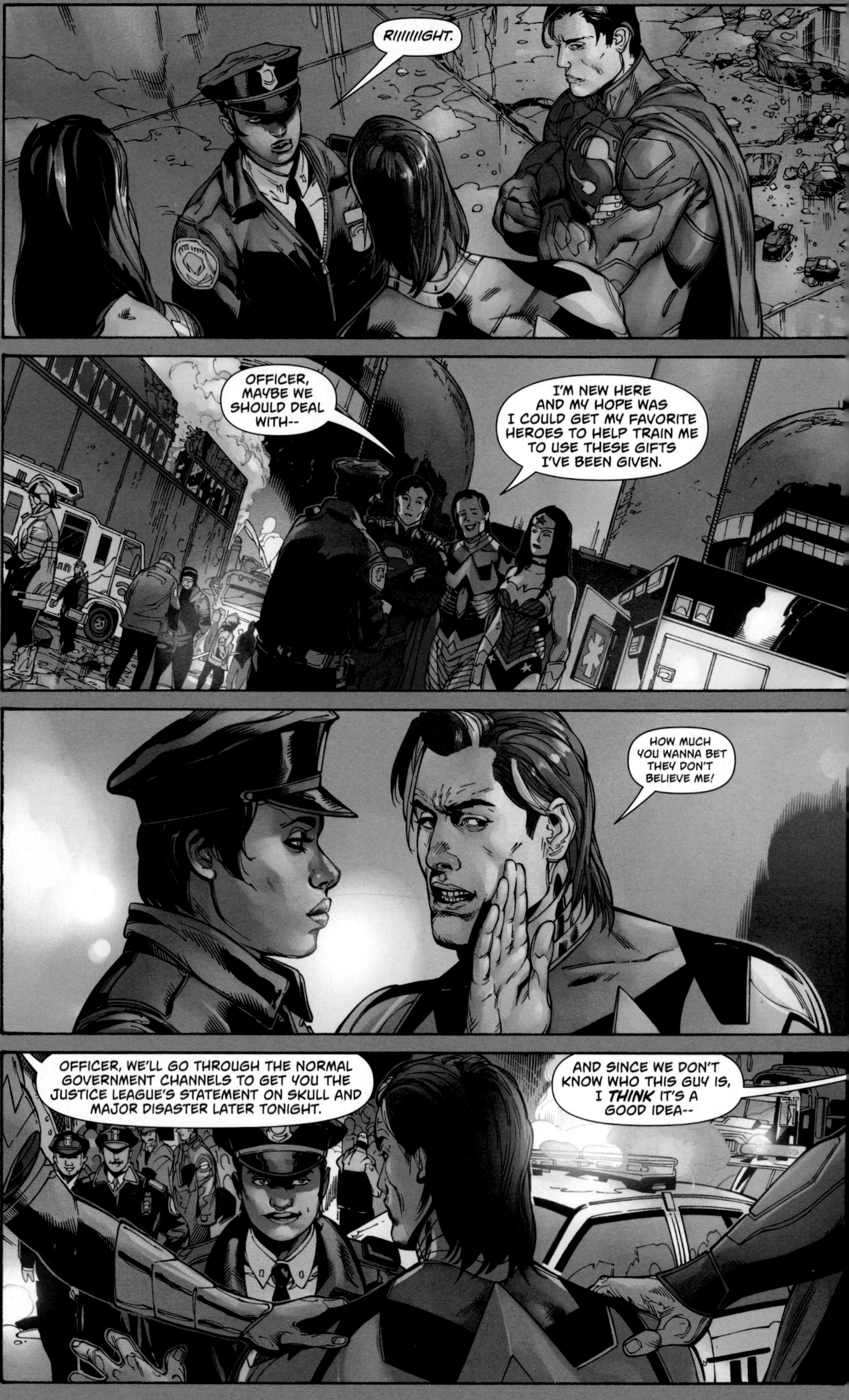
RIIIIIIGHT.
OFFICER, MAYBE WE SHOULD DEAL WITH--
I'M NEW HERE AND MY HOPE WAS I COULD GET MY FAVORITE HEROES TO HELP TRAIN ME TO USE THESE GIFTS I'VE BEEN GIVEN.
HOW MUCH YOU WANNA BET THEY DON'T BELIEVE ME!
OFFICER, WE'LL GO THROUGH THE NORMAL GOVERNMENT CHANNELS TO GET YOU THE JUSTICE LEAGUE'S STATEMENT ON SKULL AND MAJOR DISASTER LATER TONIGHT.
AND SINCE WE DON'T KNOW WHO THIS GUY IS, I *THINK* IT'S A GOOD IDEA--

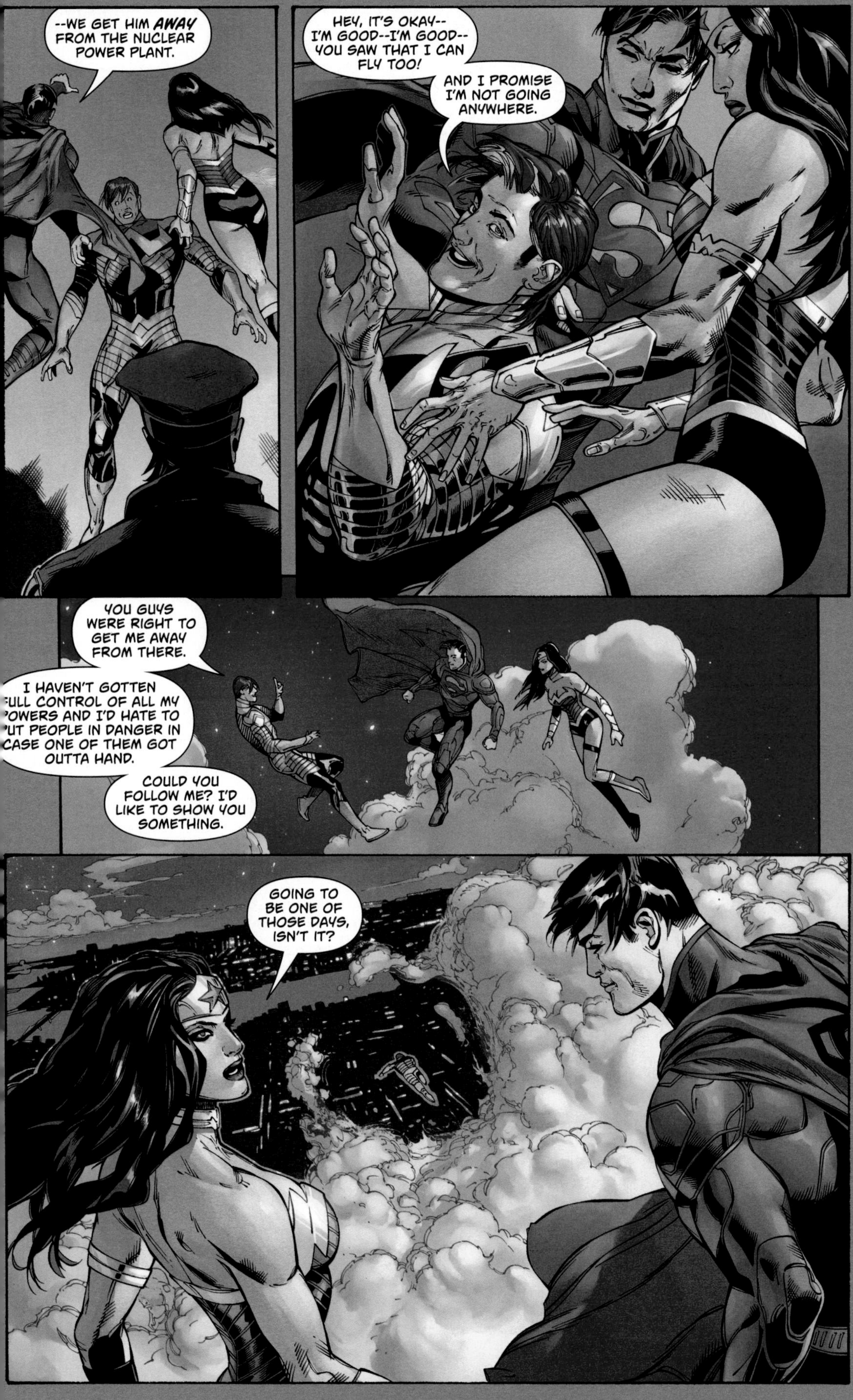
--WE GET HIM AWAY FROM THE NUCLEAR POWER PLANT.
HEY, IT'S OKAY-- I'M GOOD--I'M GOOD-- YOU SAW THAT I CAN FLY TOO!
AND I PROMISE I'M NOT GOING ANYWHERE.
YOU GUYS WERE RIGHT TO GET ME AWAY FROM THERE.
I HAVEN'T GOTTEN ULL CONTROL OF ALL MY OWERS AND I'D HATE TO UT PEOPLE IN DANGER IN CASE ONE OF THEM GOT OUTTA HAND.
COULD YOU FOLLOW ME? I'D LIKE TO SHOW YOU SOMETHING.
GOING TO BE ONE OF THOSE DAYS, ISN'T IT?

TELL US WHAT YOU *CAN* REMEMBER.

AFRAID THERE'S NOT MUCH TO TELL. I KNOW I WAS SOMEONE BEFORE *THIS*...BUT I DON'T KNOW WHO.

I WOKE UP HERE IN THIS CRATER WITH THESE POWERS AND THIS UNIFORM.

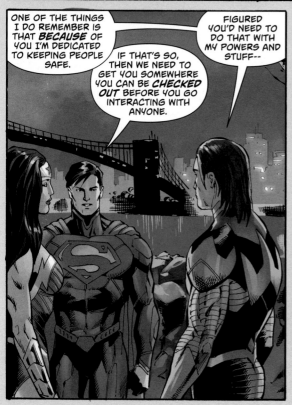

ONE OF THE THINGS I DO REMEMBER IS THAT *BECAUSE* OF YOU I'M DEDICATED TO KEEPING PEOPLE SAFE.

IF THAT'S SO, THEN WE NEED TO GET YOU SOMEWHERE YOU CAN BE *CHECKED OUT* BEFORE YOU GO INTERACTING WITH ANYONE.

FIGURED YOU'D NEED TO DO THAT WITH MY POWERS AND STUFF--

...

ARE YOU ALL RIGHT?

--GOTTA GO-- PEOPLE IN NEED!

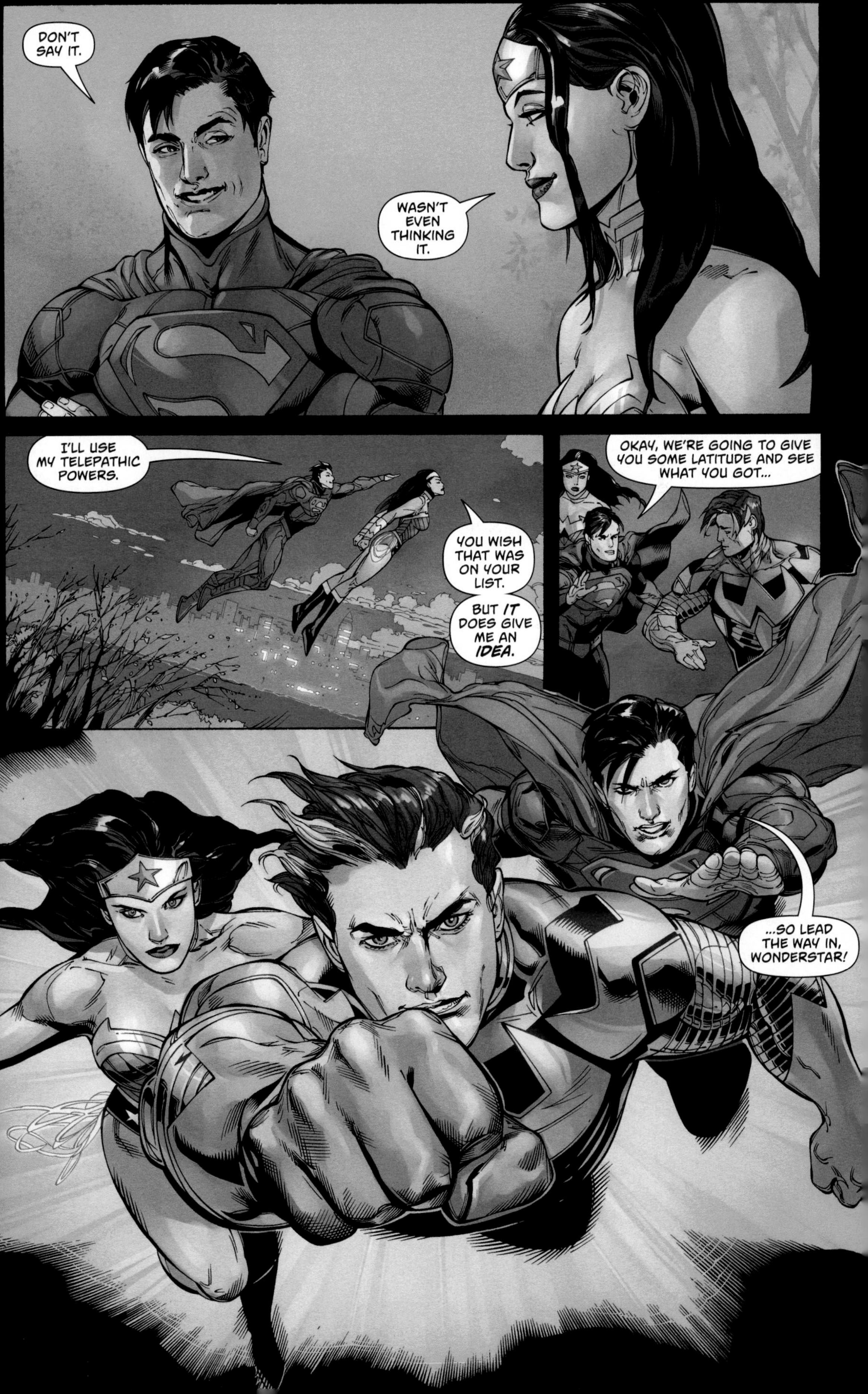
DON'T SAY IT.
WASN'T EVEN THINKING IT.
I'LL USE MY TELEPATHIC POWERS.
YOU WISH THAT WAS ON YOUR LIST.
BUT *IT* DOES GIVE ME AN *IDEA*.
OKAY, WE'RE GOING TO GIVE YOU SOME LATITUDE AND SEE WHAT YOU GOT...
...SO LEAD THE WAY IN, WONDERSTAR!

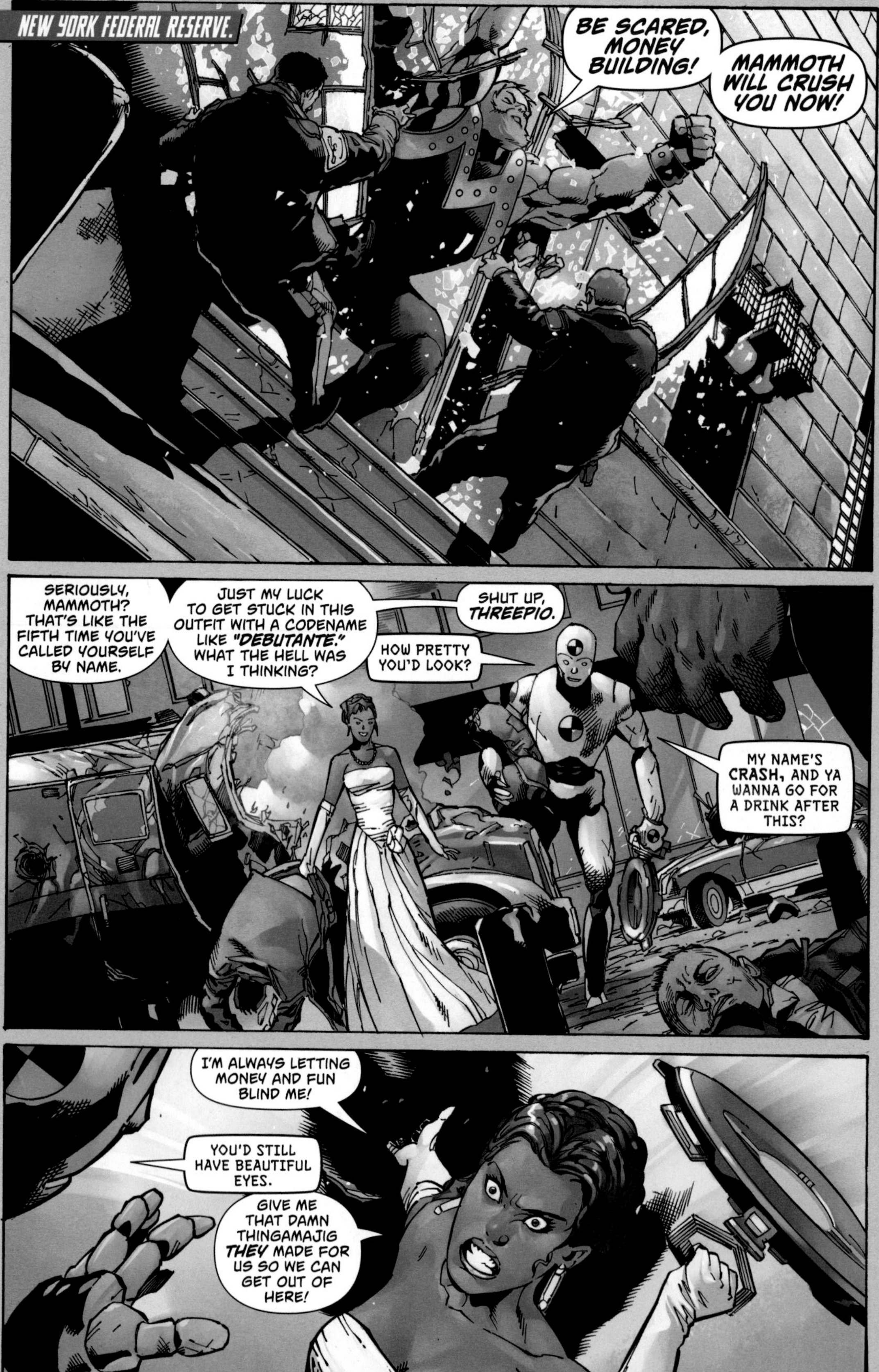
NEW YORK FEDERAL RESERVE.
BE SCARED, MONEY BUILDING!
MAMMOTH WILL CRUSH YOU NOW!
SERIOUSLY, MAMMOTH? THAT'S LIKE THE FIFTH TIME YOU'VE CALLED YOURSELF BY NAME.
JUST MY LUCK TO GET STUCK IN THIS OUTFIT WITH A CODENAME LIKE "DEBUTANTE." WHAT THE HELL WAS I THINKING?
SHUT UP, THREEPIO.
HOW PRETTY YOU'D LOOK?
MY NAME'S CRASH, AND YA WANNA GO FOR A DRINK AFTER THIS?
I'M ALWAYS LETTING MONEY AND FUN BLIND ME!
YOU'D STILL HAVE BEAUTIFUL EYES.
GIVE ME THAT DAMN THINGAMAJIG THEY MADE FOR US SO WE CAN GET OUT OF HERE!

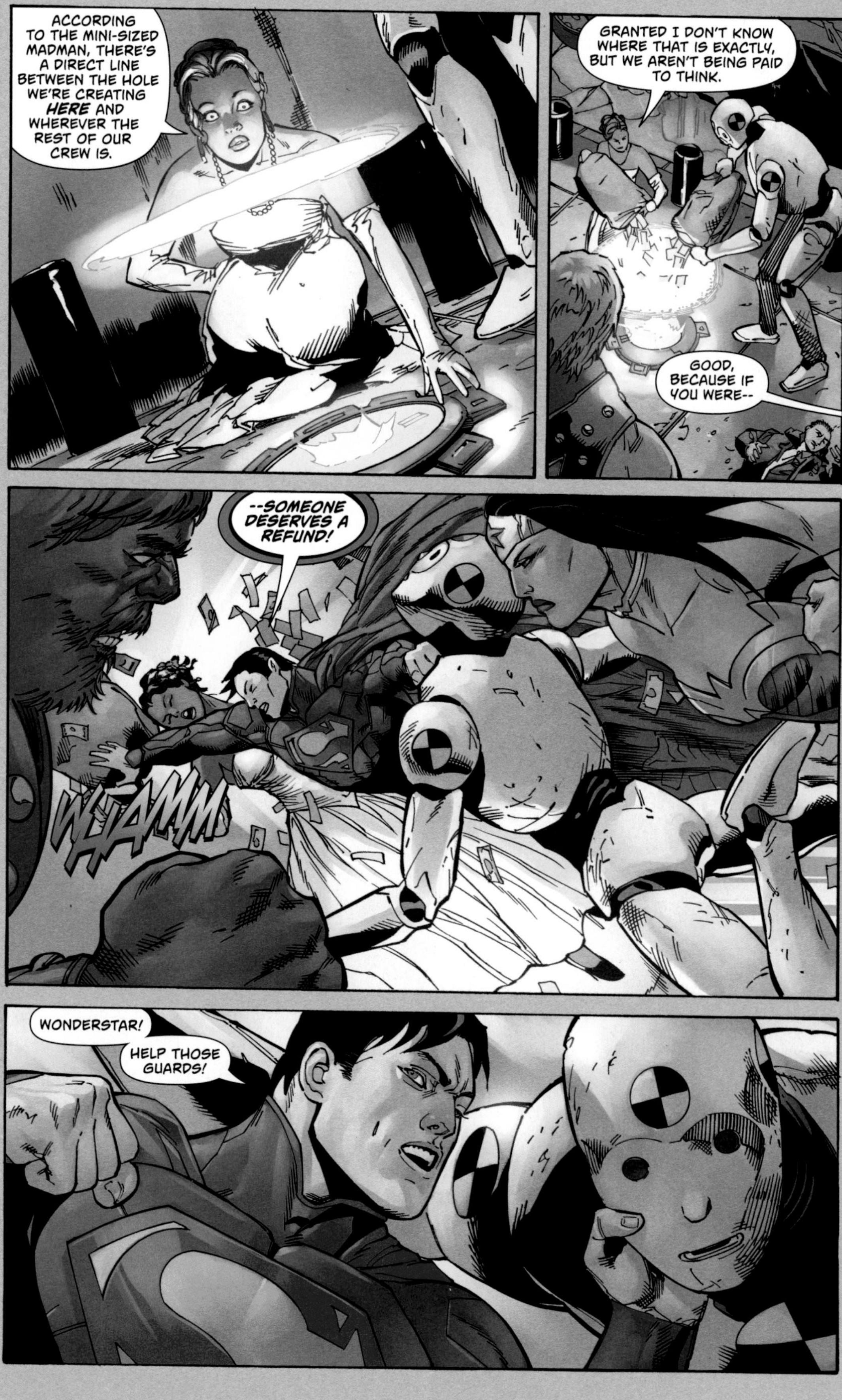
ACCORDING TO THE MINI-SIZED MADMAN, THERE'S A DIRECT LINE BETWEEN THE HOLE WE'RE CREATING HERE AND WHEREVER THE REST OF OUR CREW IS.
GRANTED I DON'T KNOW WHERE THAT IS EXACTLY, BUT WE AREN'T BEING PAID TO THINK.
GOOD, BECAUSE IF YOU WERE--
--SOMEONE DESERVES A REFUND!
WHAMM
WONDERSTAR!
HELP THOSE GUARDS!

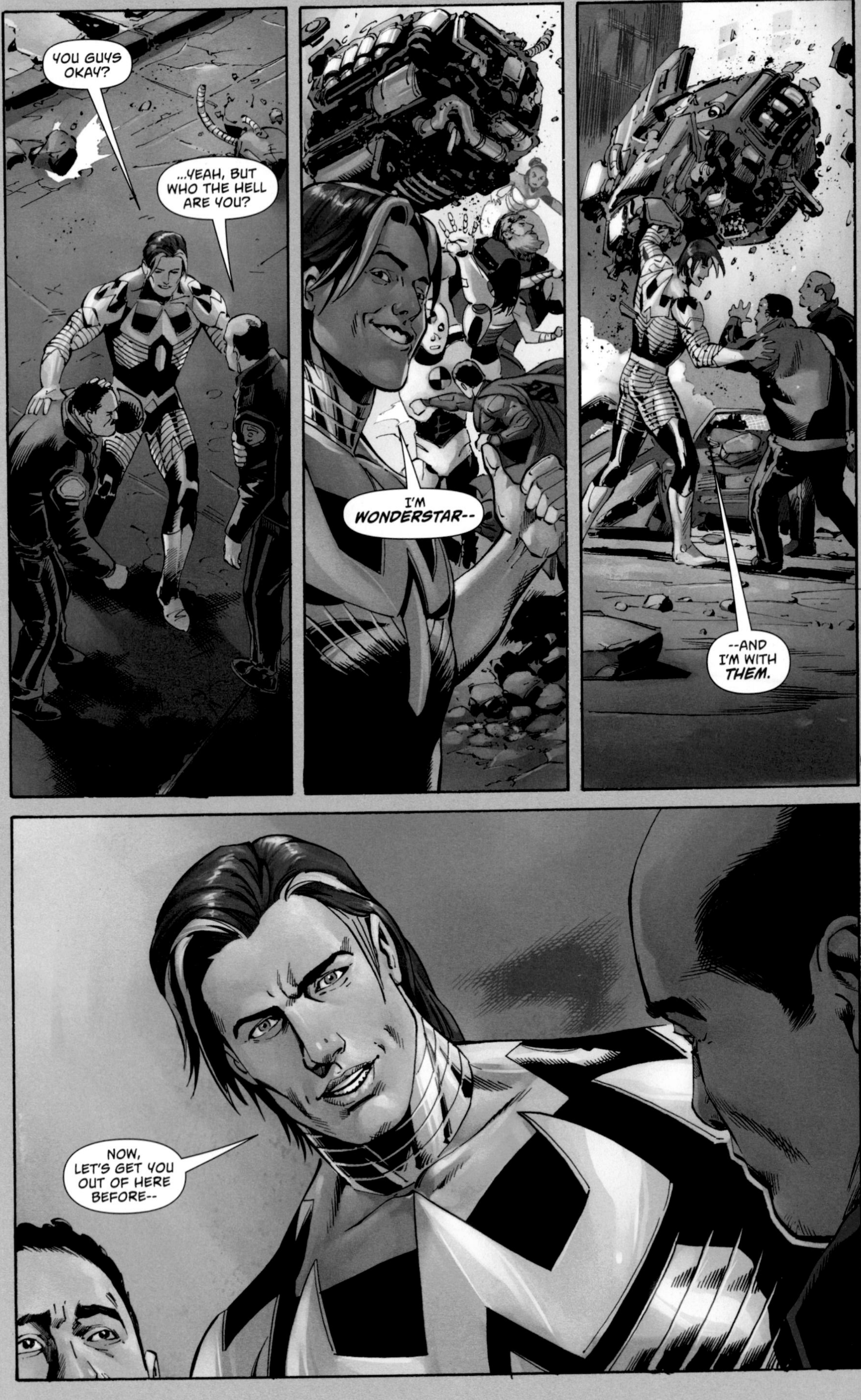
YOU GUYS OKAY?
...YEAH, BUT WHO THE HELL ARE YOU?
I'M *WONDERSTAR*--
--AND I'M WITH *THEM.*
NOW, LET'S GET YOU OUT OF HERE BEFORE--

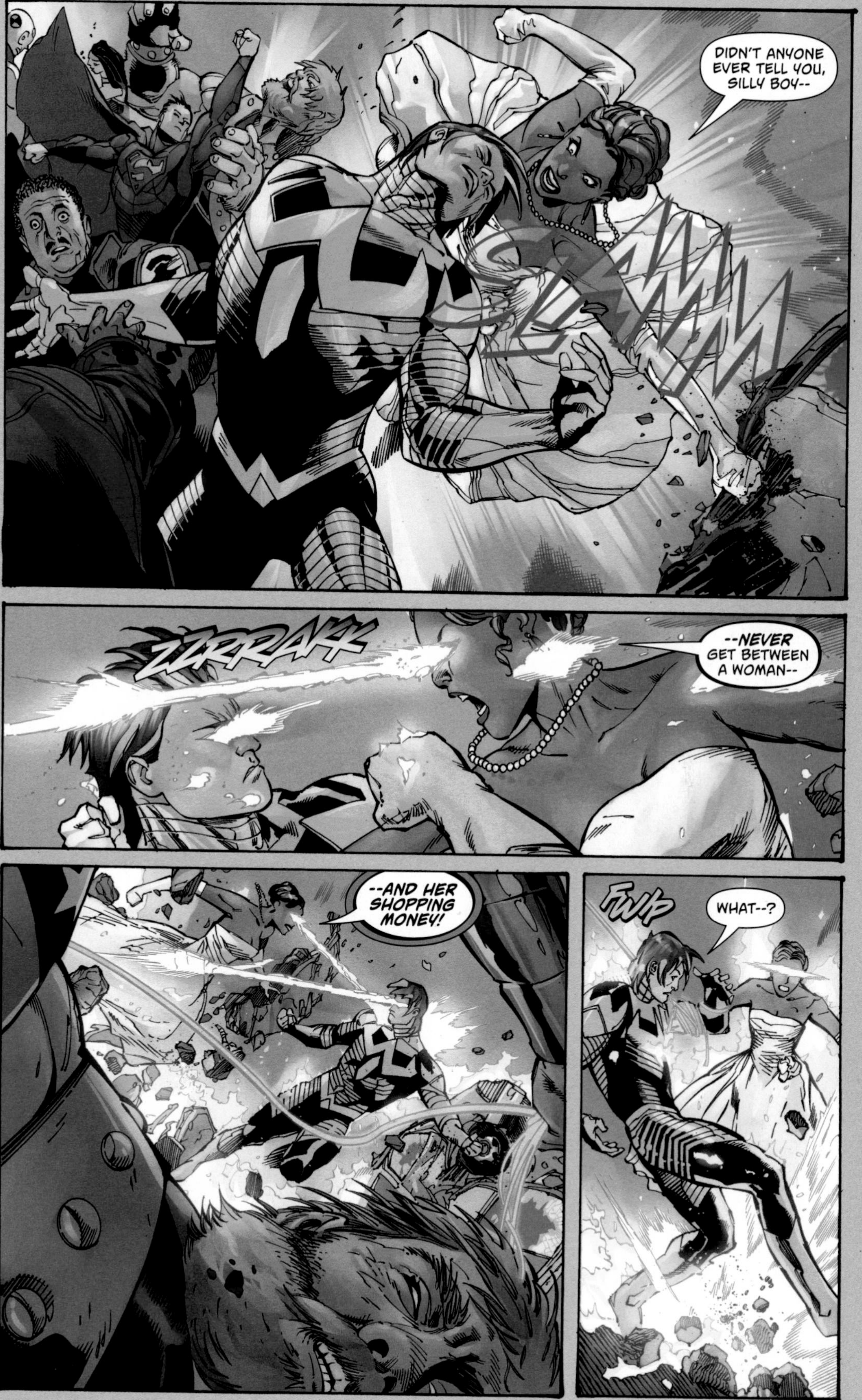
DIDN'T ANYONE EVER TELL YOU, SILLY BOY--
--NEVER GET BETWEEN A WOMAN--
--AND HER SHOPPING MONEY!
FWIP
WHAT--?

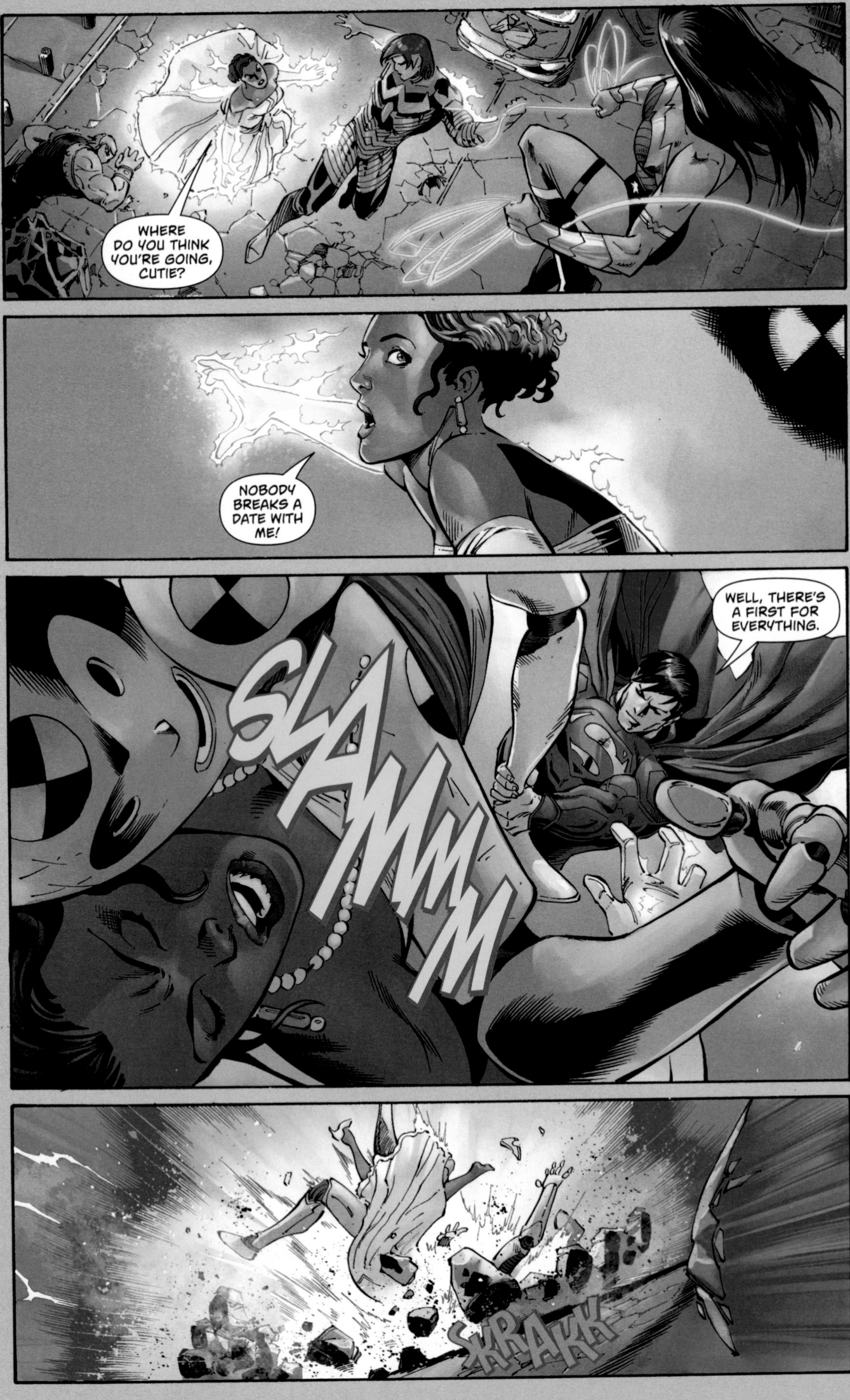
WHERE DO YOU THINK YOU'RE GOING, CUTIE?
NOBODY BREAKS A DATE WITH ME!
SLAMMM
WELL, THERE'S A FIRST FOR EVERYTHING.
SKRAKK

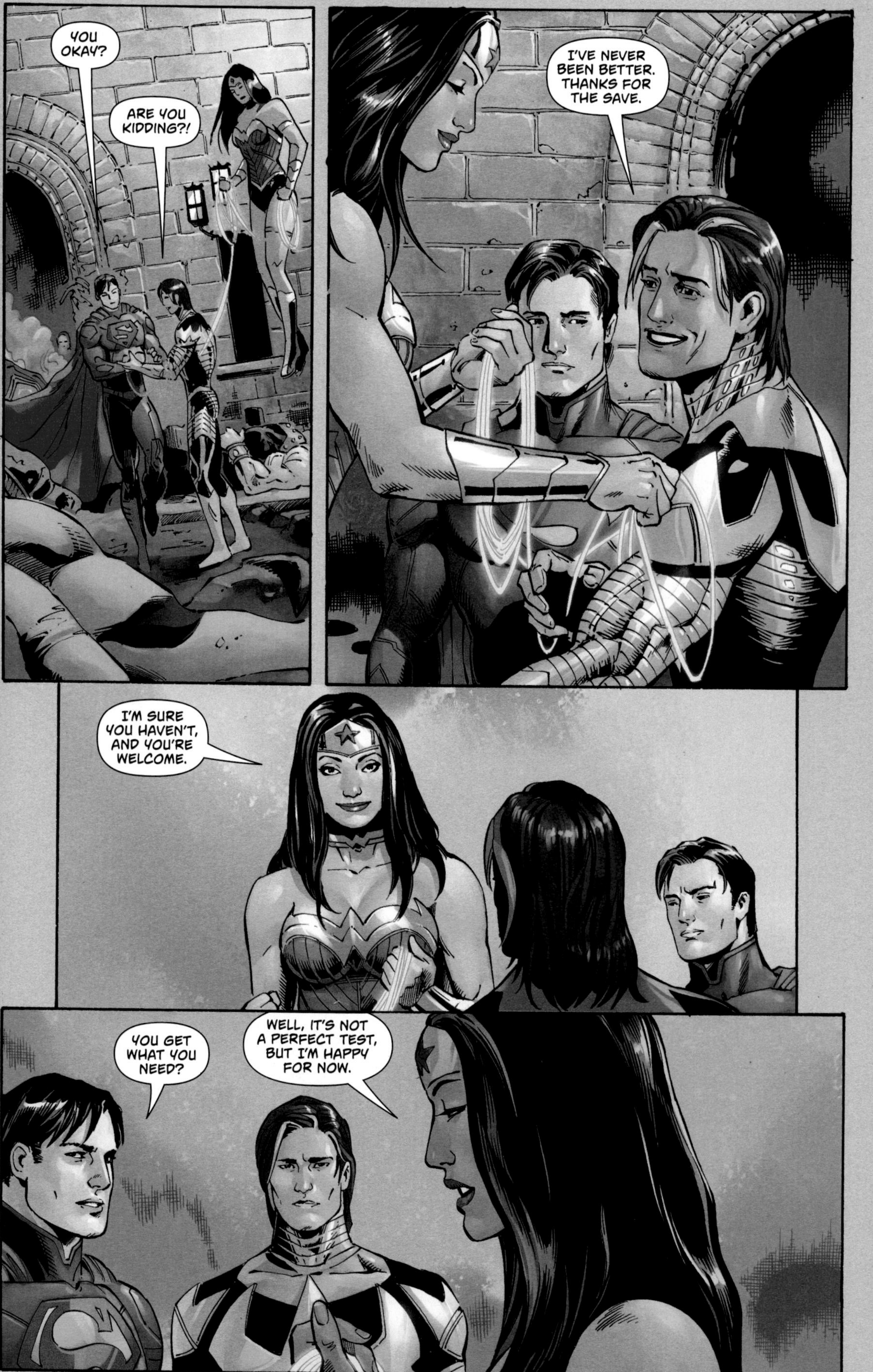
YOU OKAY?
ARE YOU KIDDING?!
I'VE NEVER BEEN BETTER. THANKS FOR THE SAVE.
I'M SURE YOU HAVEN'T, AND YOU'RE WELCOME.
YOU GET WHAT YOU NEED?
WELL, IT'S NOT A PERFECT TEST, BUT I'M HAPPY FOR NOW.

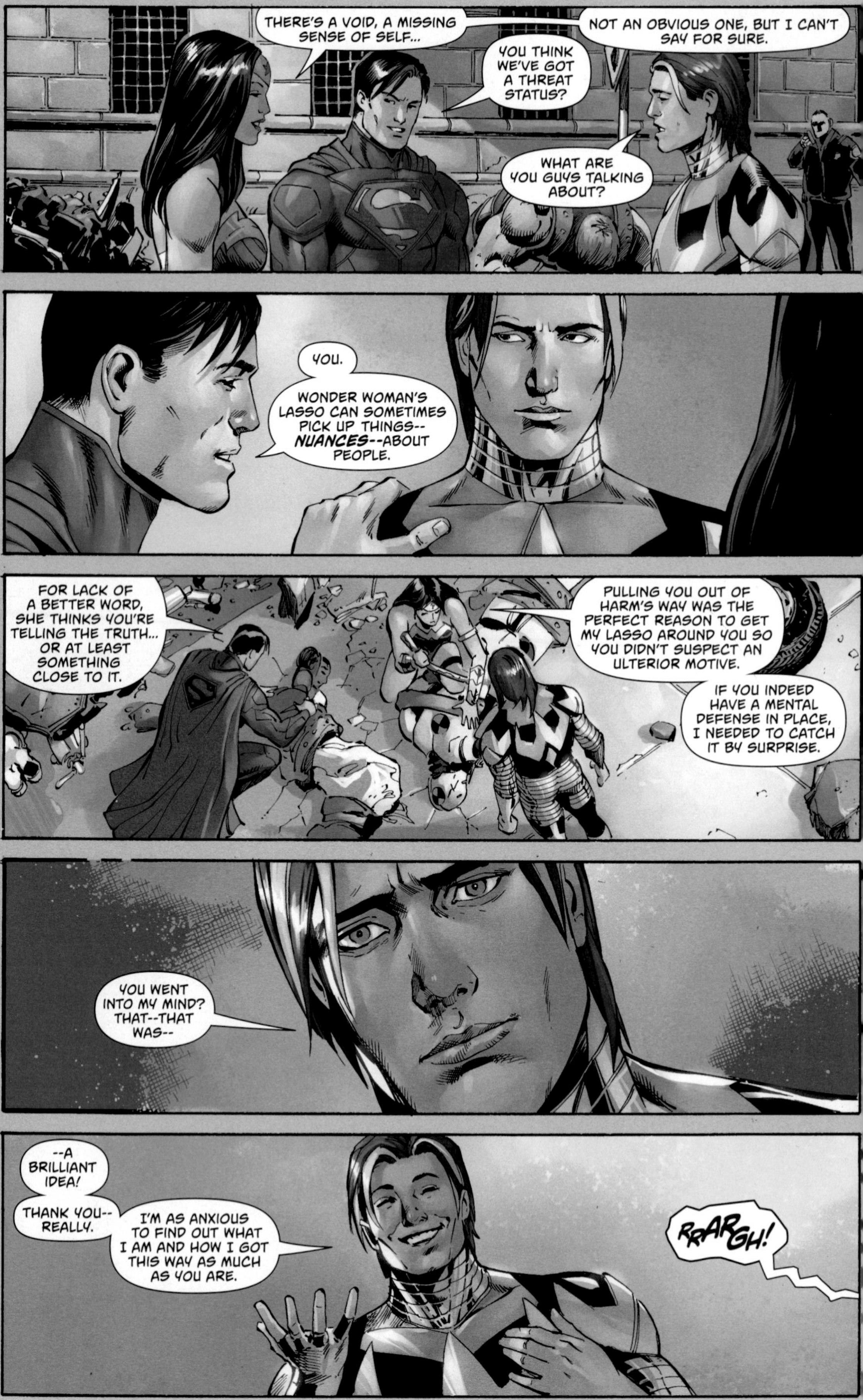
THERE'S A VOID, A MISSING SENSE OF SELF...
NOT AN OBVIOUS ONE, BUT I CAN'T SAY FOR SURE.
YOU THINK WE'VE GOT A THREAT STATUS?
WHAT ARE YOU GUYS TALKING ABOUT?
YOU.
WONDER WOMAN'S LASSO CAN SOMETIMES PICK UP THINGS--NUANCES--ABOUT PEOPLE.
FOR LACK OF A BETTER WORD, SHE THINKS YOU'RE TELLING THE TRUTH... OR AT LEAST SOMETHING CLOSE TO IT.
PULLING YOU OUT OF HARM'S WAY WAS THE PERFECT REASON TO GET MY LASSO AROUND YOU SO YOU DIDN'T SUSPECT AN ULTERIOR MOTIVE.
IF YOU INDEED HAVE A MENTAL DEFENSE IN PLACE, I NEEDED TO CATCH IT BY SURPRISE.
YOU WENT INTO MY MIND? THAT--THAT WAS--
--A BRILLIANT IDEA!
THANK YOU--REALLY.
I'M AS ANXIOUS TO FIND OUT WHAT I AM AND HOW I GOT THIS WAY AS MUCH AS YOU ARE.
RRRARGH!

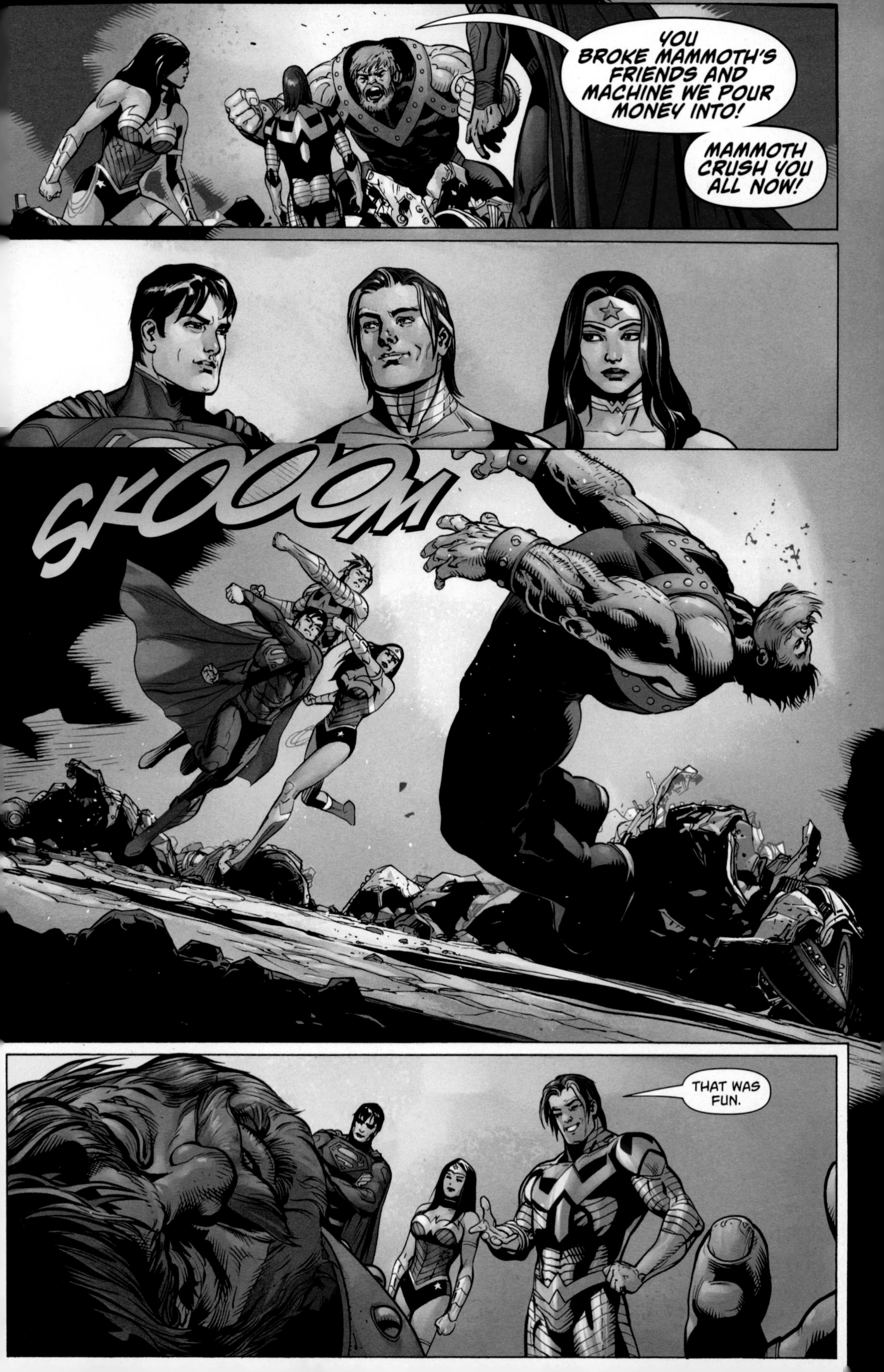
YOU BROKE MAMMOTH'S FRIENDS AND MACHINE WE POUR MONEY INTO!
MAMMOTH CRUSH YOU ALL NOW!
SKOOOM
THAT WAS FUN.

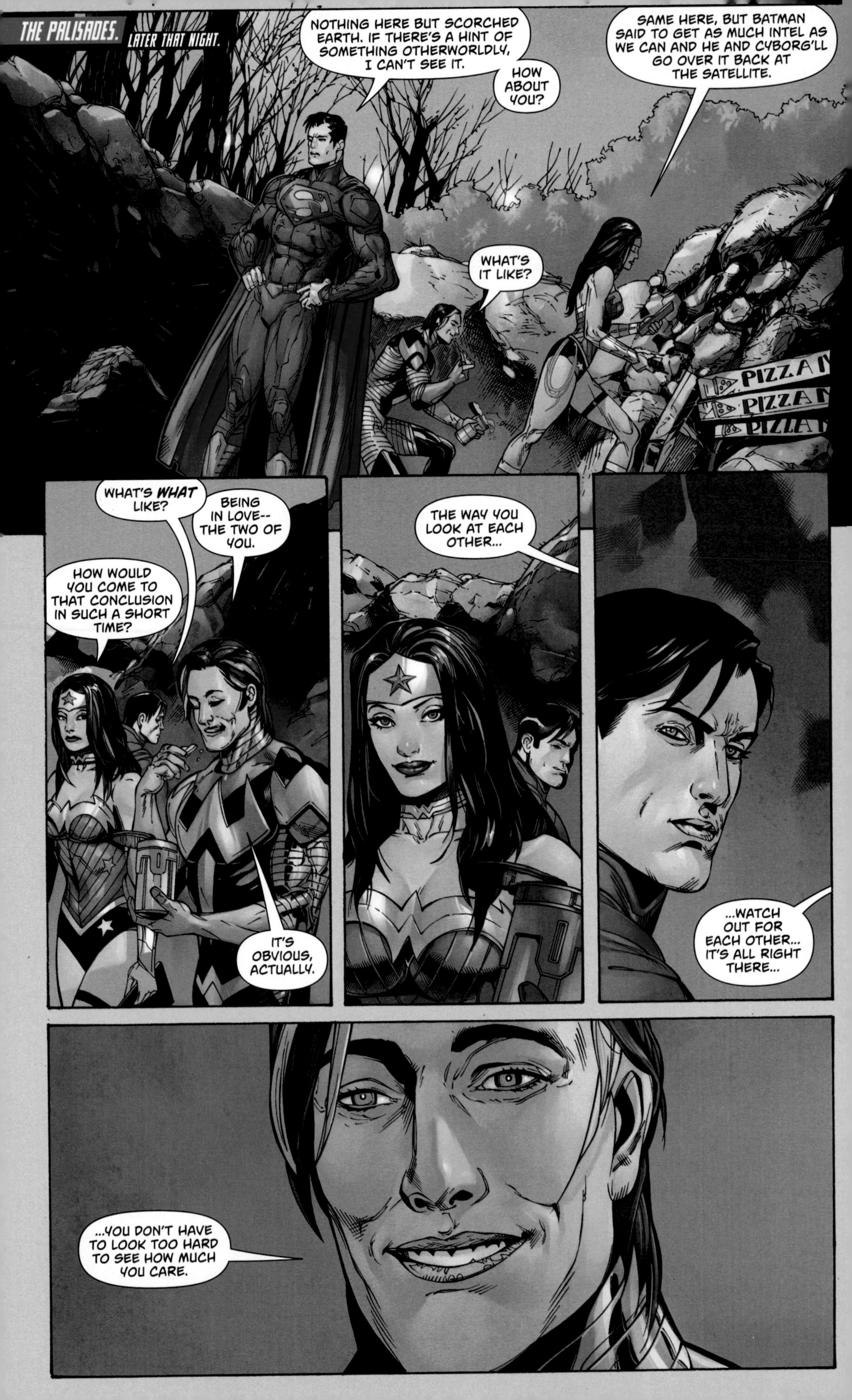
THE PALISADES. LATER THAT NIGHT.
NOTHING HERE BUT SCORCHED EARTH. IF THERE'S A HINT OF SOMETHING OTHERWORLDLY, I CAN'T SEE IT.
HOW ABOUT YOU?
SAME HERE, BUT BATMAN SAID TO GET AS MUCH INTEL AS WE CAN AND HE AND CYBORG'LL GO OVER IT BACK AT THE SATELLITE.
WHAT'S IT LIKE?
PIZZA
PIZZA
PIZZA
WHAT'S WHAT LIKE?
BEING IN LOVE-- THE TWO OF YOU.
HOW WOULD YOU COME TO THAT CONCLUSION IN SUCH A SHORT TIME?
IT'S OBVIOUS, ACTUALLY.
THE WAY YOU LOOK AT EACH OTHER...
...WATCH OUT FOR EACH OTHER... IT'S ALL RIGHT THERE...
...YOU DON'T HAVE TO LOOK TOO HARD TO SEE HOW MUCH YOU CARE.

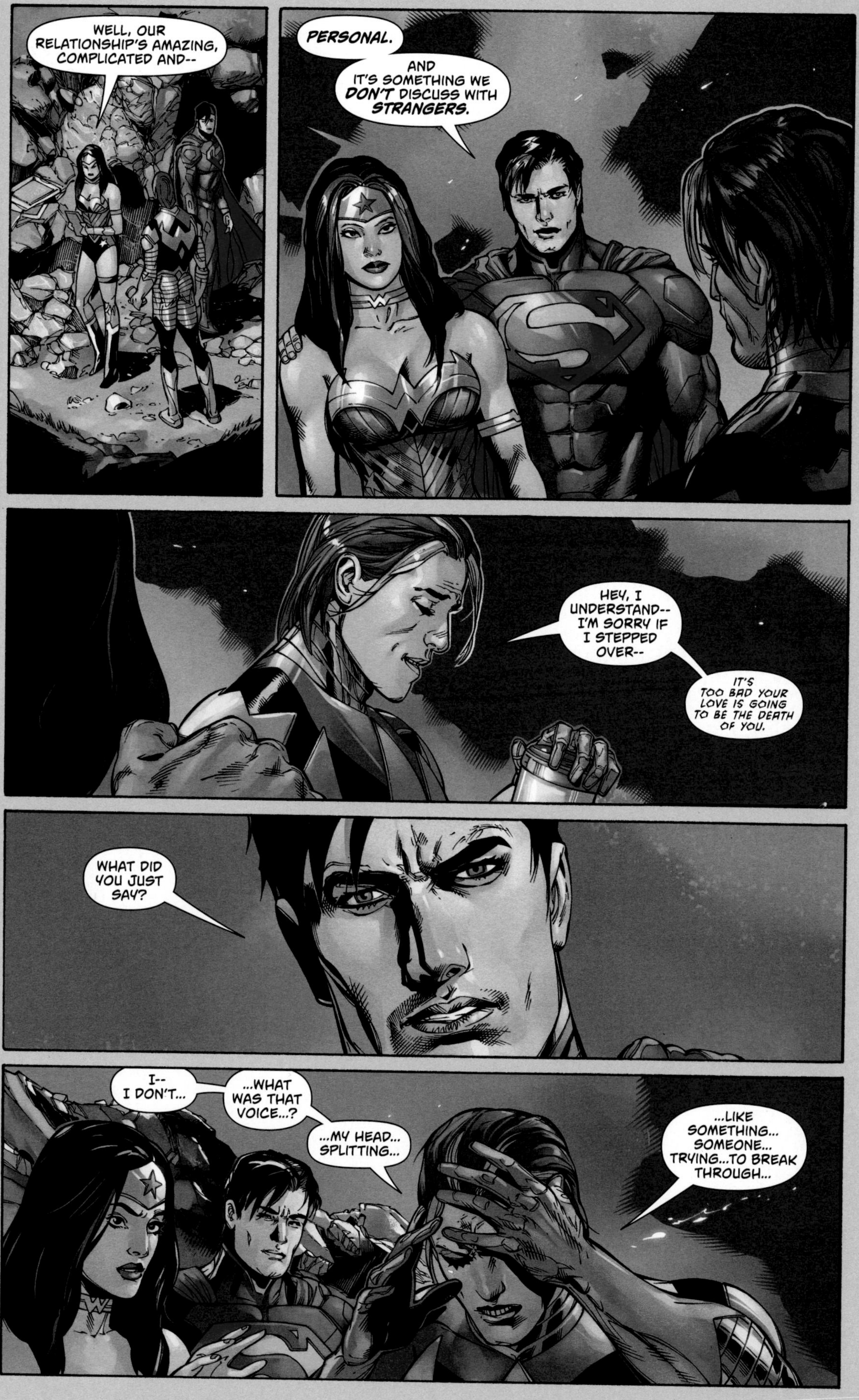
WELL, OUR RELATIONSHIP'S AMAZING, COMPLICATED AND--
PERSONAL.
AND IT'S SOMETHING WE DON'T DISCUSS WITH STRANGERS.
HEY, I UNDERSTAND-- I'M SORRY IF I STEPPED OVER--
IT'S TOO BAD YOUR LOVE IS GOING TO BE THE DEATH OF YOU.
WHAT DID YOU JUST SAY?
I-- I DON'T...
...WHAT WAS THAT VOICE...?
...MY HEAD... SPLITTING...
...LIKE SOMETHING... SOMEONE... TRYING...TO BREAK THROUGH...

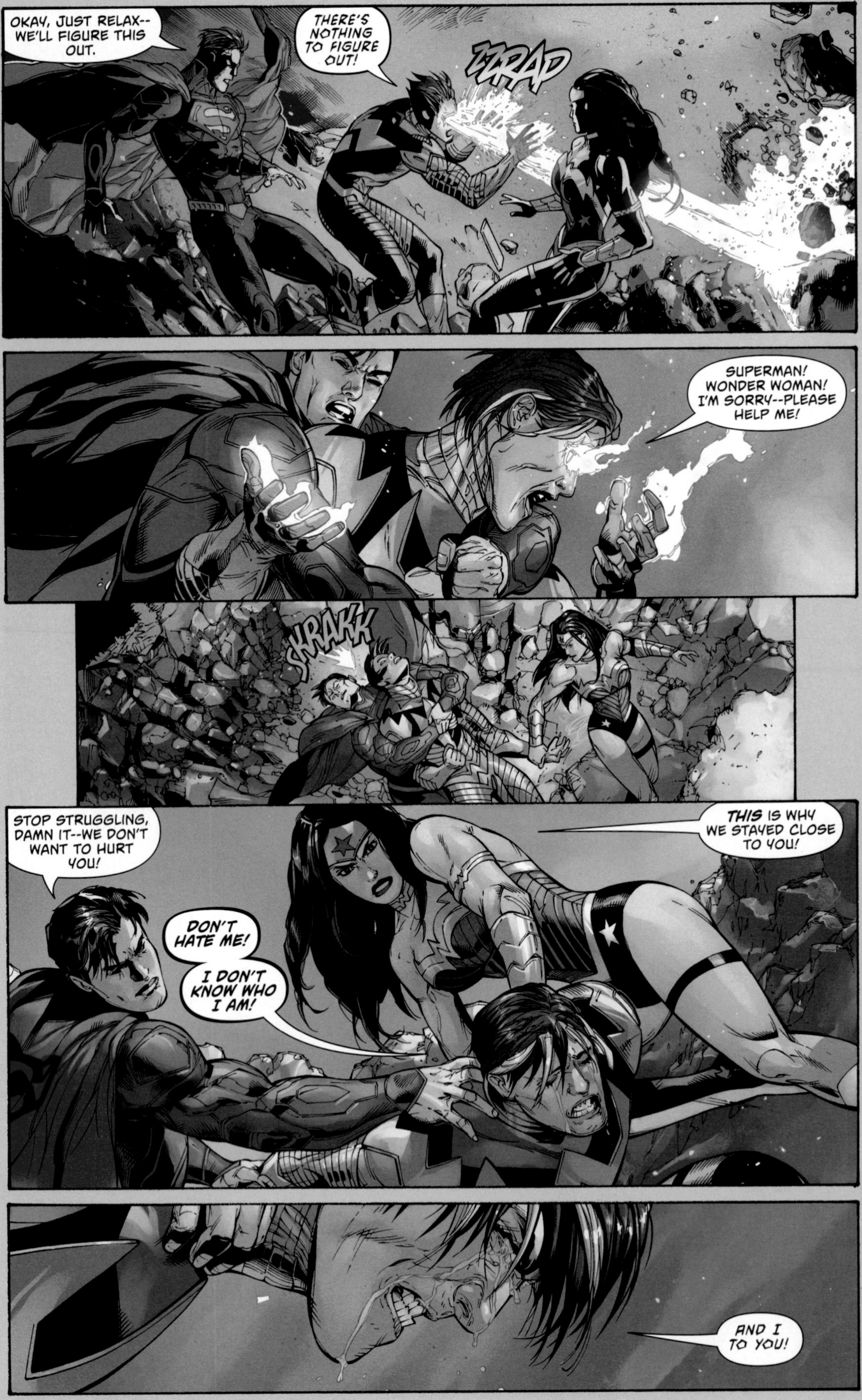

OKAY, JUST RELAX--WE'LL FIGURE THIS OUT.
THERE'S NOTHING TO FIGURE OUT!
ZZRAD
SUPERMAN! WONDER WOMAN! I'M SORRY--PLEASE HELP ME!
SKRAKK
STOP STRUGGLING, DAMN IT--WE DON'T WANT TO HURT YOU!
THIS IS WHY WE STAYED CLOSE TO YOU!
DON'T HATE ME!
I DON'T KNOW WHO I AM!
AND I TO YOU!

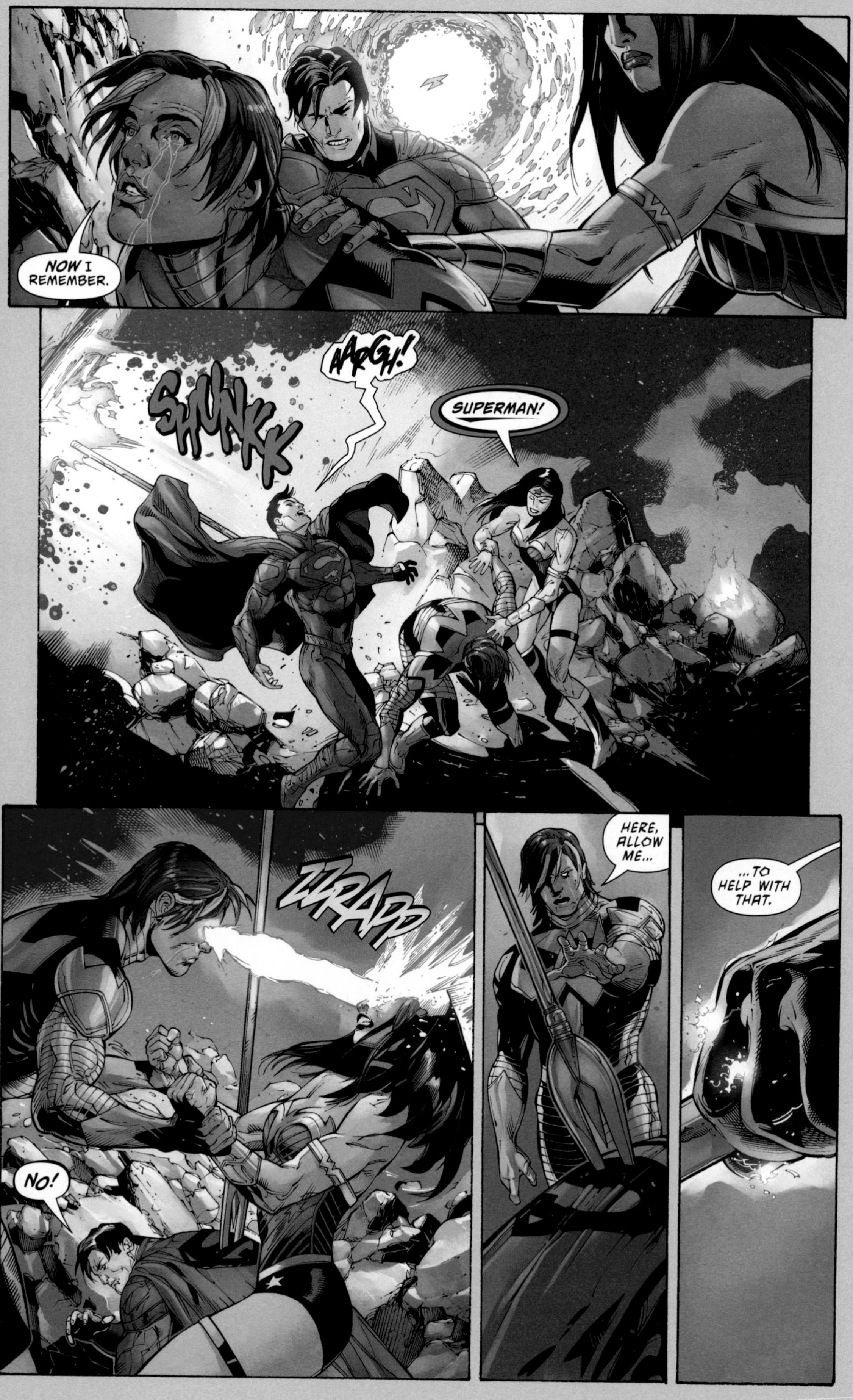
NOW I REMEMBER.
AARGH!
SHUNKK
SUPERMAN!
ZZRAPP
NO!
HERE, ALLOW ME...
...TO HELP WITH THAT.

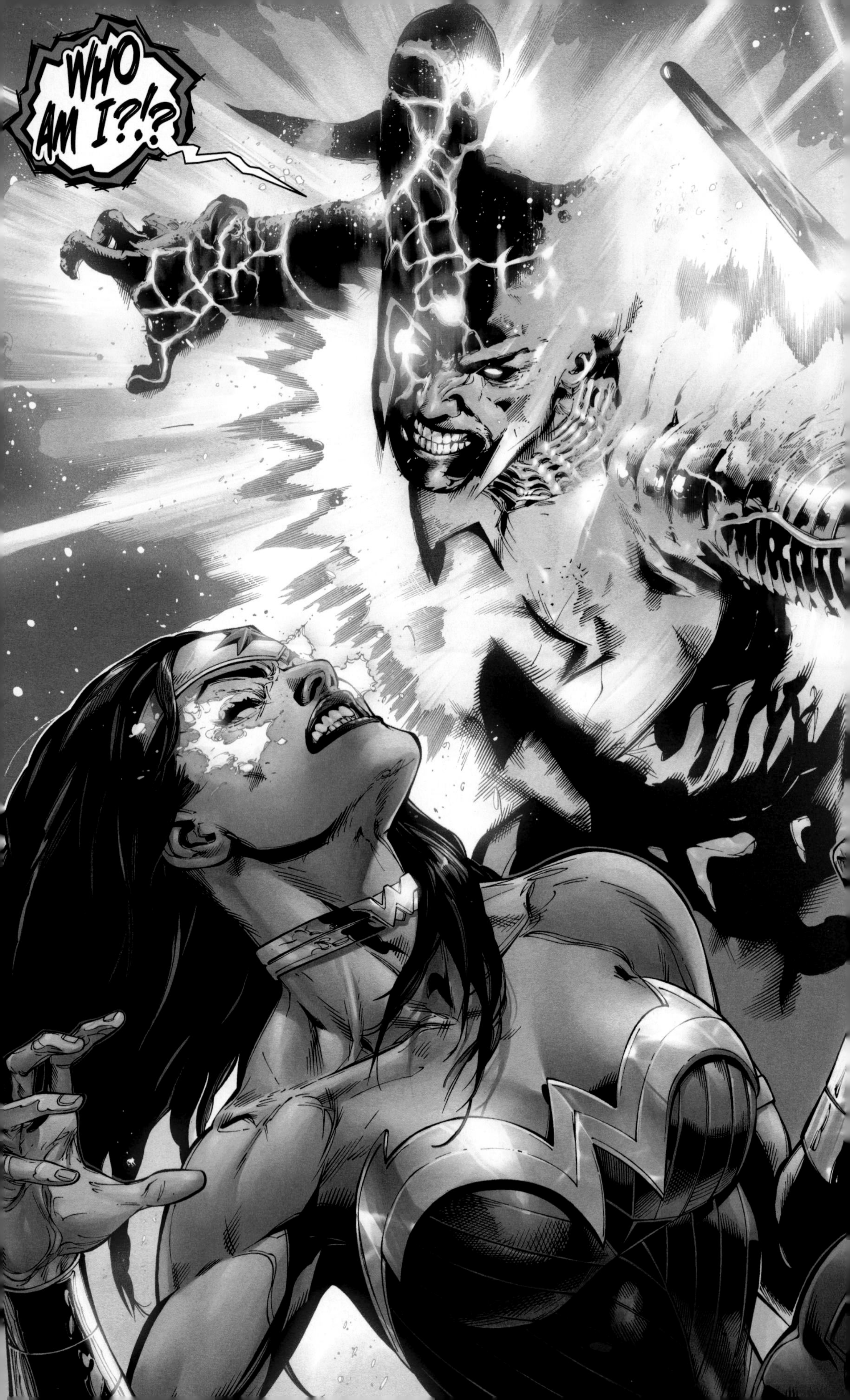
WHO AM I?!?

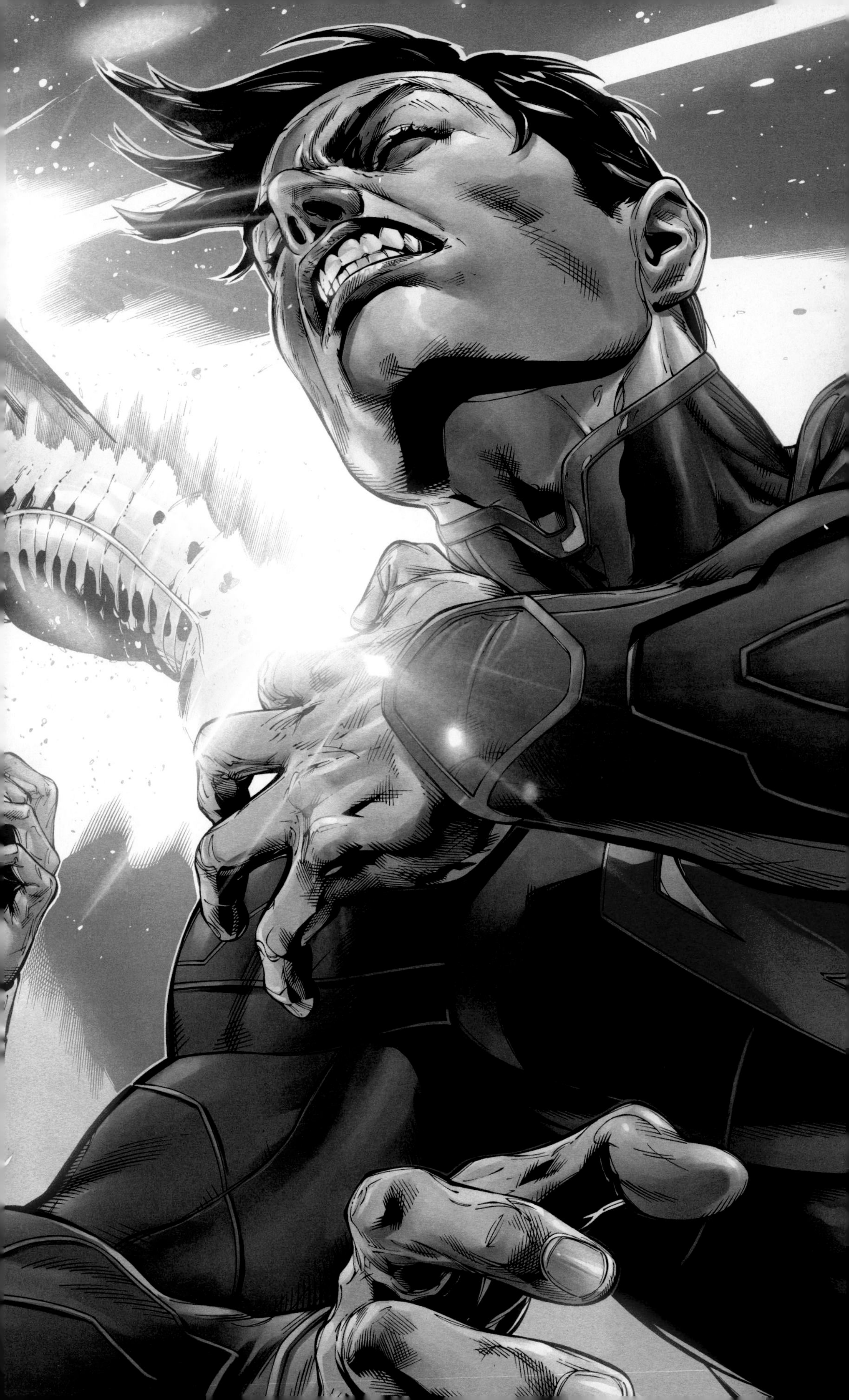

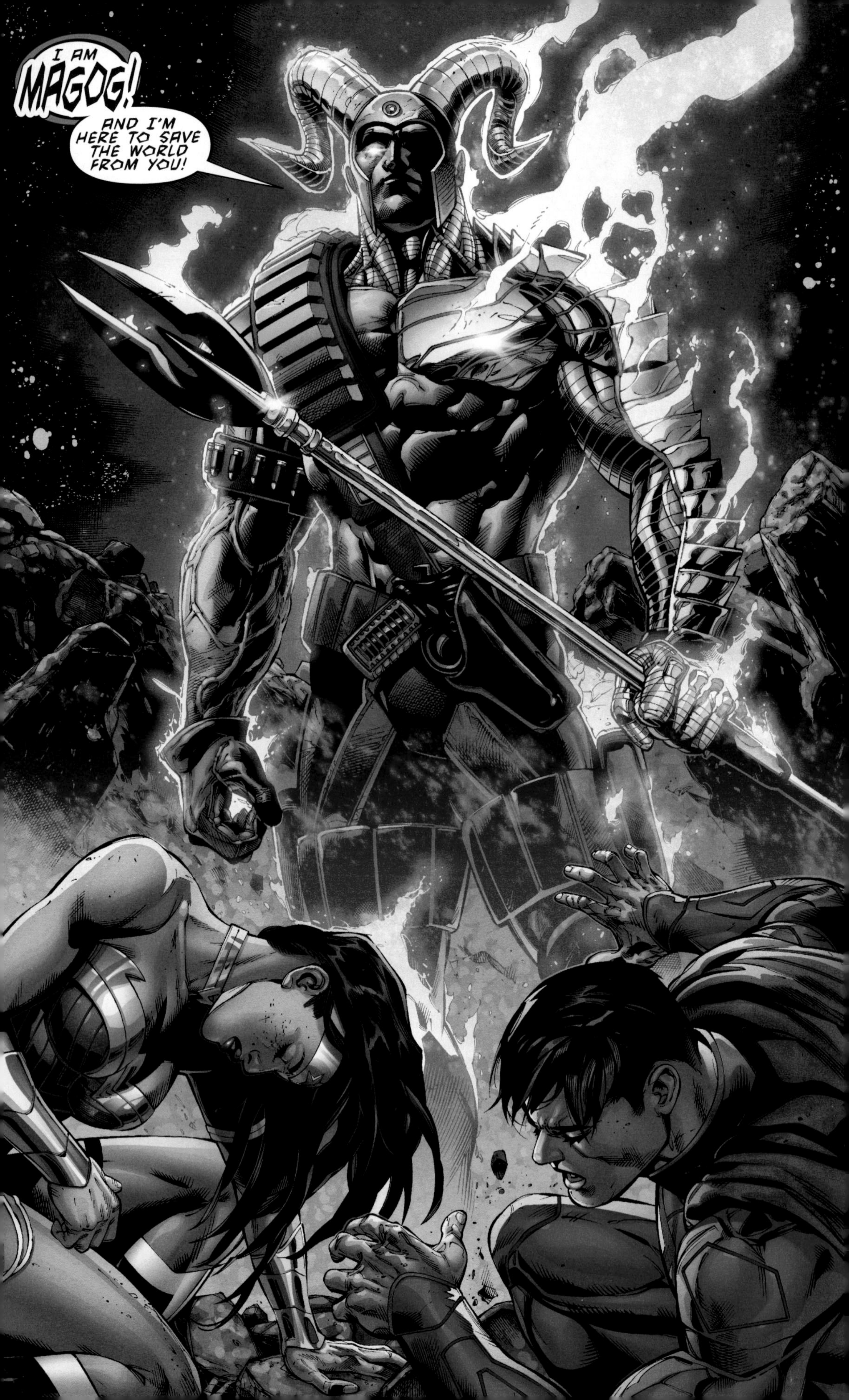
I AM MAGOG!
AND I'M HERE TO SAVE THE WORLD FROM YOU!

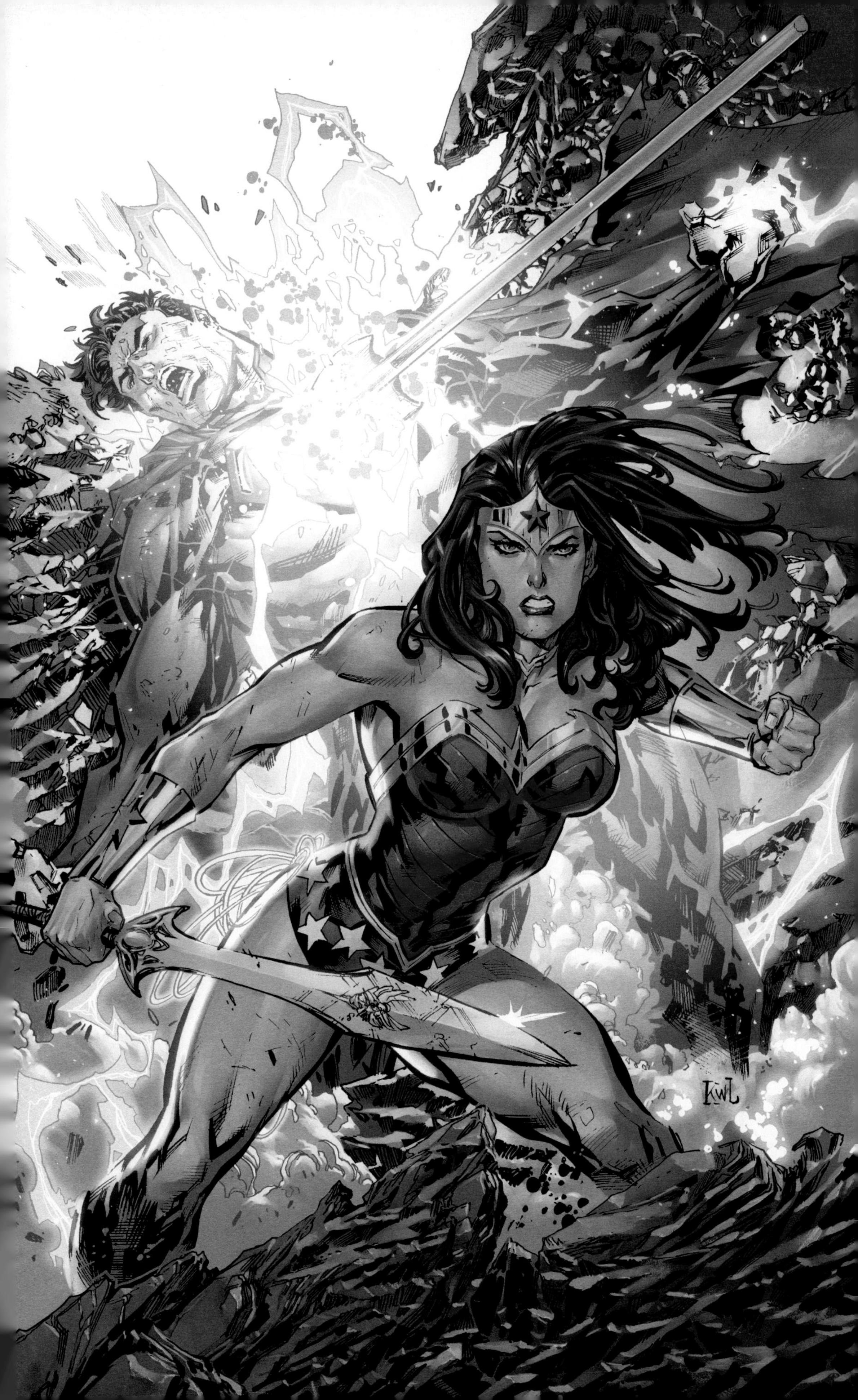

DARK TESTAMENT

PETER J. TOMASI writer ED BENES DOUG MAHNKE pencillers JAIME MENDOZA MARK IRWIN DON HO inkers TOMEU MOREY MARCELO MAIOLO PETE PANTAZIS colorists TAYLOR ESPOSITO letterer cover by KEN LASHLEY & MOREY

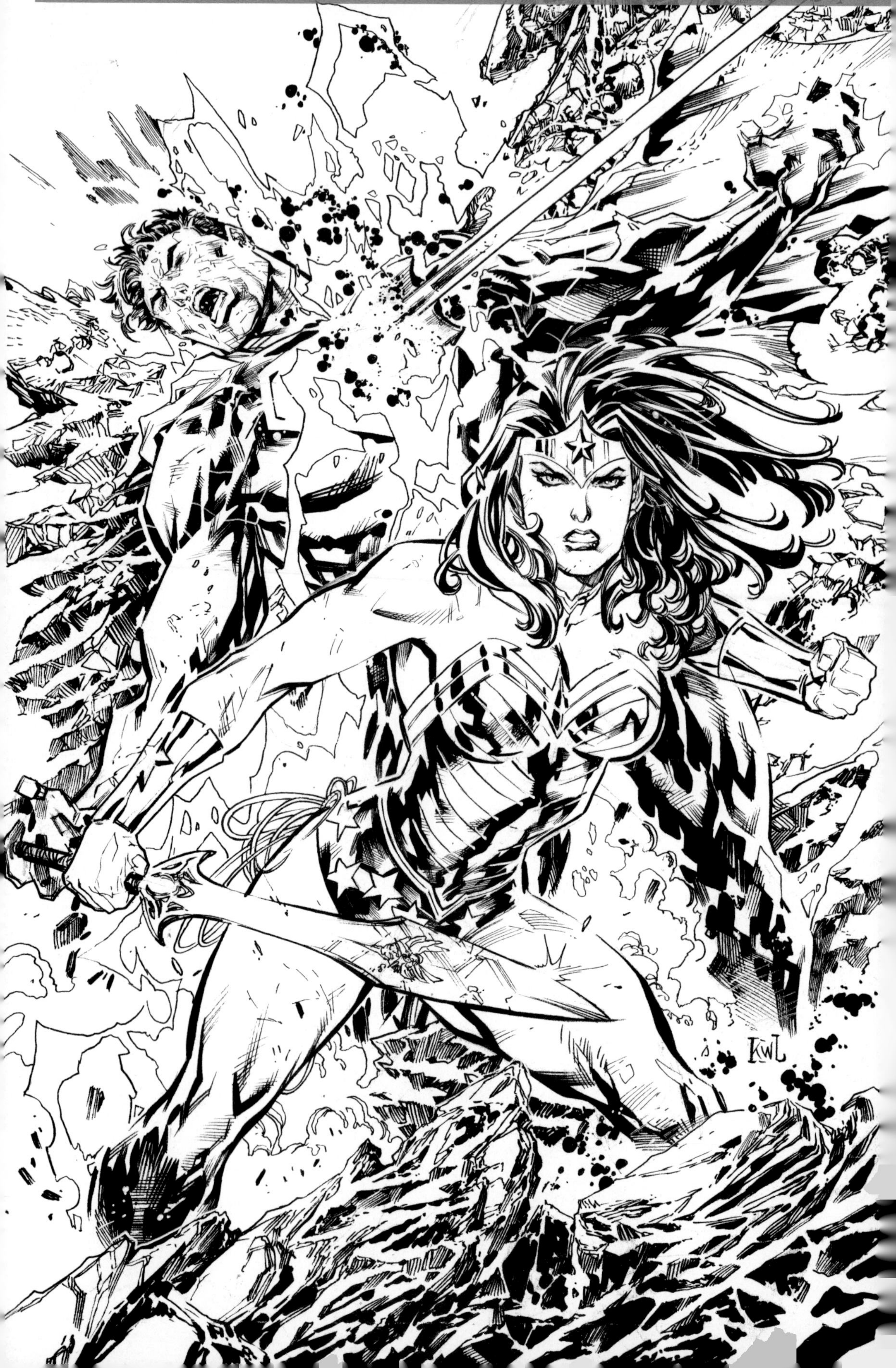

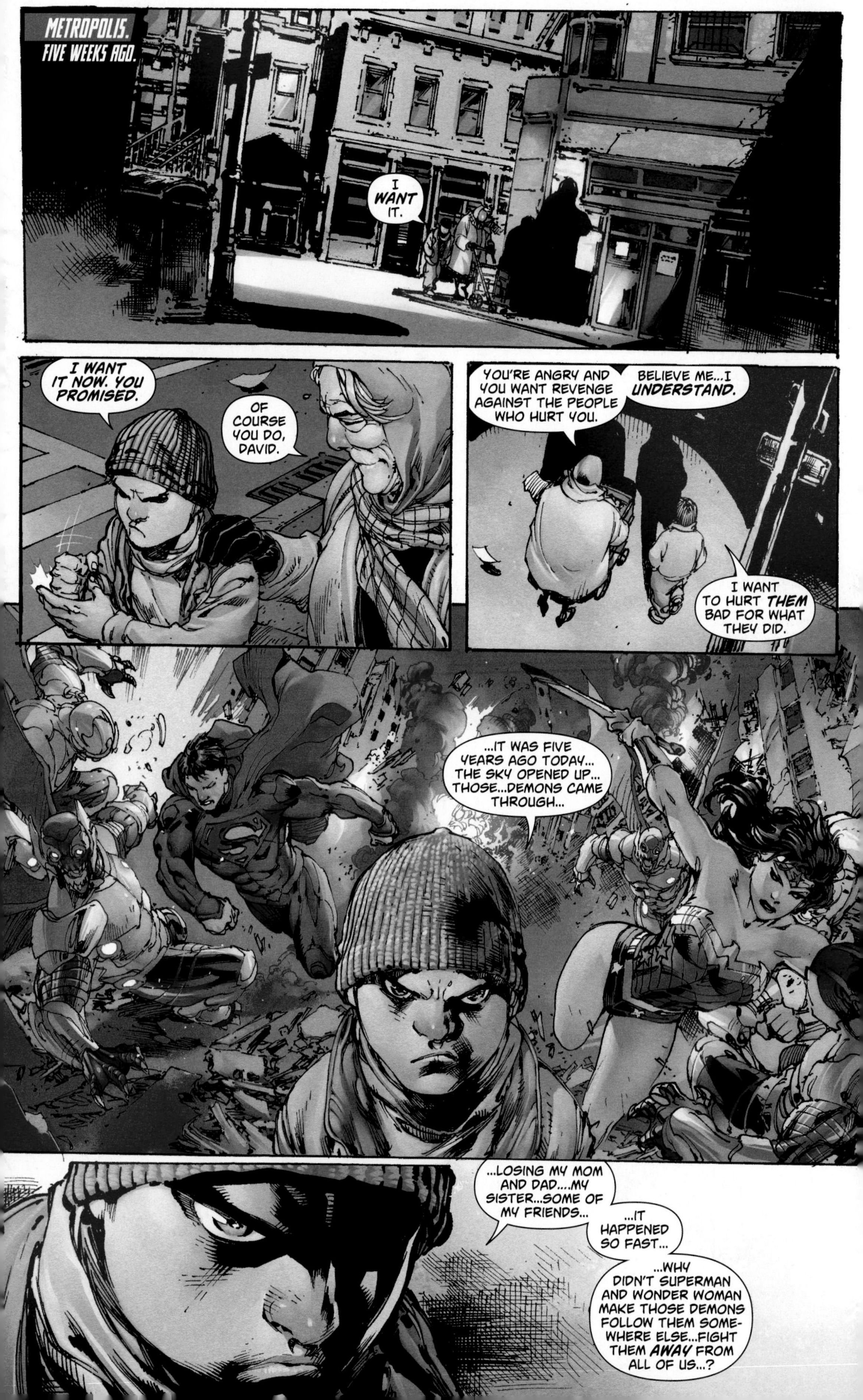

METROPOLIS.
FIVE WEEKS AGO.
I WANT IT.
I WANT IT NOW. YOU PROMISED.
OF COURSE YOU DO, DAVID.
YOU'RE ANGRY AND YOU WANT REVENGE AGAINST THE PEOPLE WHO HURT YOU.
BELIEVE ME...I UNDERSTAND.
I WANT TO HURT THEM BAD FOR WHAT THEY DID.
...IT WAS FIVE YEARS AGO TODAY... THE SKY OPENED UP... THOSE...DEMONS CAME THROUGH...
...LOSING MY MOM AND DAD....MY SISTER...SOME OF MY FRIENDS...
...IT HAPPENED SO FAST...
...WHY DIDN'T SUPERMAN AND WONDER WOMAN MAKE THOSE DEMONS FOLLOW THEM SOME-WHERE ELSE...FIGHT THEM AWAY FROM ALL OF US...?

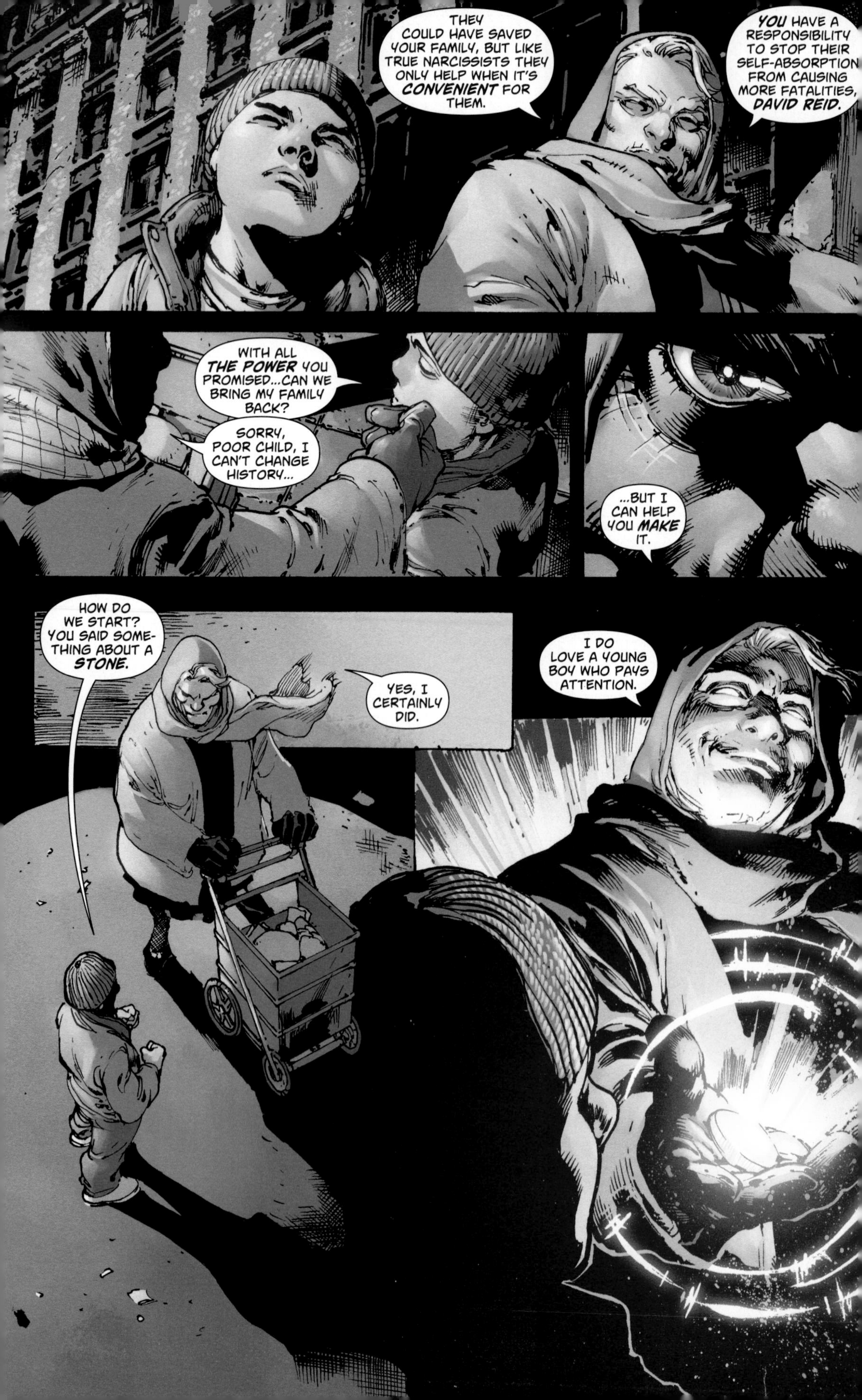

THEY COULD HAVE SAVED YOUR FAMILY, BUT LIKE TRUE NARCISSISTS THEY ONLY HELP WHEN IT'S CONVENIENT FOR THEM.
YOU HAVE A RESPONSIBILITY TO STOP THEIR SELF-ABSORPTION FROM CAUSING MORE FATALITIES, DAVID REID.
WITH ALL THE POWER YOU PROMISED...CAN WE BRING MY FAMILY BACK?
SORRY, POOR CHILD, I CAN'T CHANGE HISTORY...
...BUT I CAN HELP YOU MAKE IT.
HOW DO WE START? YOU SAID SOMETHING ABOUT A STONE.
YES, I CERTAINLY DID.
I DO LOVE A YOUNG BOY WHO PAYS ATTENTION.

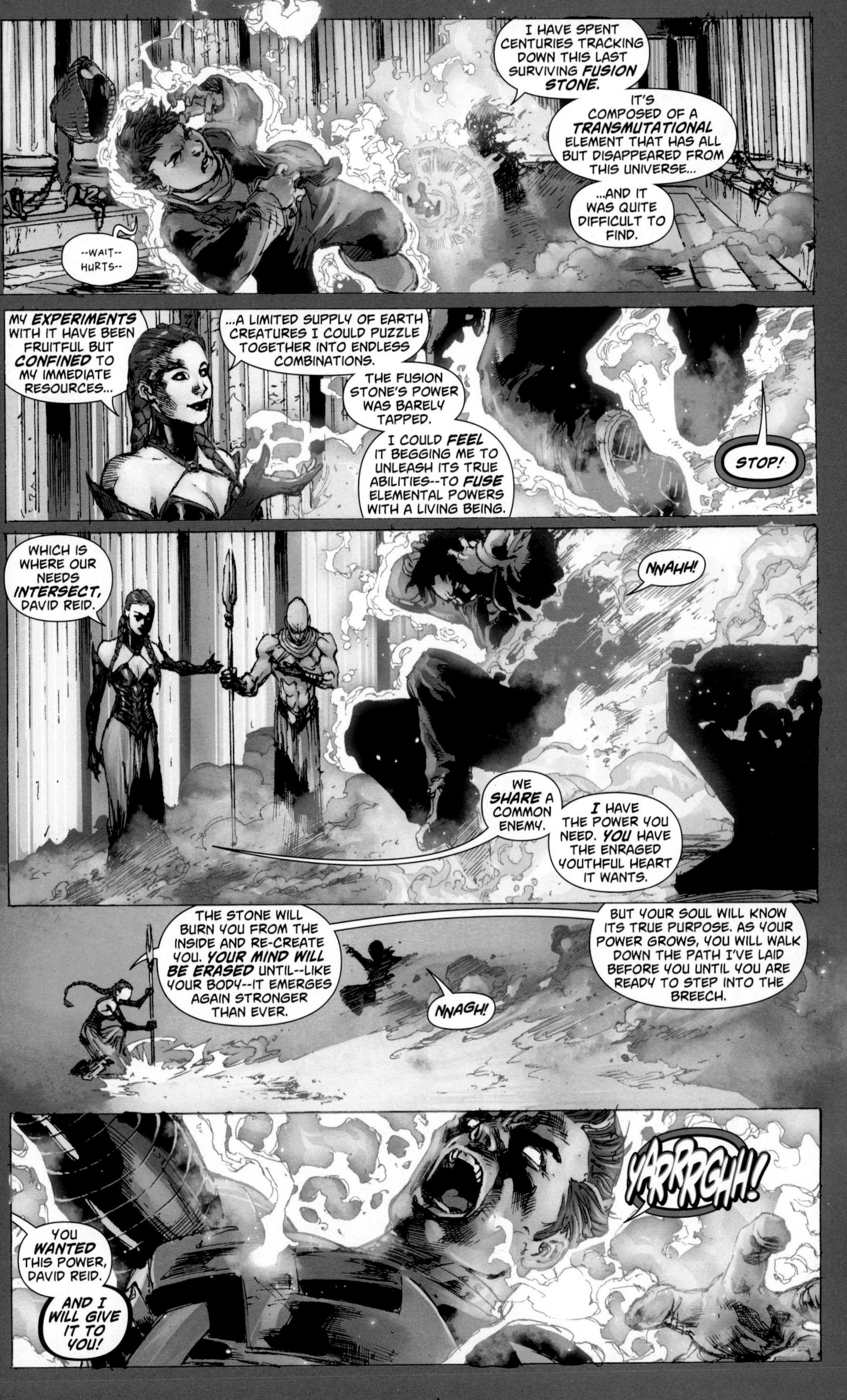
I HAVE SPENT CENTURIES TRACKING DOWN THIS LAST SURVIVING FUSION STONE.
IT'S COMPOSED OF A TRANSMUTATIONAL ELEMENT THAT HAS ALL BUT DISAPPEARED FROM THIS UNIVERSE...
...AND IT WAS QUITE DIFFICULT TO FIND.
--WAIT-- HURTS--
MY EXPERIMENTS WITH IT HAVE BEEN FRUITFUL BUT CONFINED TO MY IMMEDIATE RESOURCES...
...A LIMITED SUPPLY OF EARTH CREATURES I COULD PUZZLE TOGETHER INTO ENDLESS COMBINATIONS.
THE FUSION STONE'S POWER WAS BARELY TAPPED.
I COULD FEEL IT BEGGING ME TO UNLEASH ITS TRUE ABILITIES--TO FUSE ELEMENTAL POWERS WITH A LIVING BEING.
STOP!
WHICH IS WHERE OUR NEEDS INTERSECT, DAVID REID.
NNAHH!
WE SHARE A COMMON ENEMY.
I HAVE THE POWER YOU NEED. YOU HAVE THE ENRAGED YOUTHFUL HEART IT WANTS.
THE STONE WILL BURN YOU FROM THE INSIDE AND RE-CREATE YOU. YOUR MIND WILL BE ERASED UNTIL--LIKE YOUR BODY--IT EMERGES AGAIN STRONGER THAN EVER.
NNAGH!
BUT YOUR SOUL WILL KNOW ITS TRUE PURPOSE. AS YOUR POWER GROWS, YOU WILL WALK DOWN THE PATH I'VE LAID BEFORE YOU UNTIL YOU ARE READY TO STEP INTO THE BREECH.
YARRRGHH!
YOU WANTED THIS POWER, DAVID REID.
AND I WILL GIVE IT TO YOU!

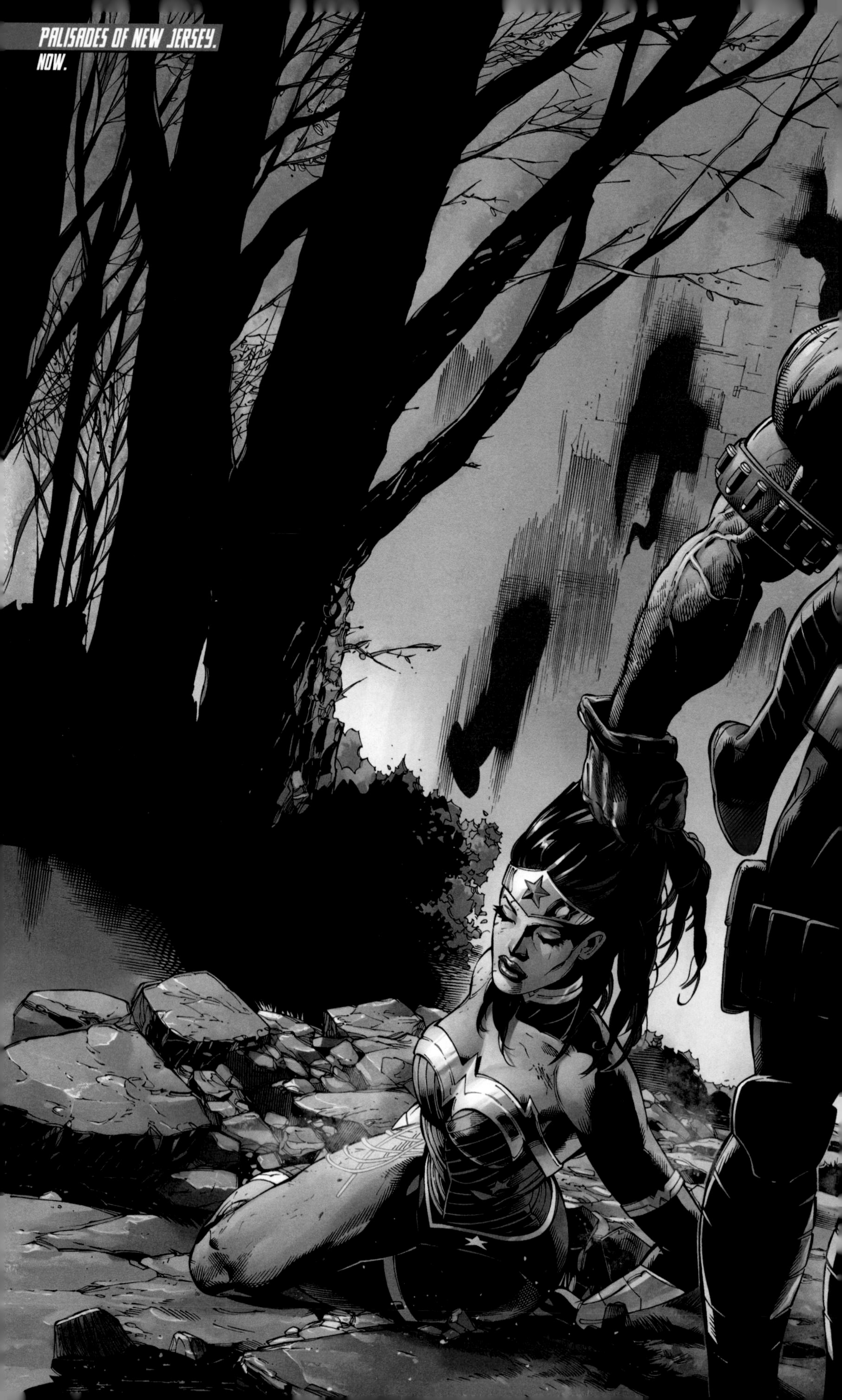
PALISADES OF NEW JERSEY.
NOW.

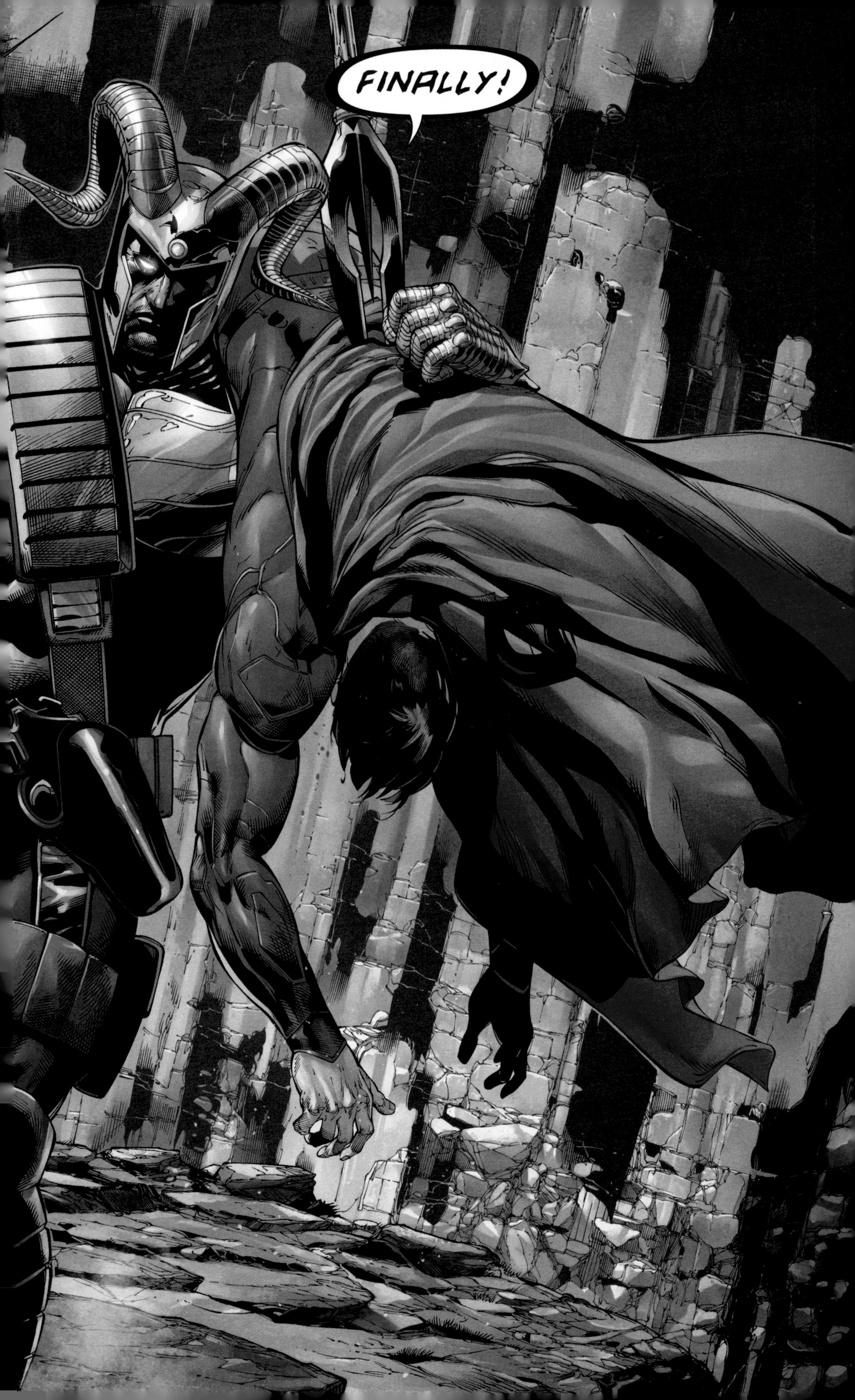
FINALLY!

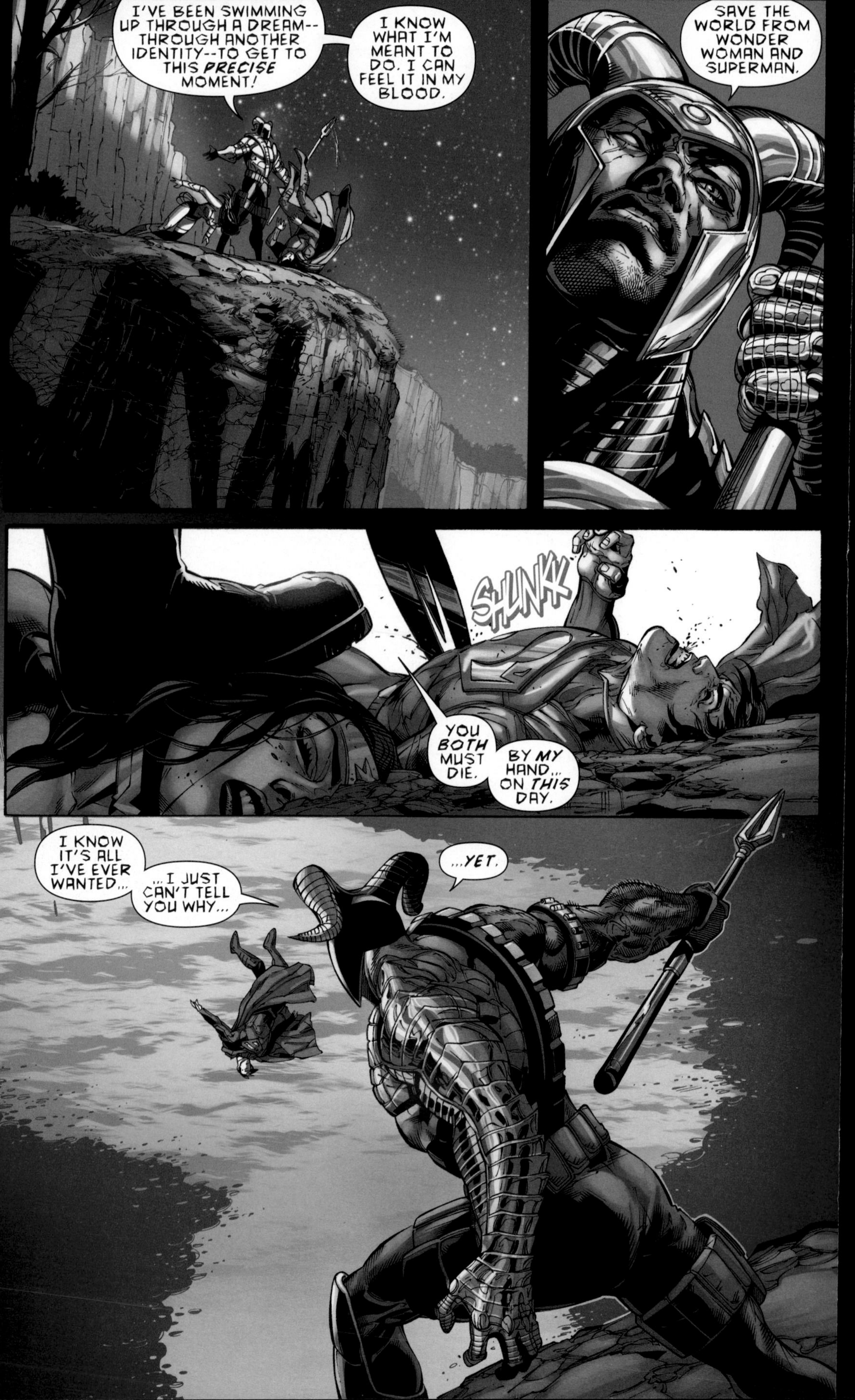
I'VE BEEN SWIMMING UP THROUGH A DREAM--THROUGH ANOTHER IDENTITY--TO GET TO THIS PRECISE MOMENT!
I KNOW WHAT I'M MEANT TO DO. I CAN FEEL IT IN MY BLOOD.
SAVE THE WORLD FROM WONDER WOMAN AND SUPERMAN.
SHUNK!
YOU BOTH MUST DIE.
BY MY HAND... ON THIS DAY.
I KNOW IT'S ALL I'VE EVER WANTED...
...I JUST CAN'T TELL YOU WHY...
...YET.

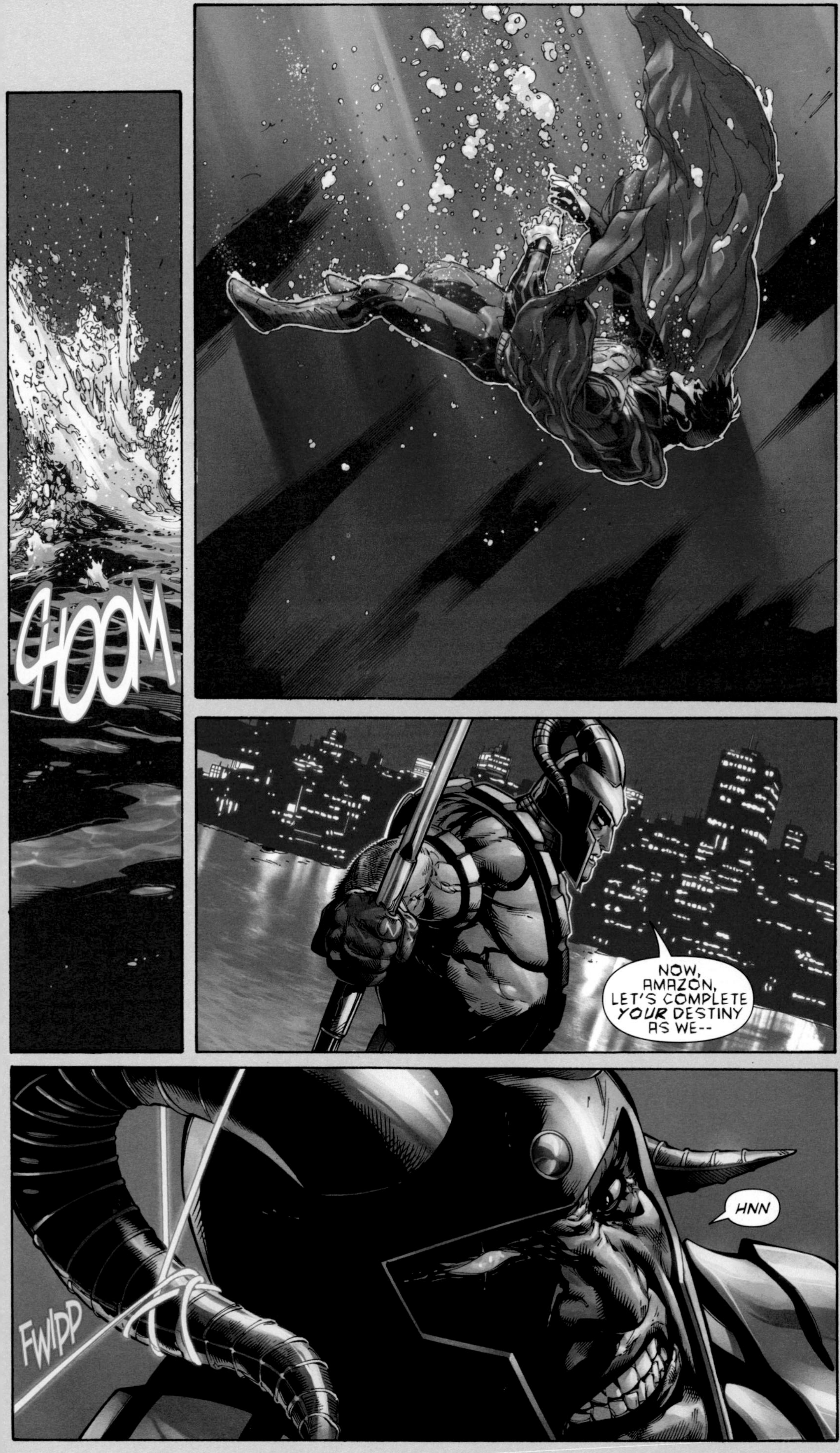
CHOOM
NOW, AMAZON, LET'S COMPLETE *YOUR* DESTINY AS WE--
HNN
FWIPP

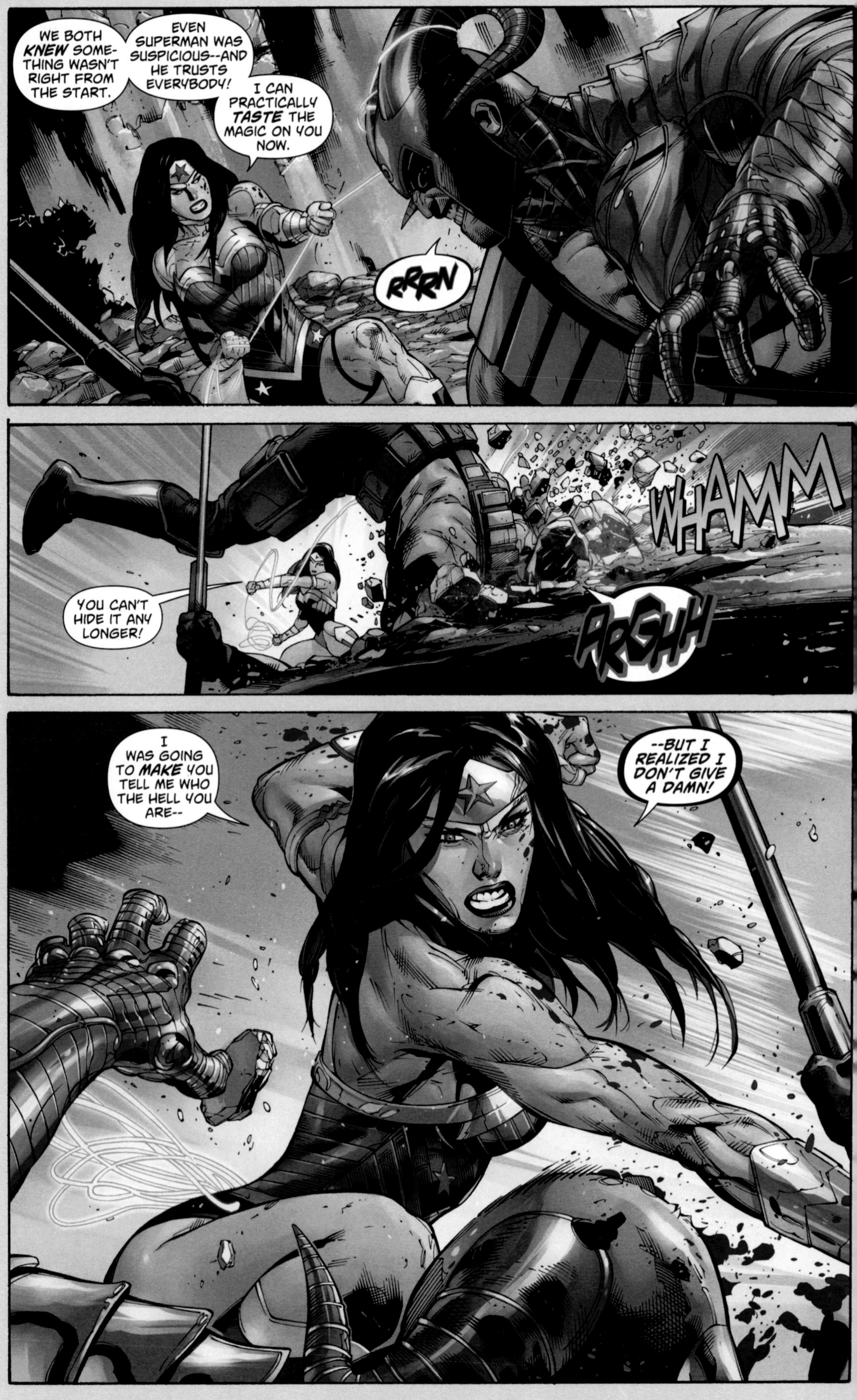
WE BOTH KNEW SOMETHING WASN'T RIGHT FROM THE START.
EVEN SUPERMAN WAS SUSPICIOUS--AND HE TRUSTS EVERYBODY!
I CAN PRACTICALLY TASTE THE MAGIC ON YOU NOW.
RRRN
WHAMM
YOU CAN'T HIDE IT ANY LONGER!
ARGHH
I WAS GOING TO MAKE YOU TELL ME WHO THE HELL YOU ARE--
--BUT I REALIZED I DON'T GIVE A DAMN!

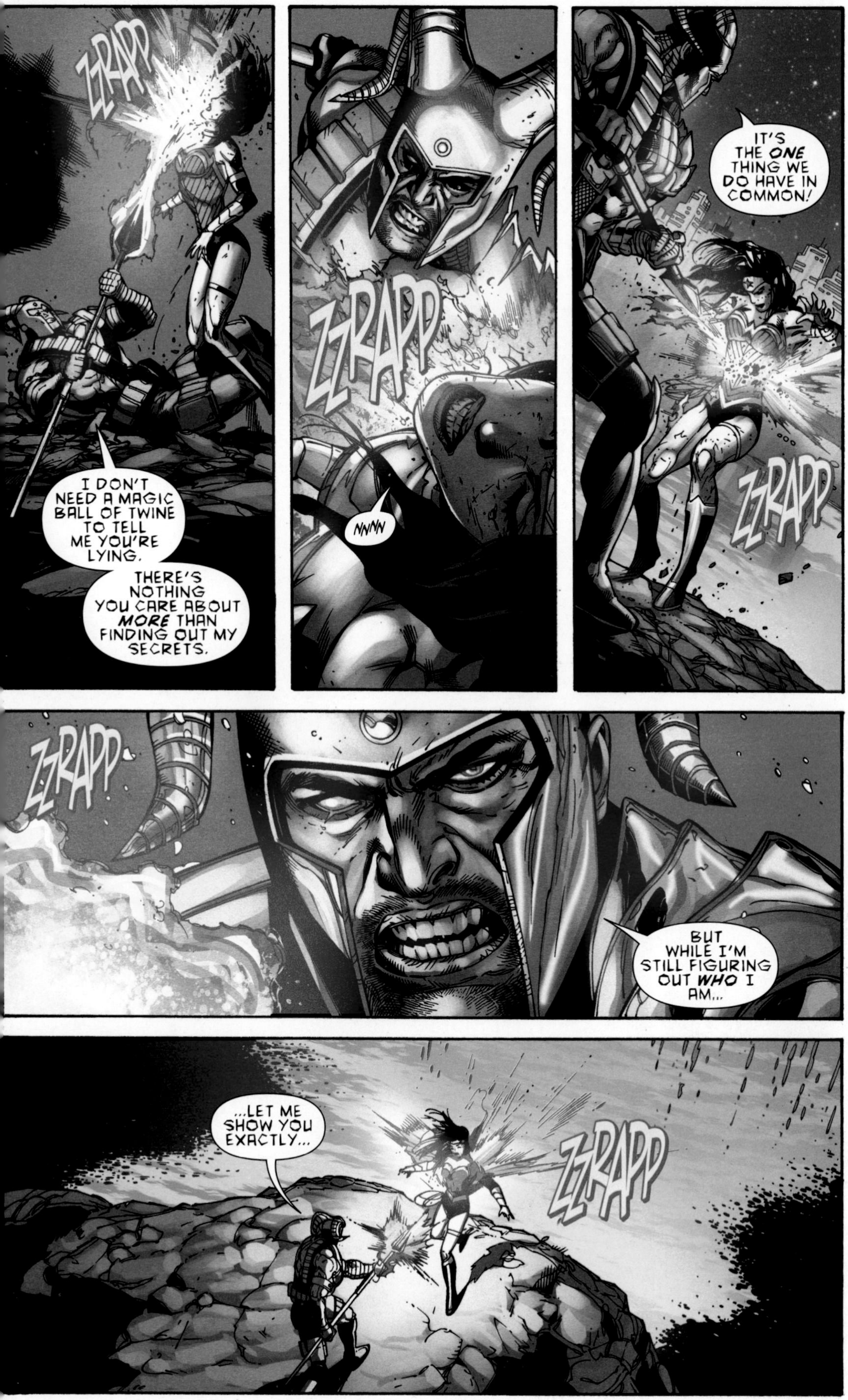
ZZRAPP
I DON'T NEED A MAGIC BALL OF TWINE TO TELL ME YOU'RE LYING.
THERE'S NOTHING YOU CARE ABOUT MORE THAN FINDING OUT MY SECRETS.
ZZRAPP
NNNN
IT'S THE ONE THING WE DO HAVE IN COMMON!
ZZRAPP
ZZRAPP
BUT WHILE I'M STILL FIGURING OUT WHO I AM...
...LET ME SHOW YOU EXACTLY...
ZZRAPP

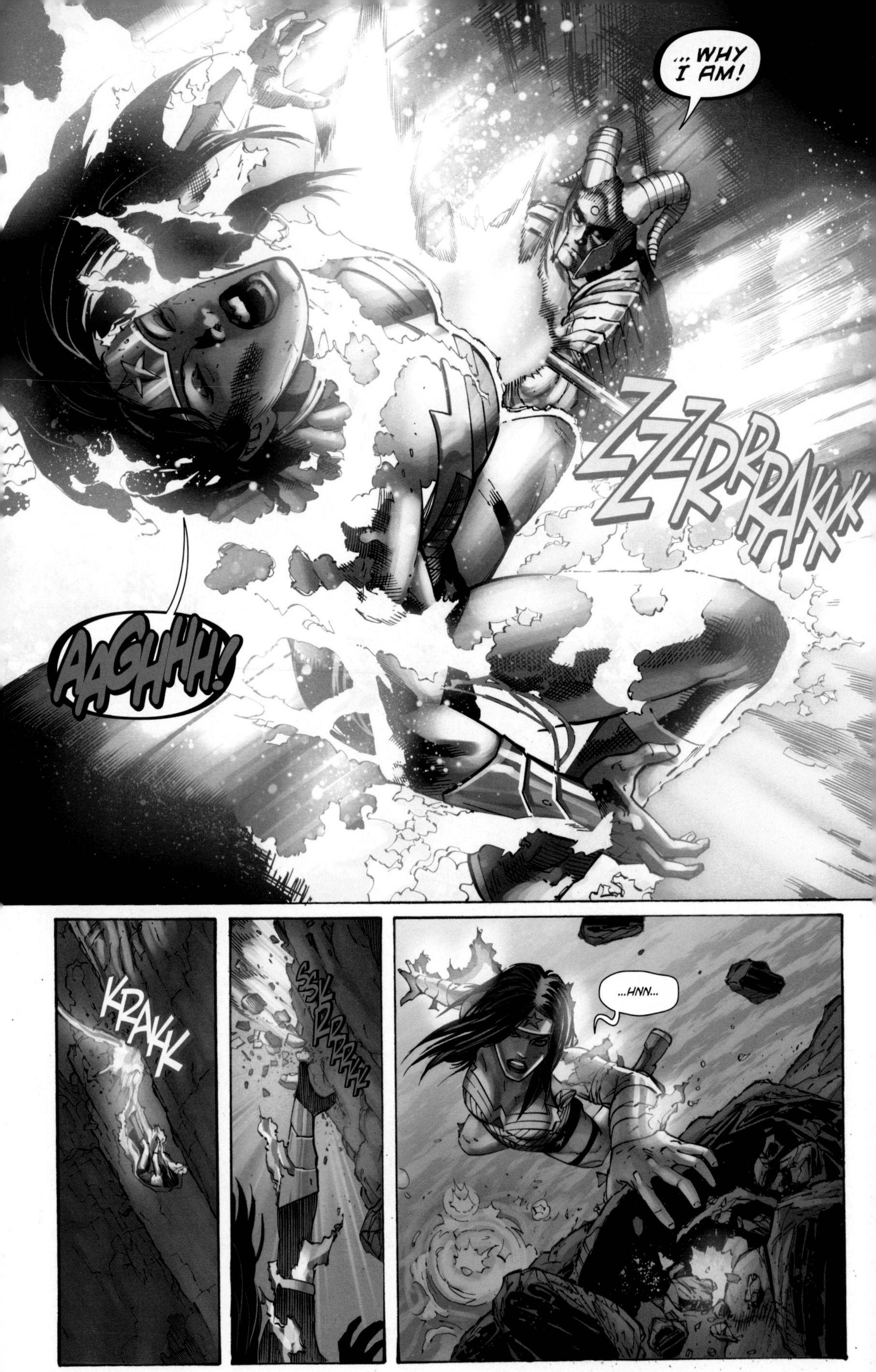
...WHY I AM!
ZZZRRRAKKK
AAGHHH!
KRAKKK
SSKRRRAKK
...HNN...

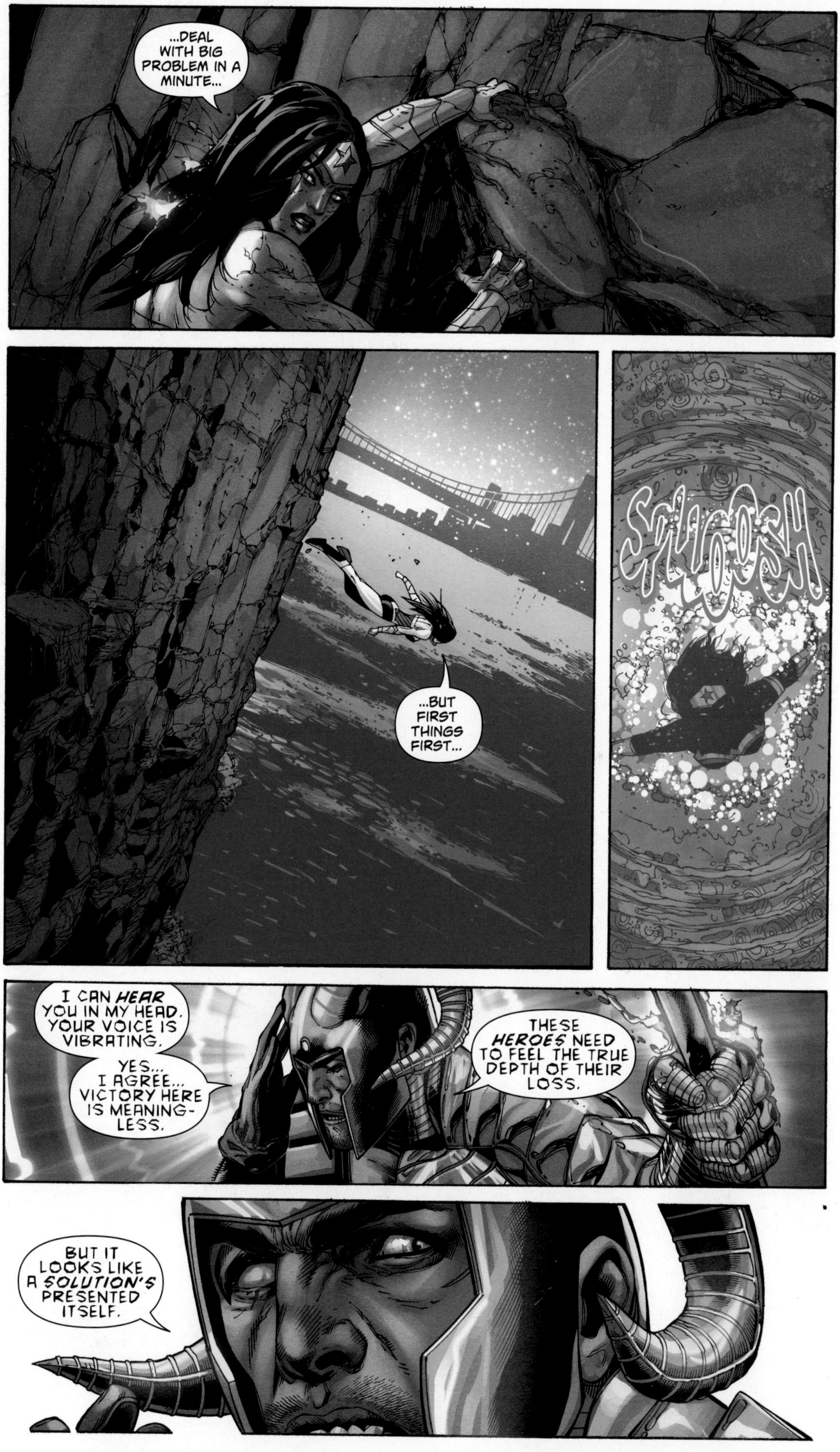
...DEAL WITH BIG PROBLEM IN A MINUTE...
...BUT FIRST THINGS FIRST...
SPLOOSH
I CAN HEAR YOU IN MY HEAD. YOUR VOICE IS VIBRATING.
YES... I AGREE... VICTORY HERE IS MEANING-LESS.
THESE HEROES NEED TO FEEL THE TRUE DEPTH OF THEIR LOSS.
BUT IT LOOKS LIKE A SOLUTION'S PRESENTED ITSELF.

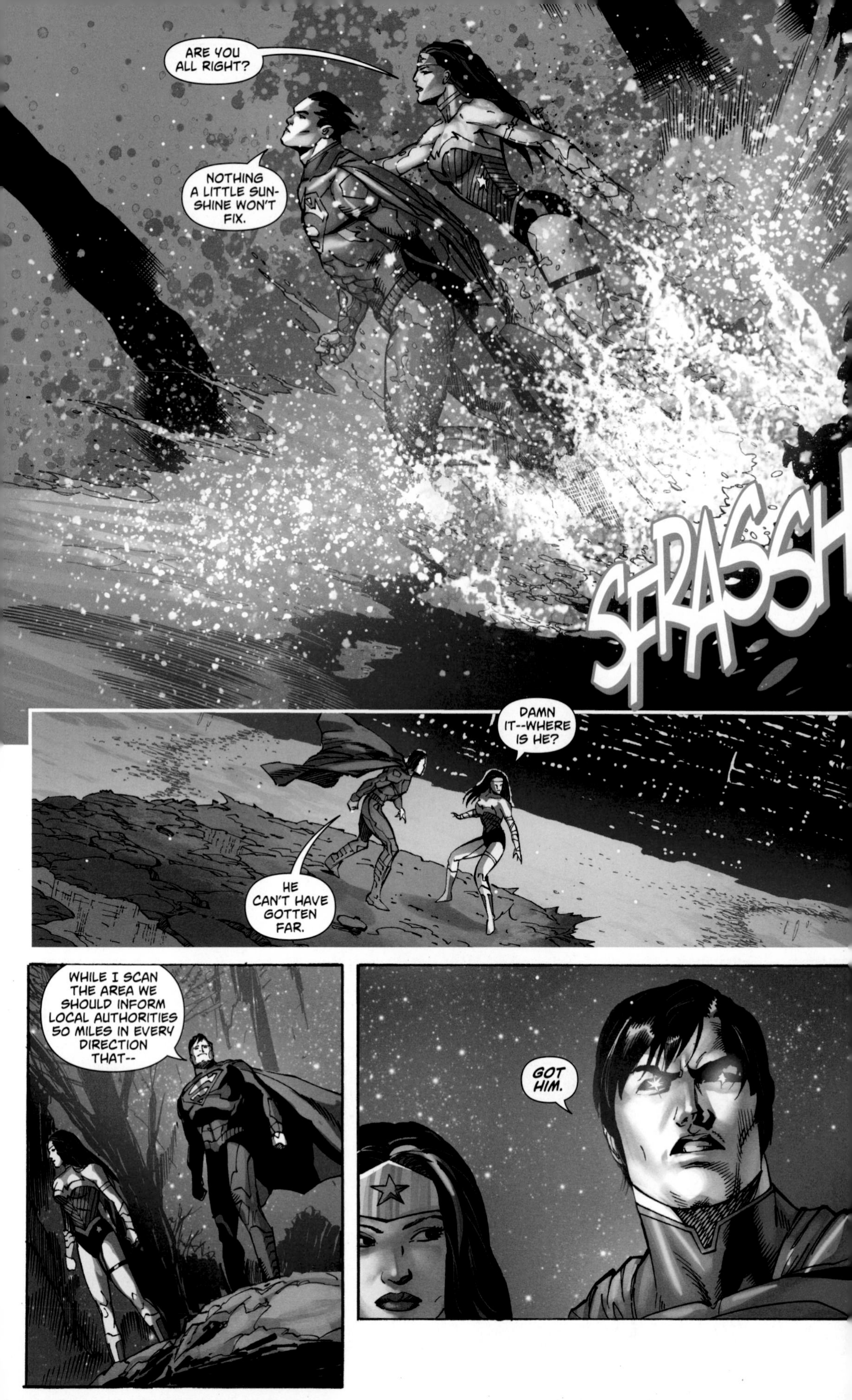

ARE YOU ALL RIGHT?
NOTHING A LITTLE SUN-SHINE WON'T FIX.
SFRASSH
DAMN IT--WHERE IS HE?
HE CAN'T HAVE GOTTEN FAR.
WHILE I SCAN THE AREA WE SHOULD INFORM LOCAL AUTHORITIES 50 MILES IN EVERY DIRECTION THAT--
GOT HIM.

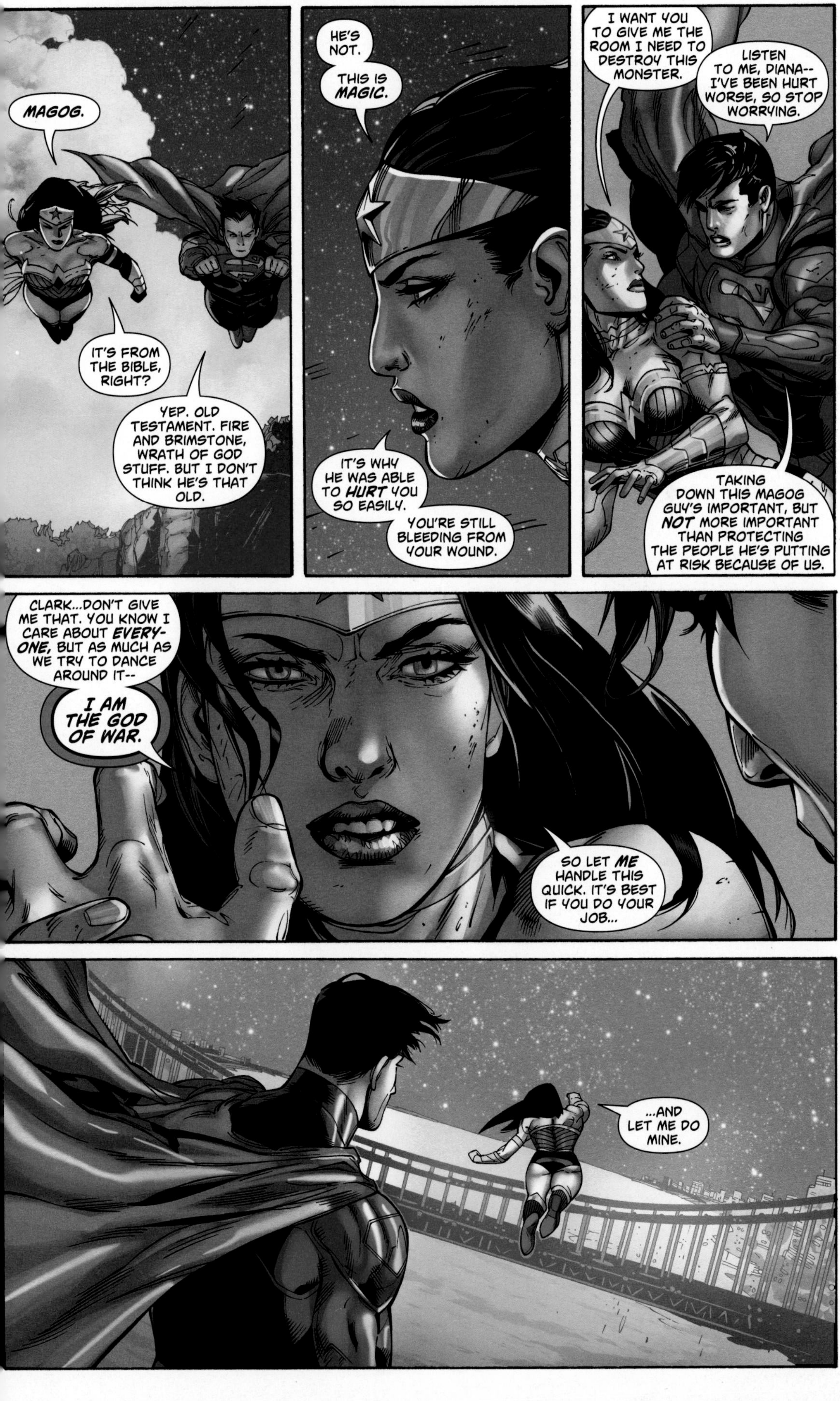
MAGOG.
IT'S FROM THE BIBLE, RIGHT?
YEP. OLD TESTAMENT. FIRE AND BRIMSTONE, WRATH OF GOD STUFF. BUT I DON'T THINK HE'S THAT OLD.
HE'S NOT.
THIS IS MAGIC.
IT'S WHY HE WAS ABLE TO HURT YOU SO EASILY.
YOU'RE STILL BLEEDING FROM YOUR WOUND.
I WANT YOU TO GIVE ME THE ROOM I NEED TO DESTROY THIS MONSTER.
LISTEN TO ME, DIANA-- I'VE BEEN HURT WORSE, SO STOP WORRYING.
TAKING DOWN THIS MAGOG GUY'S IMPORTANT, BUT NOT MORE IMPORTANT THAN PROTECTING THE PEOPLE HE'S PUTTING AT RISK BECAUSE OF US.
CLARK...DON'T GIVE ME THAT. YOU KNOW I CARE ABOUT EVERY-ONE, BUT AS MUCH AS WE TRY TO DANCE AROUND IT--
I AM THE GOD OF WAR.
SO LET ME HANDLE THIS QUICK. IT'S BEST IF YOU DO YOUR JOB...
...AND LET ME DO MINE.

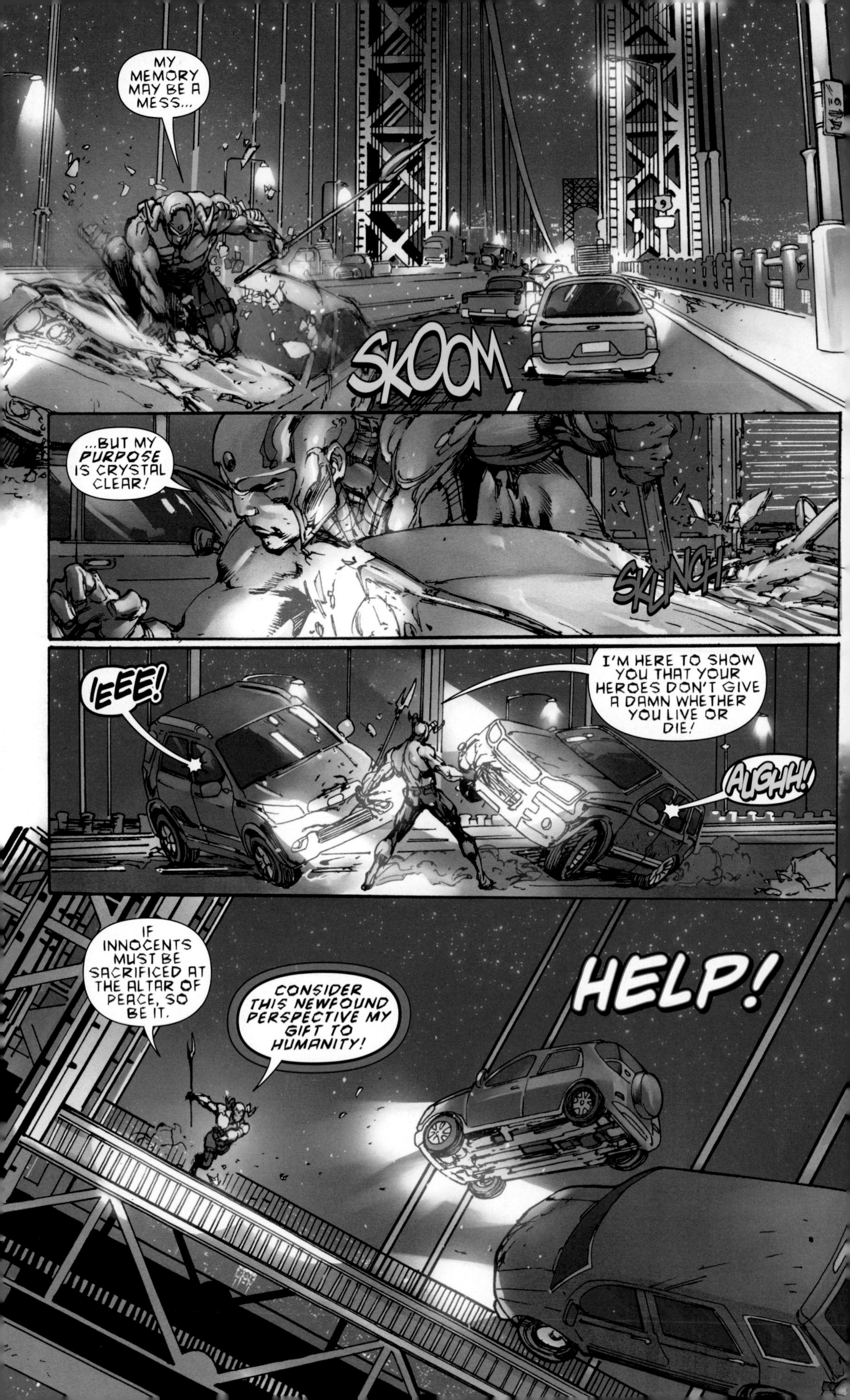
MY MEMORY MAY BE A MESS...
SKOOM
...BUT MY PURPOSE IS CRYSTAL CLEAR!
SKLUNCH
IEEE!
I'M HERE TO SHOW YOU THAT YOUR HEROES DON'T GIVE A DAMN WHETHER YOU LIVE OR DIE!
AUGHH!
IF INNOCENTS MUST BE SACRIFICED AT THE ALTAR OF PEACE, SO BE IT.
CONSIDER THIS NEWFOUND PERSPECTIVE MY GIFT TO HUMANITY!
HELP!

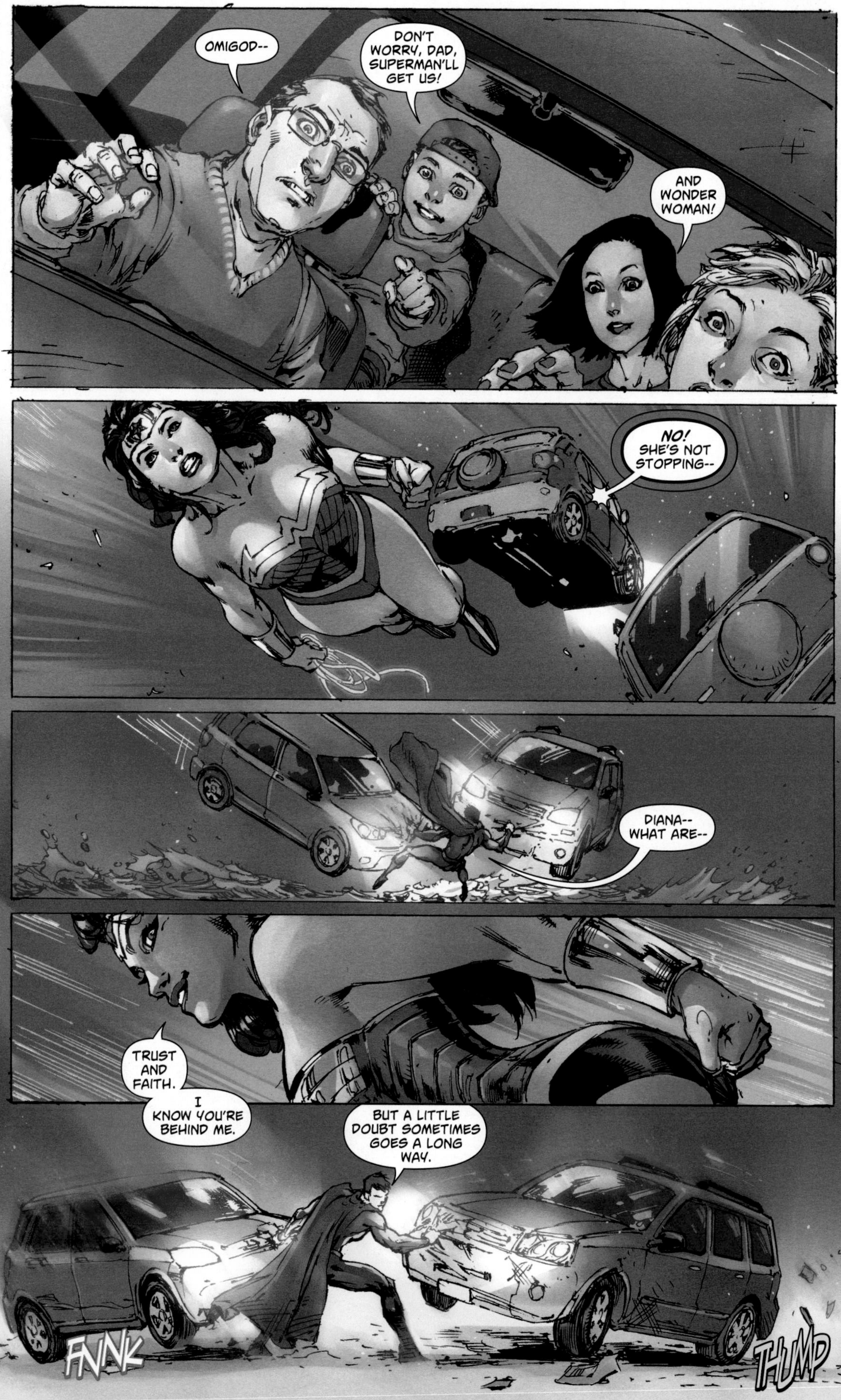
OMIGOD--
DON'T WORRY, DAD, SUPERMAN'LL GET US!
AND WONDER WOMAN!
NO! SHE'S NOT STOPPING--
DIANA-- WHAT ARE--
TRUST AND FAITH.
I KNOW YOU'RE BEHIND ME.
BUT A LITTLE DOUBT SOMETIMES GOES A LONG WAY.
FNNK
THUMP

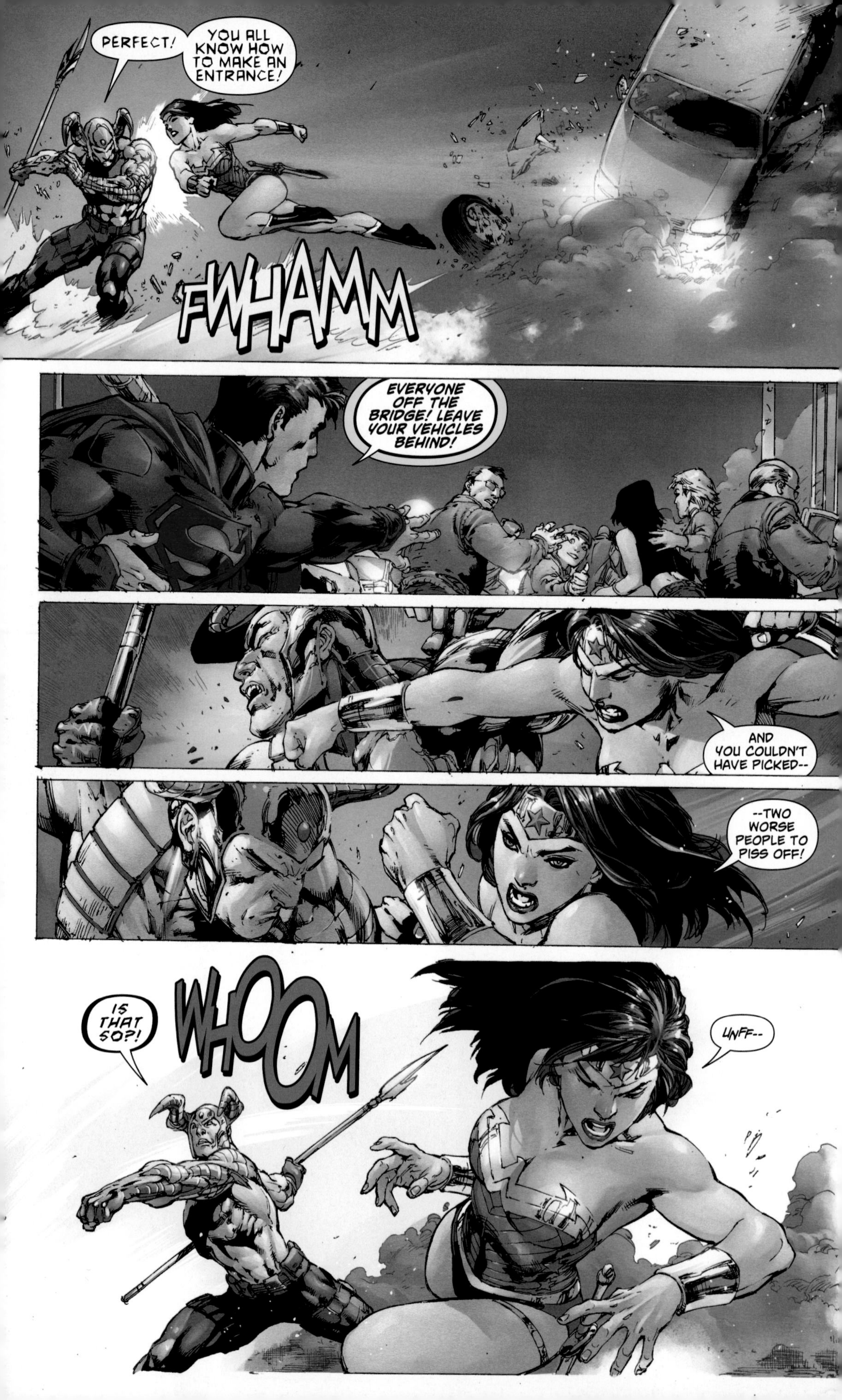
PERFECT!
YOU ALL KNOW HOW TO MAKE AN ENTRANCE!
FWHAMM
EVERYONE OFF THE BRIDGE! LEAVE YOUR VEHICLES BEHIND!
AND YOU COULDN'T HAVE PICKED--
--TWO WORSE PEOPLE TO PISS OFF!
IS THAT SO?!
WHOOM
UNFF--

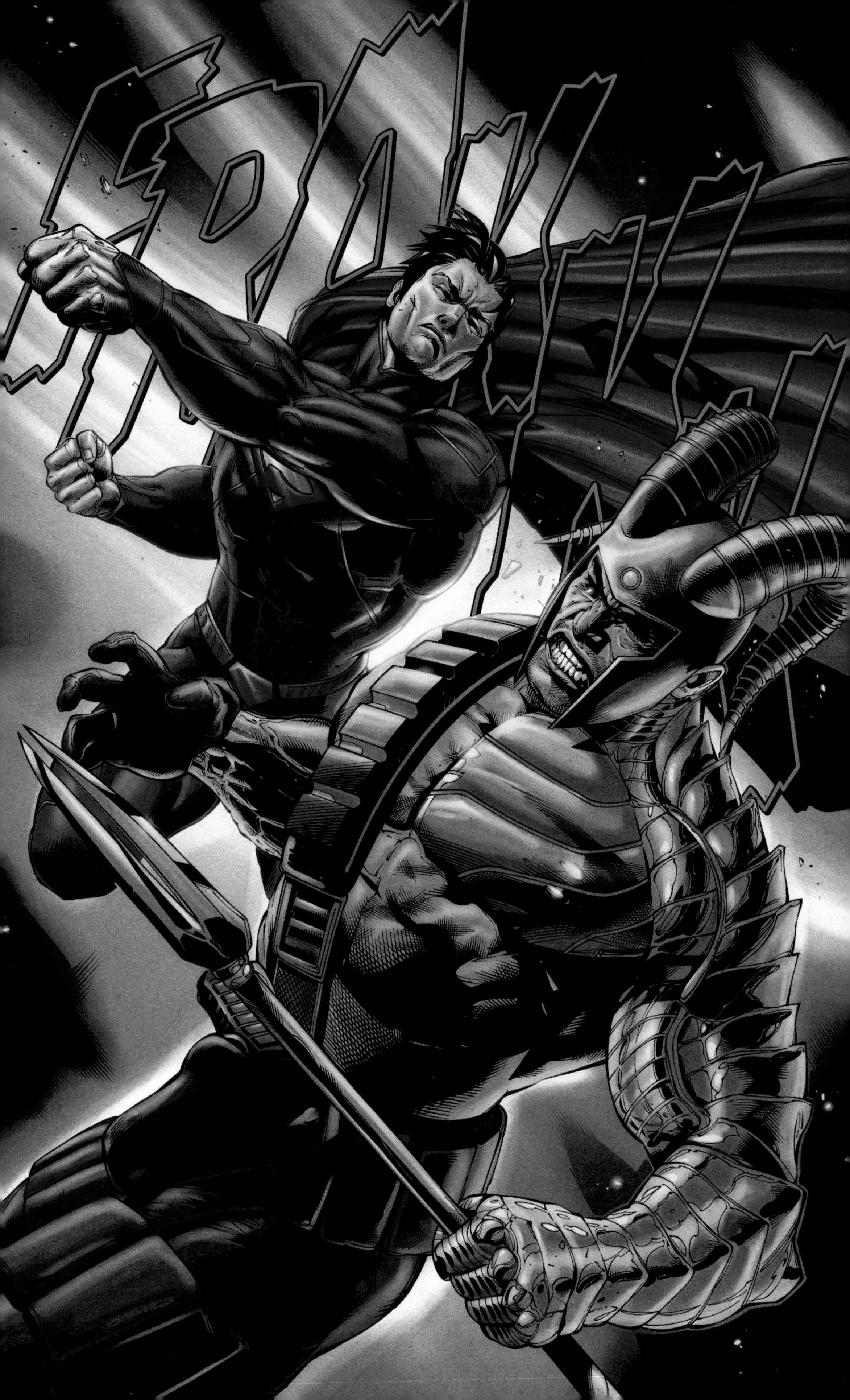

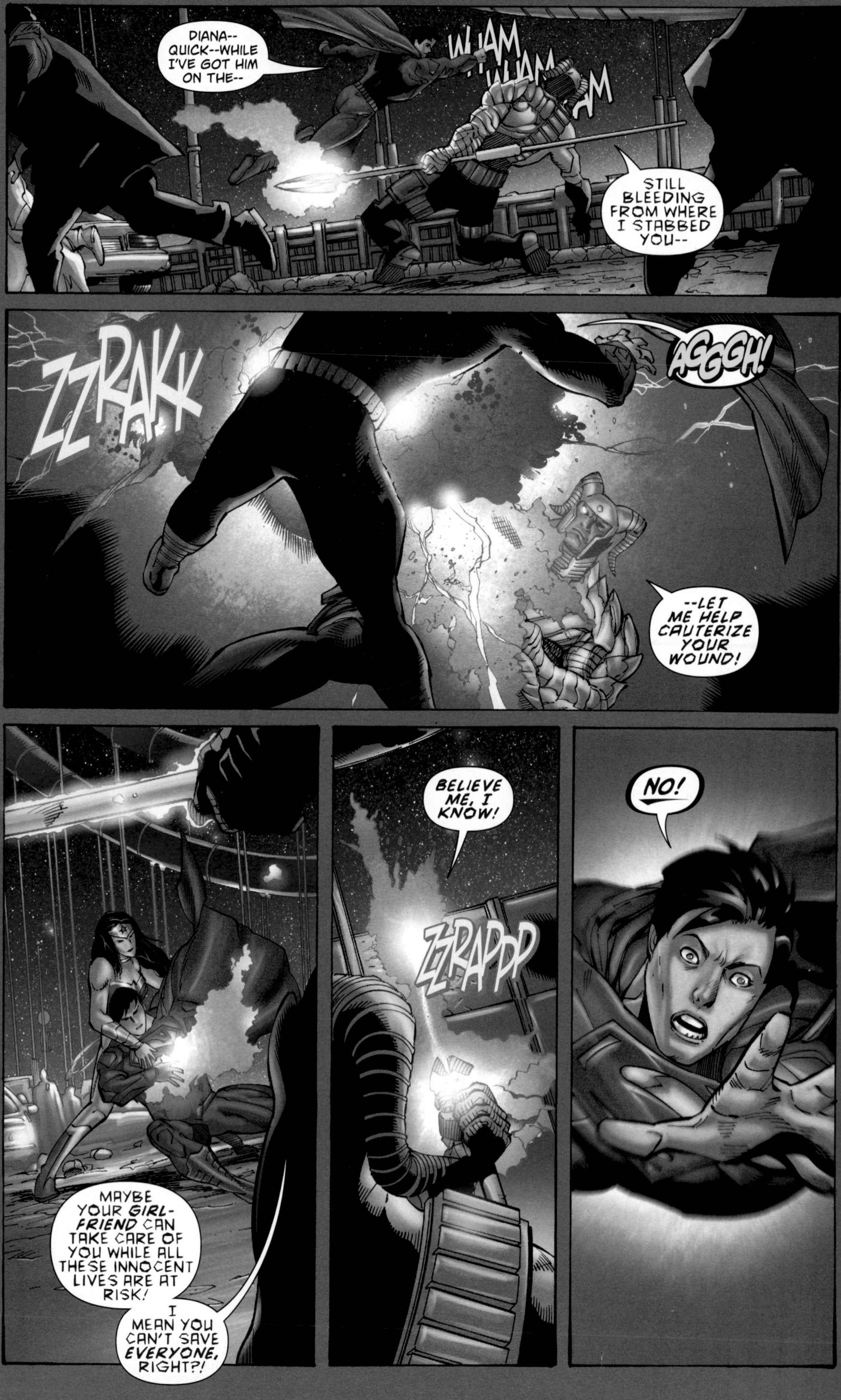
DIANA--
QUICK--WHILE I'VE GOT HIM ON THE--
WHAM
WHAM
WHAM
STILL BLEEDING FROM WHERE I STABBED YOU--
ZZRAKK
AGGGH!
--LET ME HELP CAUTERIZE YOUR WOUND!
MAYBE YOUR GIRL-FRIEND CAN TAKE CARE OF YOU WHILE ALL THESE INNOCENT LIVES ARE AT RISK!
I MEAN YOU CAN'T SAVE EVERYONE, RIGHT?!
BELIEVE ME, I KNOW!
ZZRAPPP
NO!

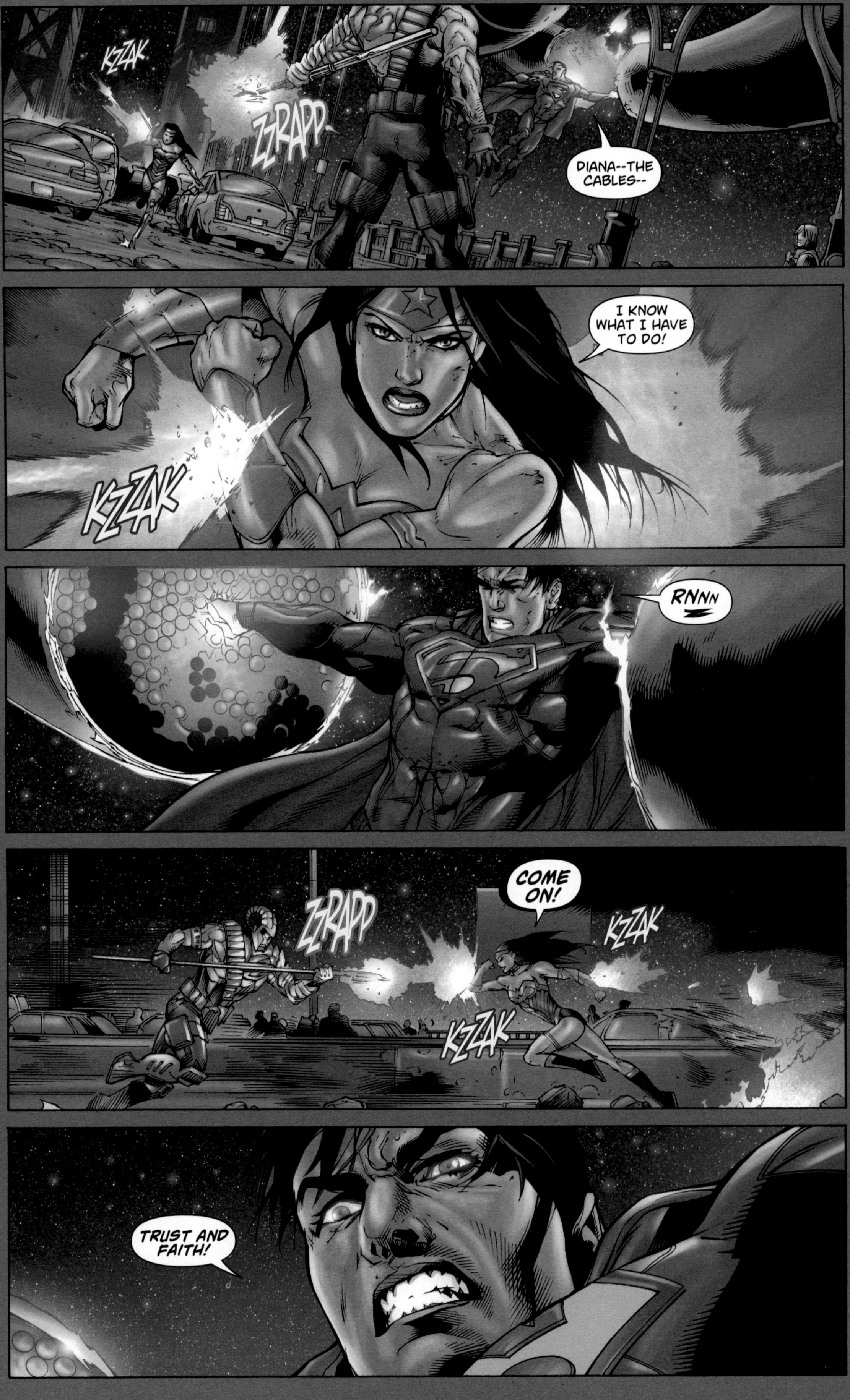
KZZAK
ZZRAPP
DIANA--THE CABLES--
I KNOW WHAT I HAVE TO DO!
KZZAK
RNNN
ZZRAPP
COME ON!
KZZAK
KZZAK
TRUST AND FAITH!

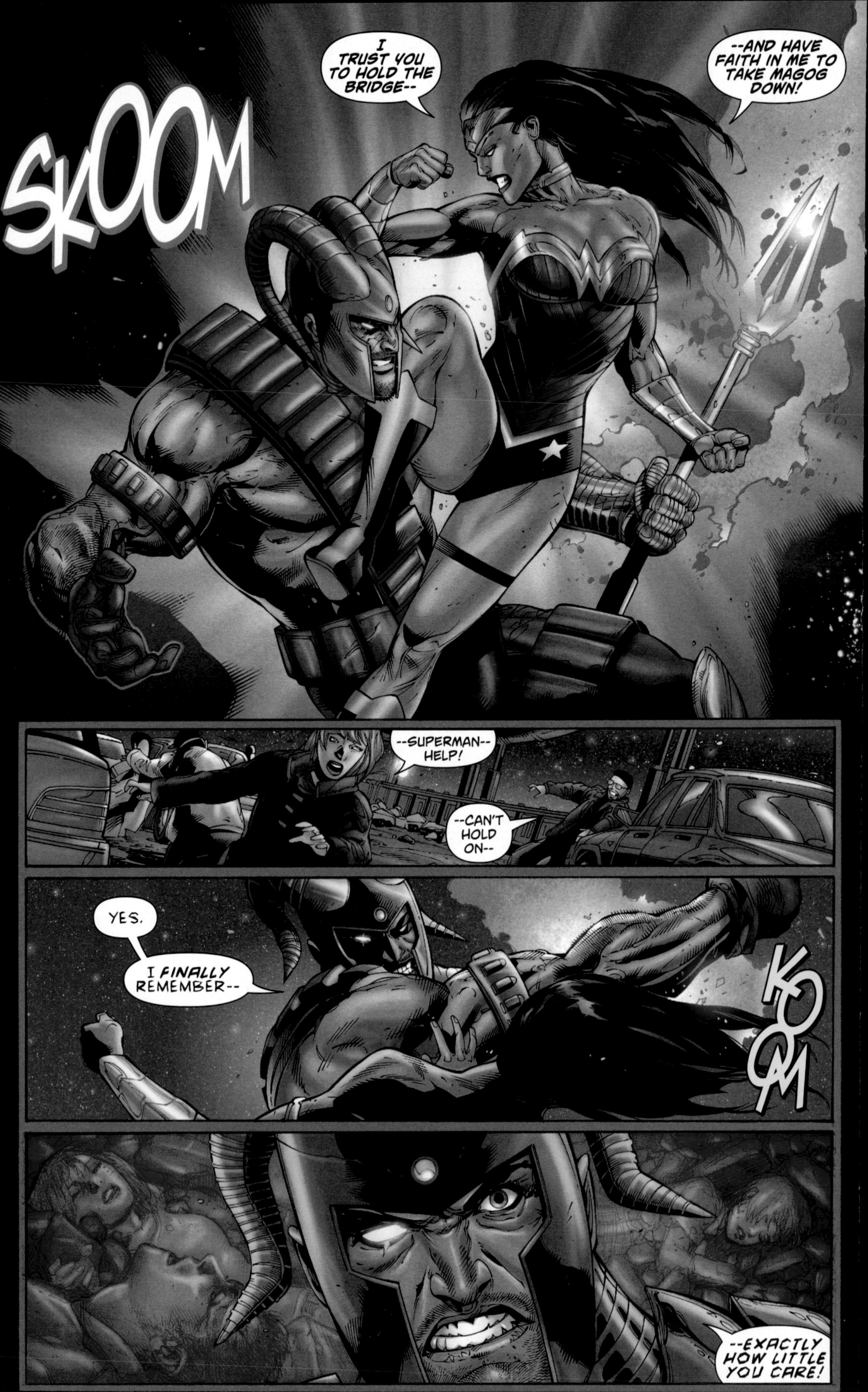
SKOOM
I TRUST YOU TO HOLD THE BRIDGE--
--AND HAVE FAITH IN ME TO TAKE MAGOG DOWN!
--SUPERMAN-- HELP!
--CAN'T HOLD ON--
YES.
I FINALLY REMEMBER--
KOOM
--EXACTLY HOW LITTLE YOU CARE!

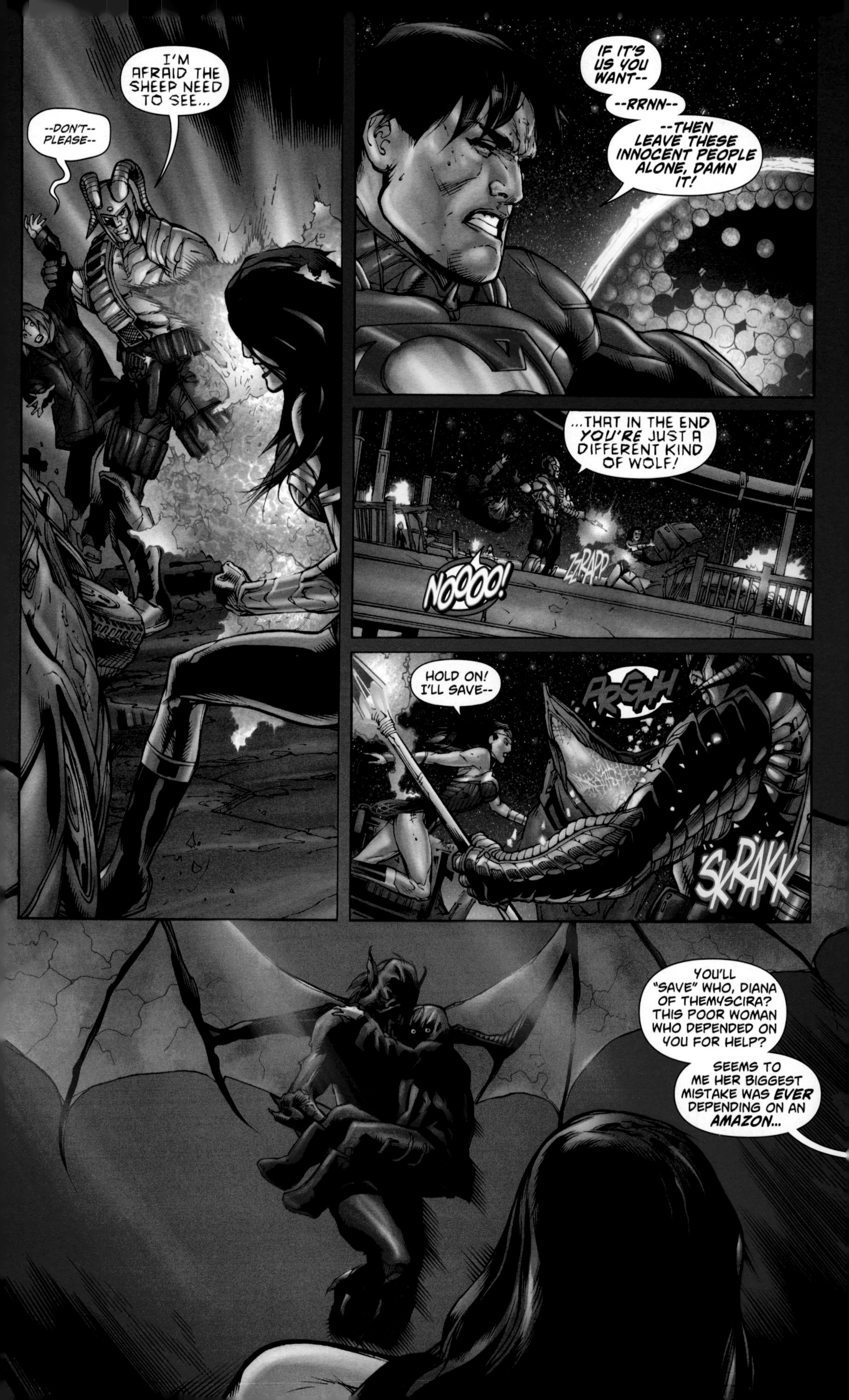

I'M AFRAID THE SHEEP NEED TO SEE...
--DON'T-- PLEASE--
IF IT'S US YOU WANT--
--RRNN--
--THEN LEAVE THESE INNOCENT PEOPLE ALONE, DAMN IT!
...THAT IN THE END YOU'RE JUST A DIFFERENT KIND OF WOLF!
NOOOO!
ZZRAPP
HOLD ON! I'LL SAVE--
ARGHH
SKRAKK
YOU'LL "SAVE" WHO, DIANA OF THEMYSCIRA? THIS POOR WOMAN WHO DEPENDED ON YOU FOR HELP?
SEEMS TO ME HER BIGGEST MISTAKE WAS EVER DEPENDING ON AN AMAZON...

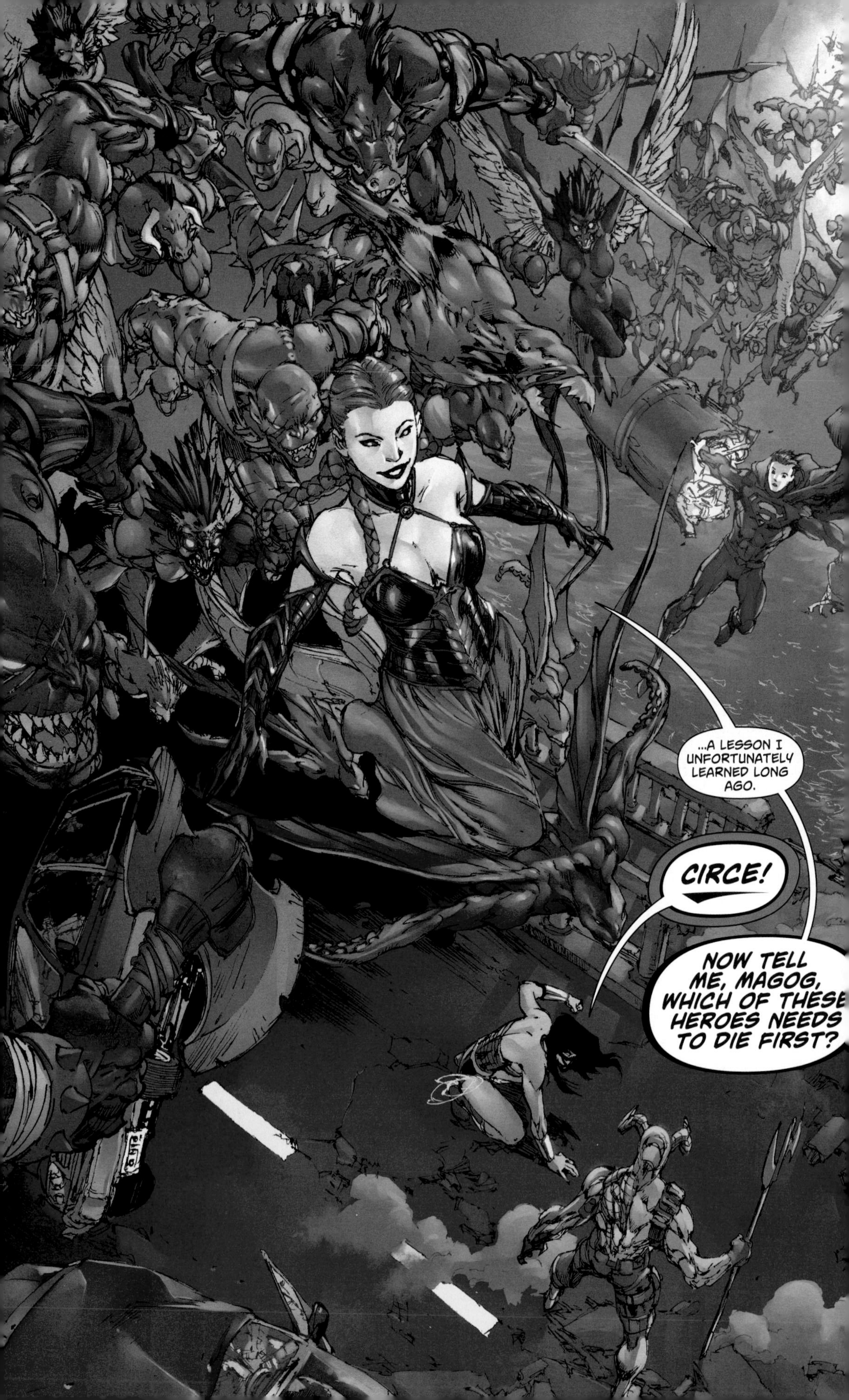
...A LESSON I UNFORTUNATELY LEARNED LONG AGO.
CIRCE!
NOW TELL ME, MAGOG, WHICH OF THESE HEROES NEEDS TO DIE FIRST?

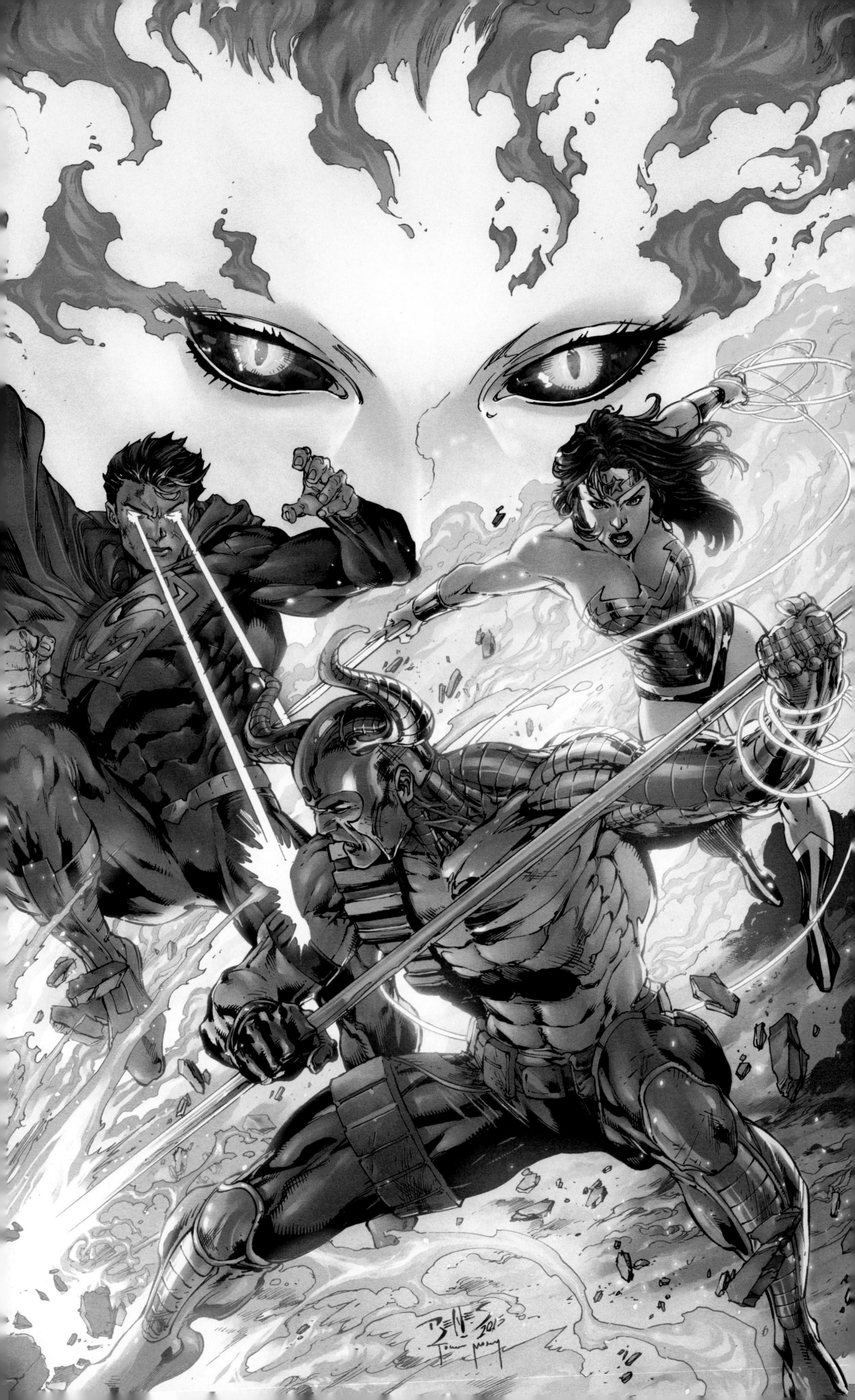

VENGEANCE SO DEAR

PETER J. TOMASI writer DOUG MAHNKE ED BENES pencillers JAIME MENDOZA ED BENES DOUG MAHNKE MARK IRWIN inkers TOMEU MOREY colorist
ROB LEIGH letterer cover by BENES & MOREY

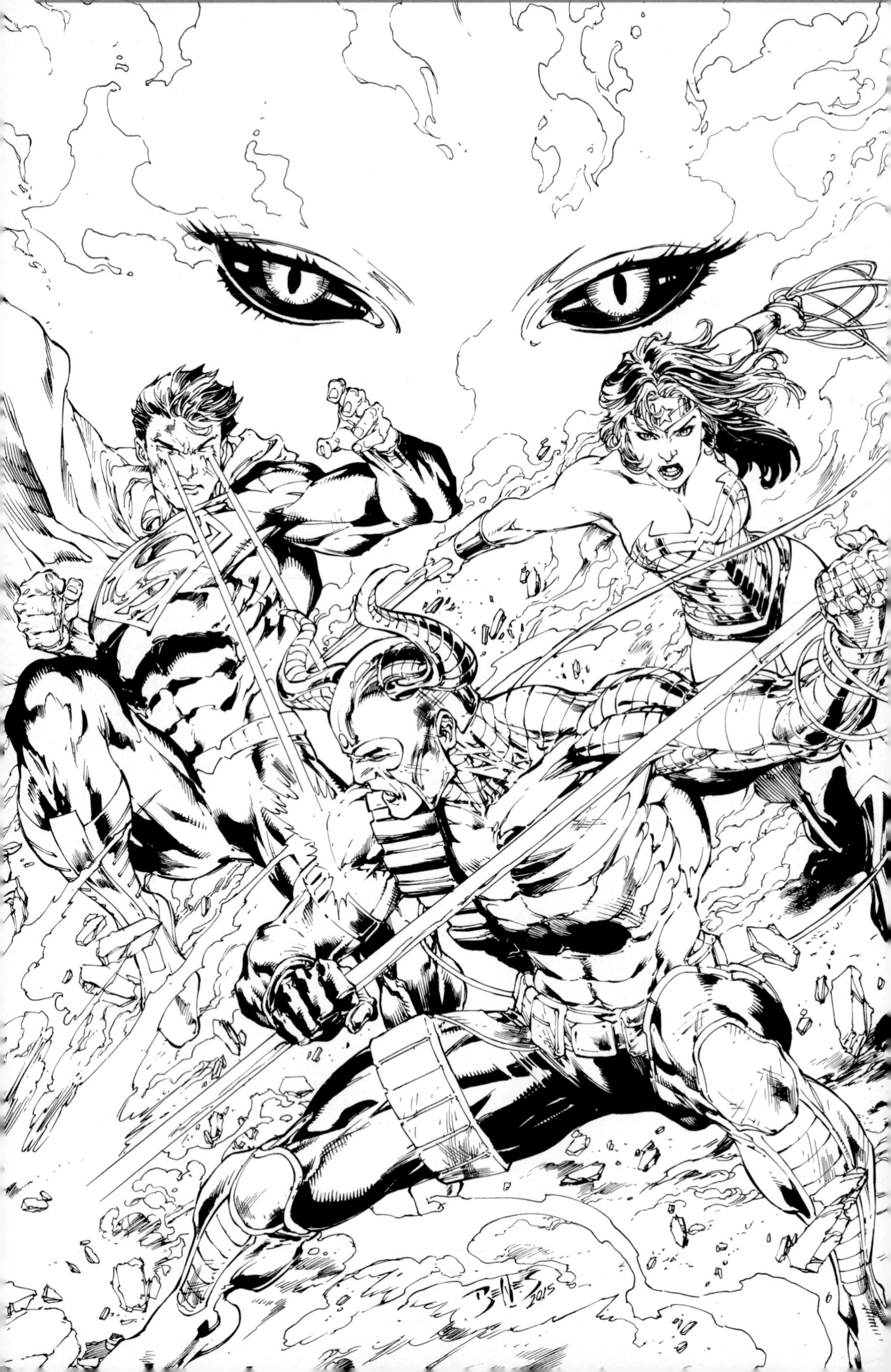

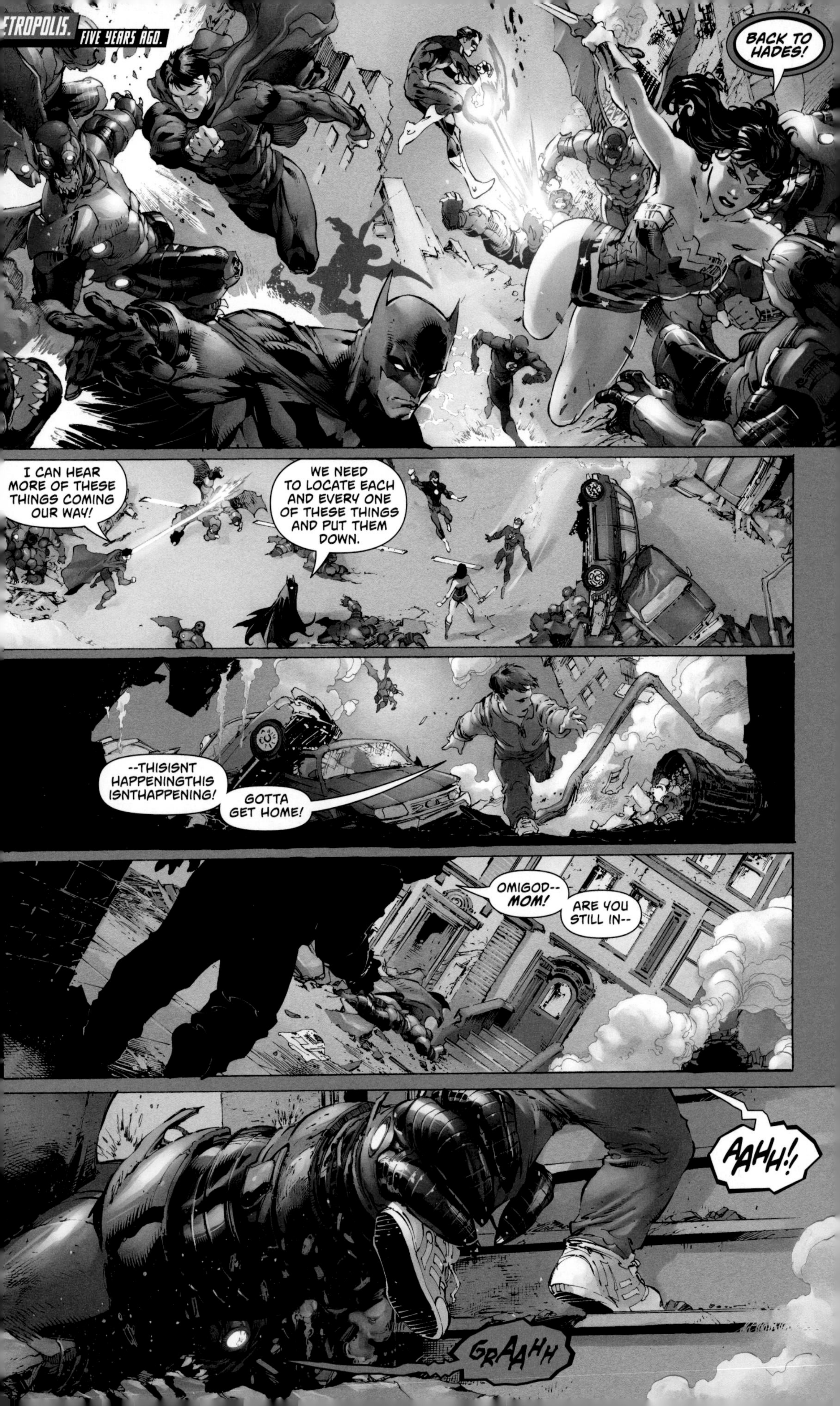
ETROPOLIS. FIVE YEARS AGO.
BACK TO HADES!
I CAN HEAR MORE OF THESE THINGS COMING OUR WAY!
WE NEED TO LOCATE EACH AND EVERY ONE OF THESE THINGS AND PUT THEM DOWN.
--THISISNT HAPPENINGTHIS ISNTHAPPENING!
GOTTA GET HOME!
OMIGOD-- MOM!
ARE YOU STILL IN--
AAHH!!
GRAAHH

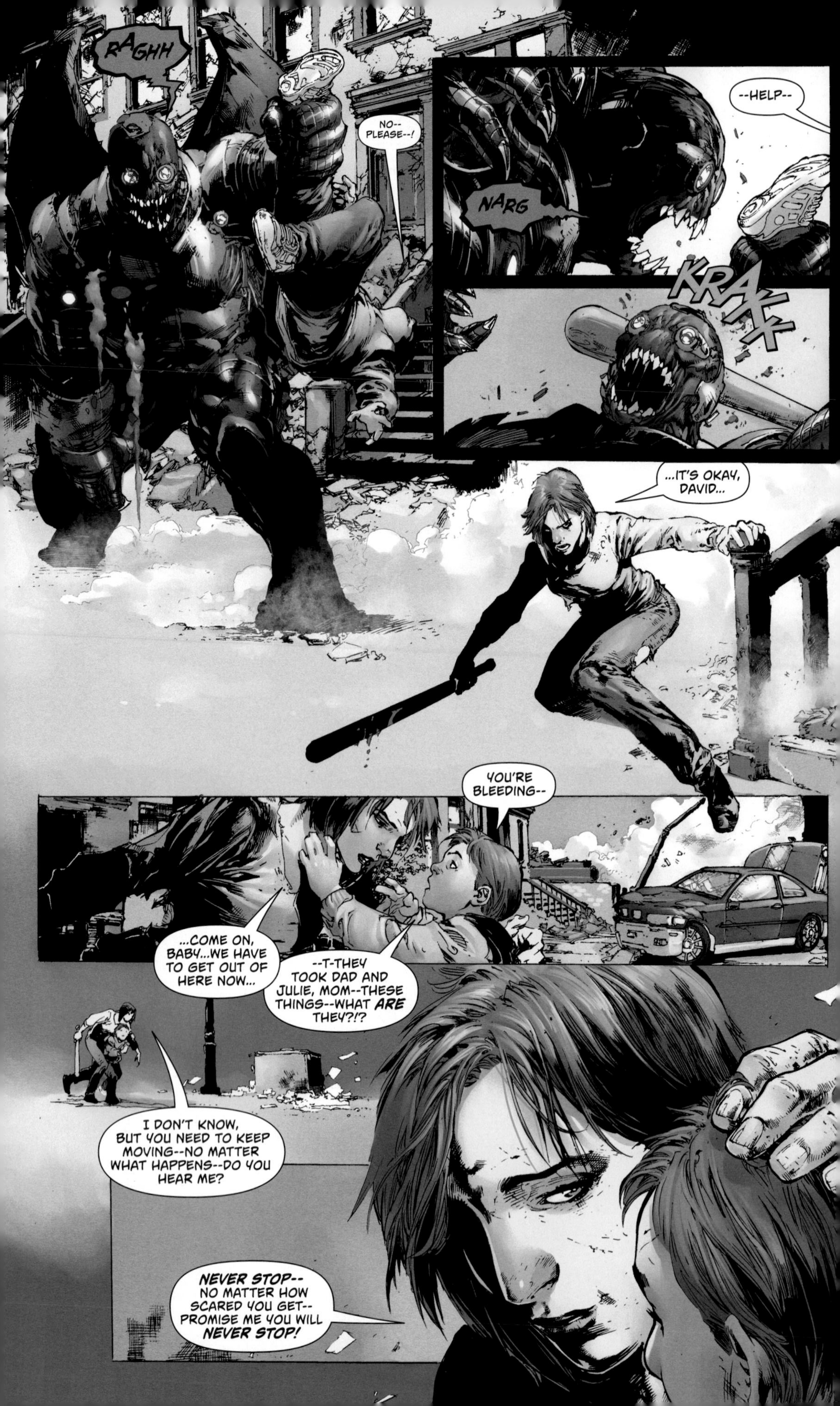
RAGHH
NO--
PLEASE--!
--HELP--
NARG
KRAKK
...IT'S OKAY, DAVID...
YOU'RE BLEEDING--
...COME ON, BABY...WE HAVE TO GET OUT OF HERE NOW...
--T-THEY TOOK DAD AND JULIE, MOM--THESE THINGS--WHAT **ARE** THEY?!?
I DON'T KNOW, BUT YOU NEED TO KEEP MOVING--NO MATTER WHAT HAPPENS--DO YOU HEAR ME?
NEVER STOP-- NO MATTER HOW SCARED YOU GET--PROMISE ME YOU WILL **NEVER STOP!**

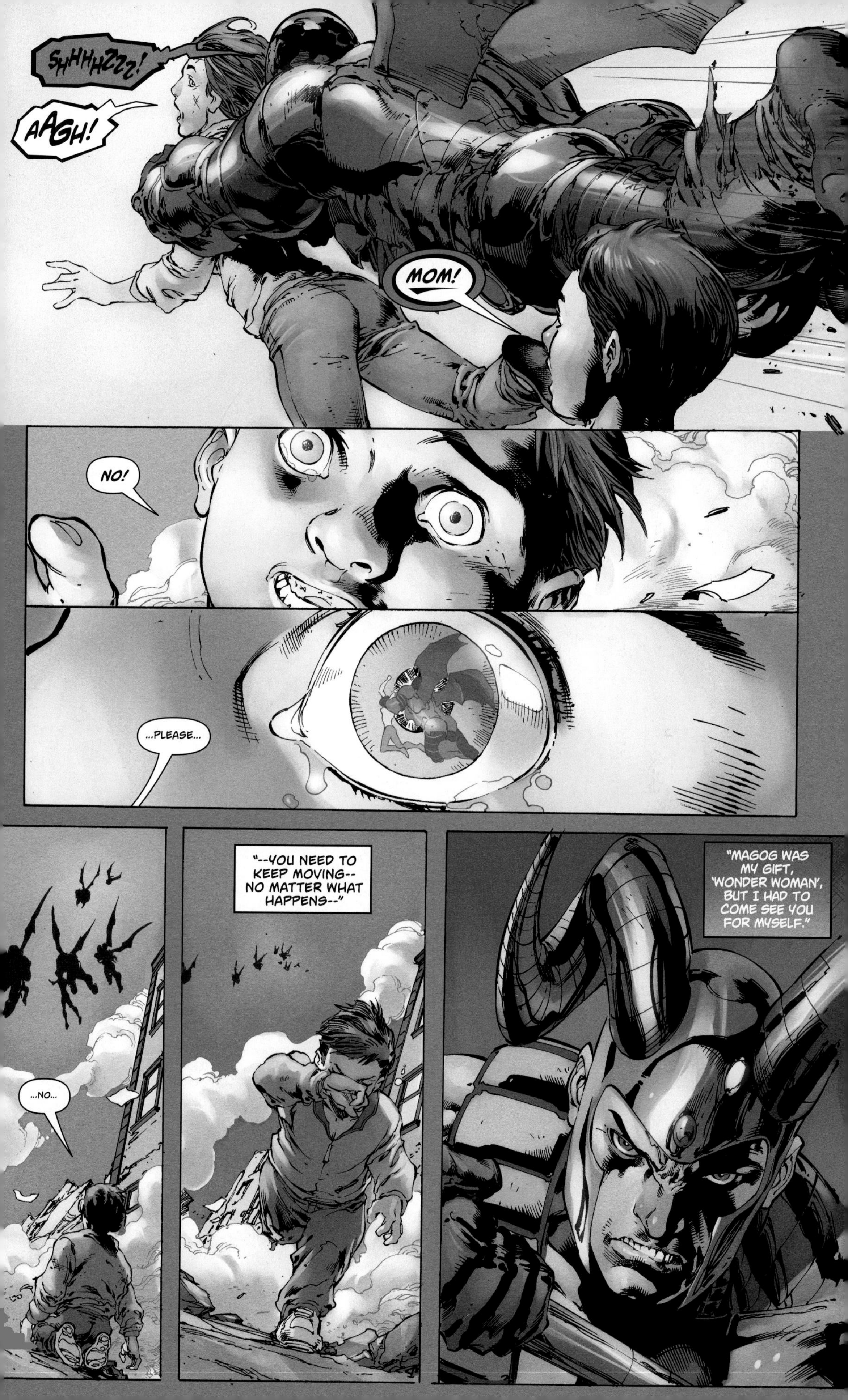
SHHHHZZZZ!
AAGH!
MOM!
NO!
...PLEASE...
...NO...
"--YOU NEED TO KEEP MOVING-- NO MATTER WHAT HAPPENS--"
"MAGOG WAS MY GIFT, 'WONDER WOMAN', BUT I HAD TO COME SEE YOU FOR MYSELF."

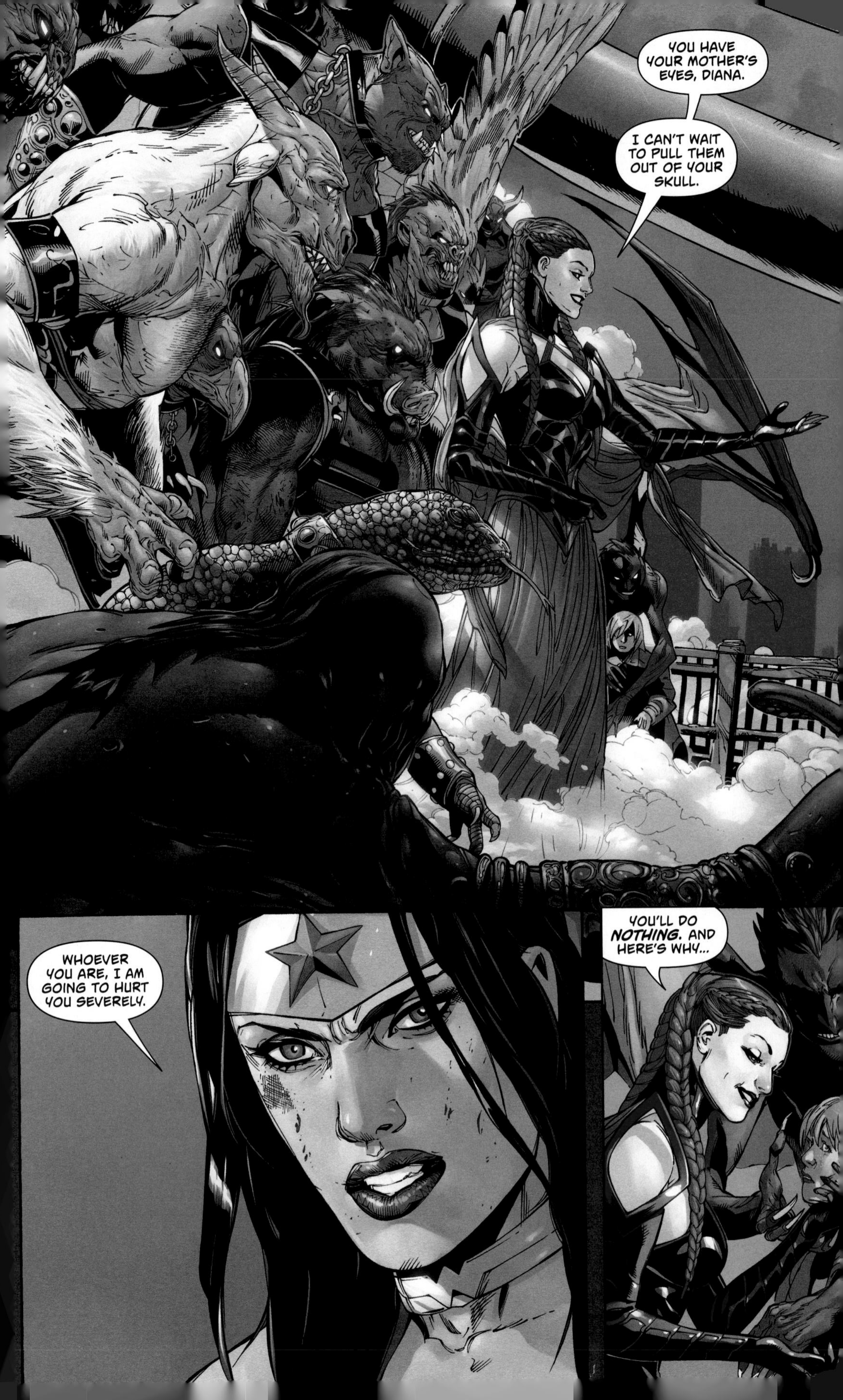
YOU HAVE YOUR MOTHER'S EYES, DIANA.
I CAN'T WAIT TO PULL THEM OUT OF YOUR SKULL.
WHOEVER YOU ARE, I AM GOING TO HURT YOU SEVERELY.
YOU'LL DO *NOTHING.* AND HERE'S WHY...

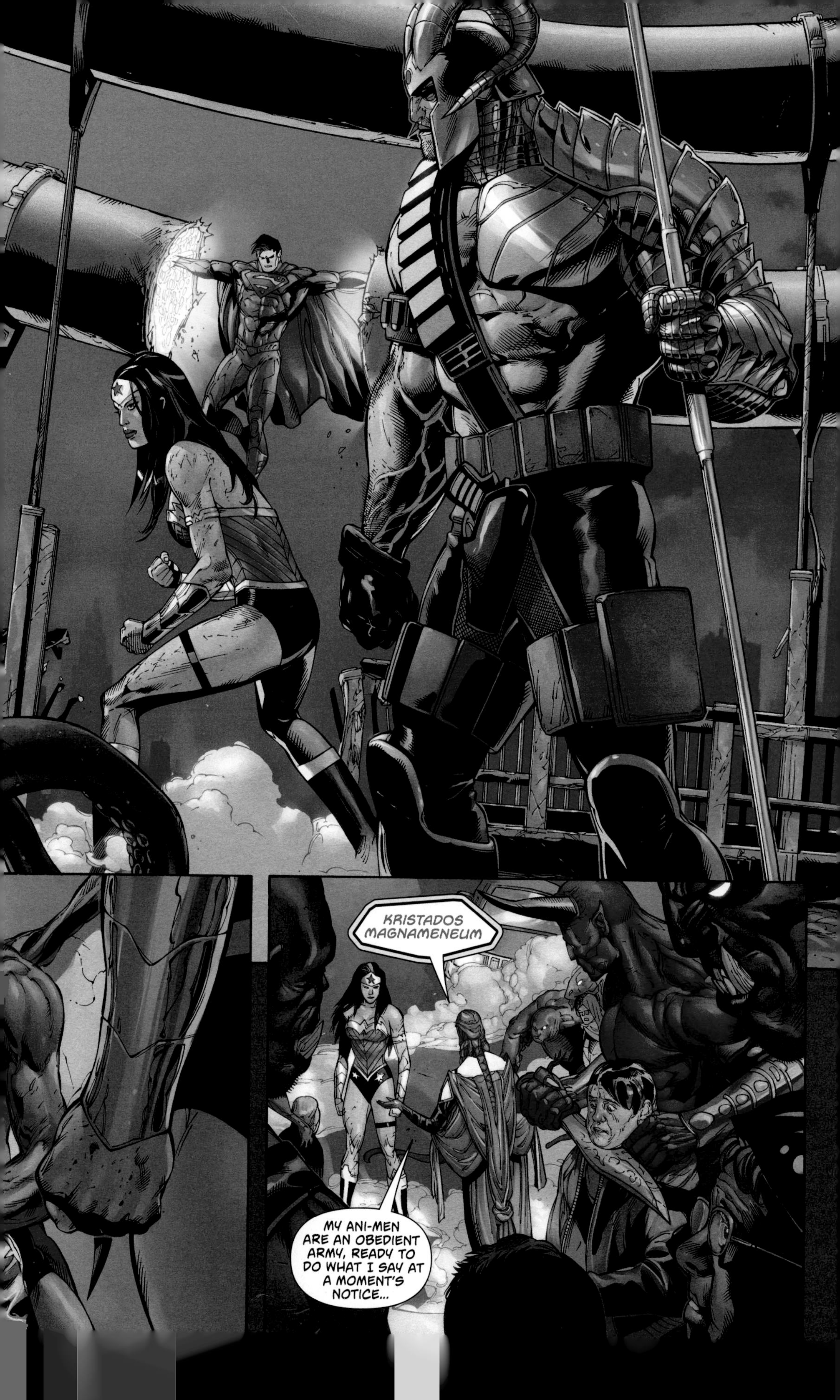
KRISTADOS MAGNAMENEUM
MY ANI-MEN ARE AN OBEDIENT ARMY, READY TO DO WHAT I SAY AT A MOMENT'S NOTICE...

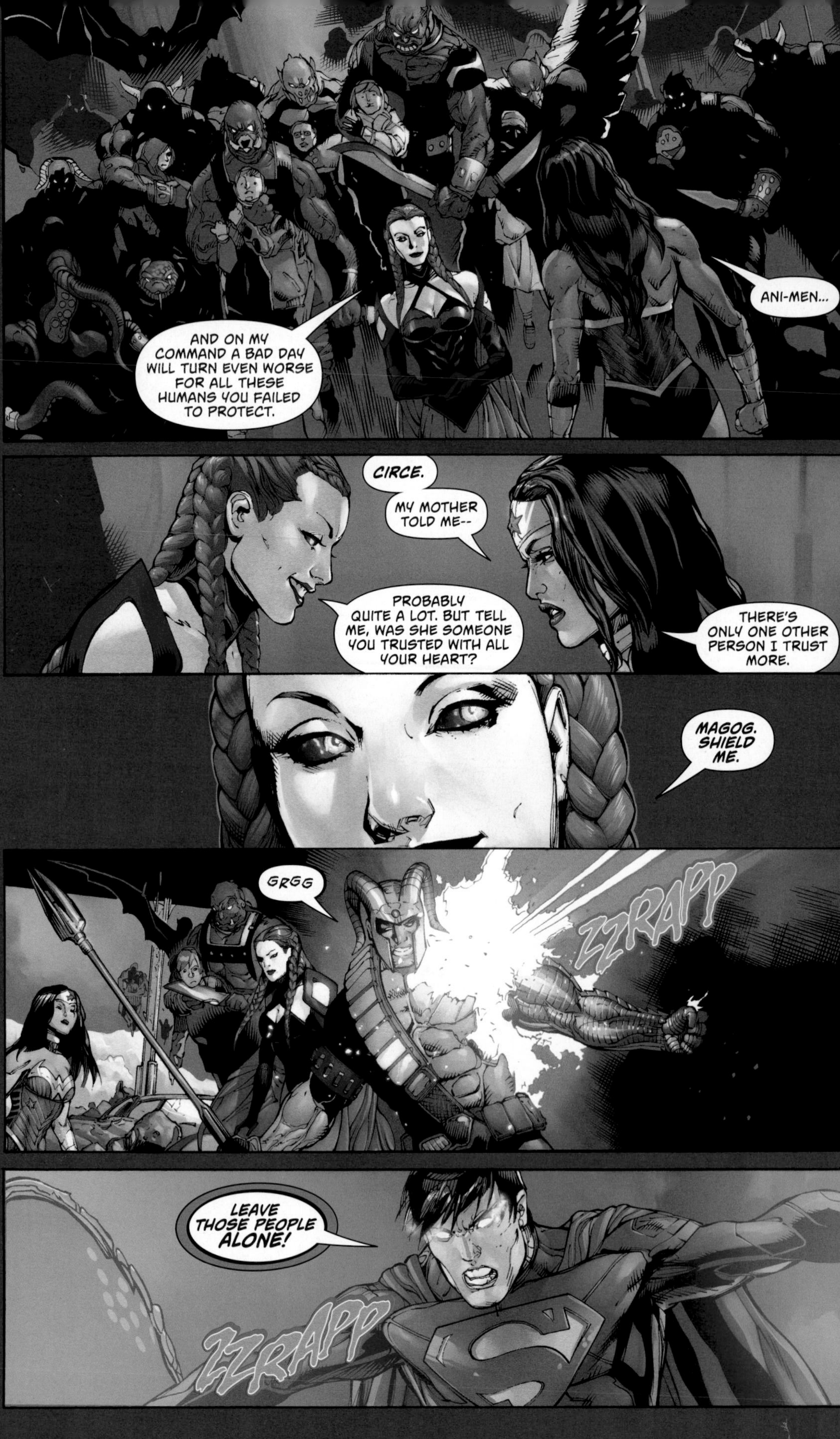
AND ON MY COMMAND A BAD DAY WILL TURN EVEN WORSE FOR ALL THESE HUMANS YOU FAILED TO PROTECT.
ANI-MEN...
CIRCE.
MY MOTHER TOLD ME--
PROBABLY QUITE A LOT. BUT TELL ME, WAS SHE SOMEONE YOU TRUSTED WITH ALL YOUR HEART?
THERE'S ONLY ONE OTHER PERSON I TRUST MORE.
MAGOG. SHIELD ME.
GRGG
ZZRAPP
LEAVE THOSE PEOPLE ALONE!
ZZRAPP

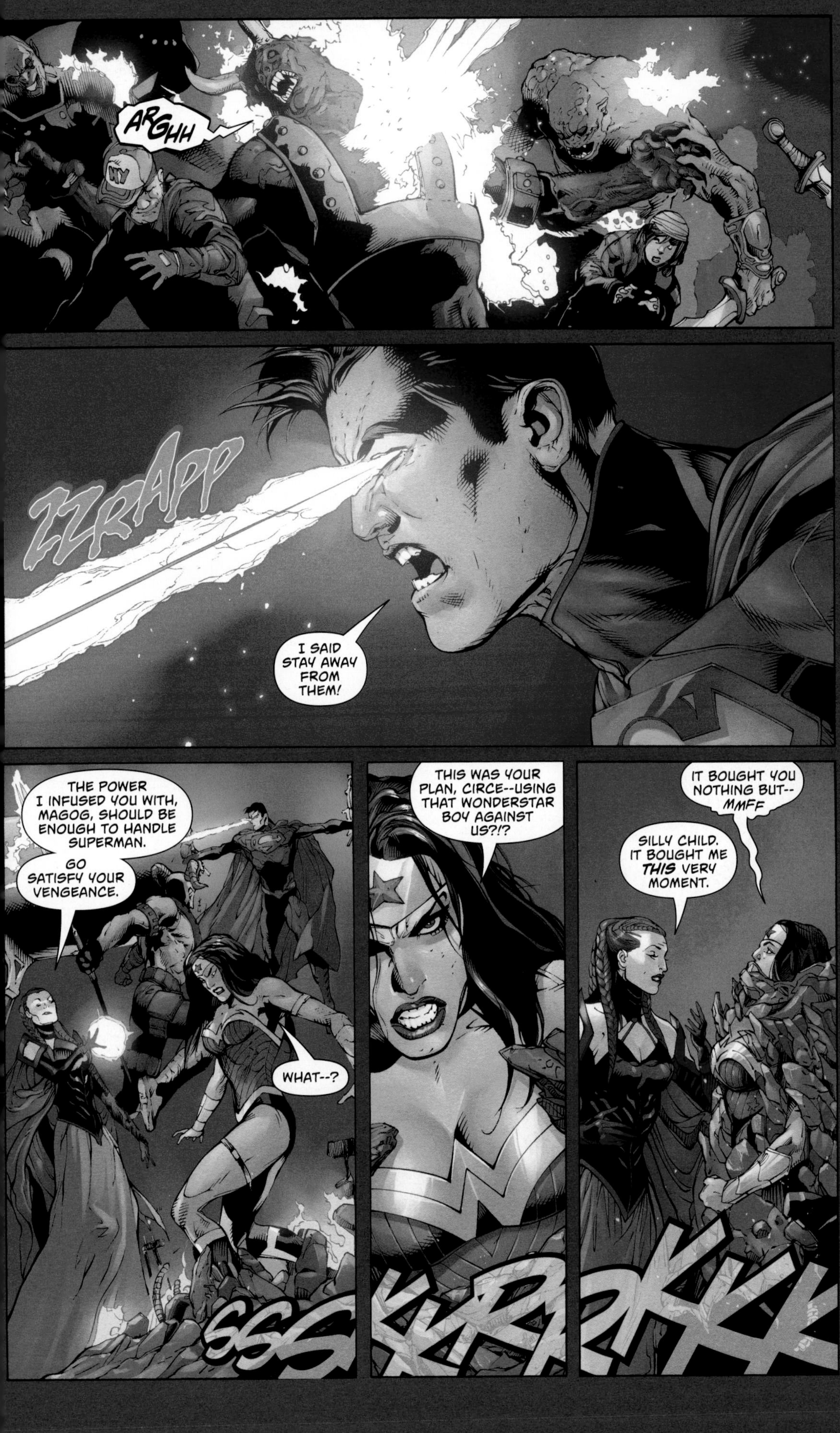
ARGHH
ZZRAPP
I SAID STAY AWAY FROM THEM!
THE POWER I INFUSED YOU WITH, MAGOG, SHOULD BE ENOUGH TO HANDLE SUPERMAN.
GO SATISFY YOUR VENGEANCE.
WHAT--?
THIS WAS YOUR PLAN, CIRCE--USING THAT WONDERSTAR BOY AGAINST US?!?
IT BOUGHT YOU NOTHING BUT--
SILLY CHILD. IT BOUGHT ME THIS VERY MOMENT.
MMFF
SSSKKRRKK

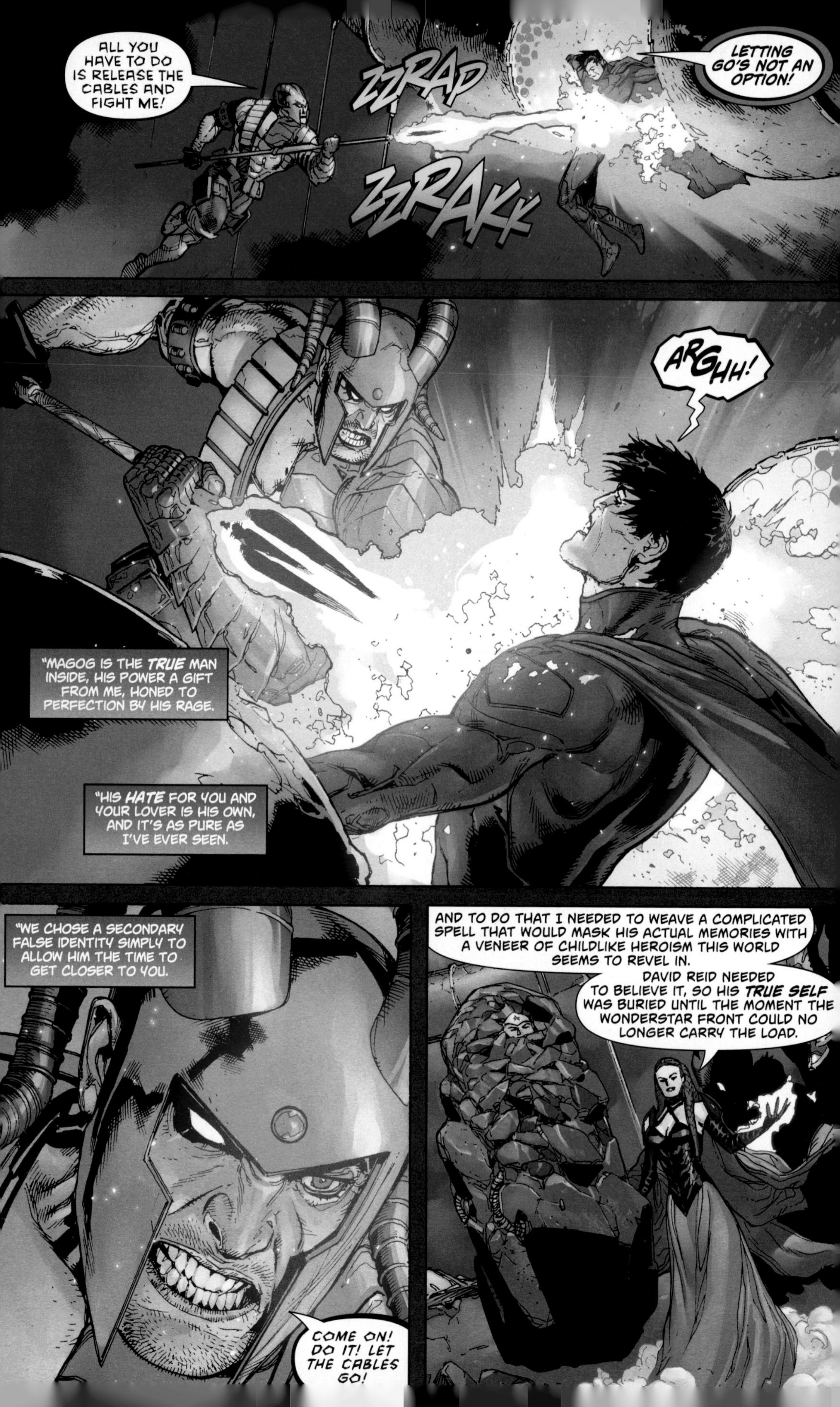
ALL YOU HAVE TO DO IS RELEASE THE CABLES AND FIGHT ME!
ZZRAP
LETTING GO'S NOT AN OPTION!
ZZRAKK
ARGHH!
"MAGOG IS THE TRUE MAN INSIDE, HIS POWER A GIFT FROM ME, HONED TO PERFECTION BY HIS RAGE.
"HIS HATE FOR YOU AND YOUR LOVER IS HIS OWN, AND IT'S AS PURE AS I'VE EVER SEEN.
"WE CHOSE A SECONDARY FALSE IDENTITY SIMPLY TO ALLOW HIM THE TIME TO GET CLOSER TO YOU.
COME ON! DO IT! LET THE CABLES GO!
AND TO DO THAT I NEEDED TO WEAVE A COMPLICATED SPELL THAT WOULD MASK HIS ACTUAL MEMORIES WITH A VENEER OF CHILDLIKE HEROISM THIS WORLD SEEMS TO REVEL IN.
DAVID REID NEEDED TO BELIEVE IT, SO HIS TRUE SELF WAS BURIED UNTIL THE MOMENT THE WONDERSTAR FRONT COULD NO LONGER CARRY THE LOAD.

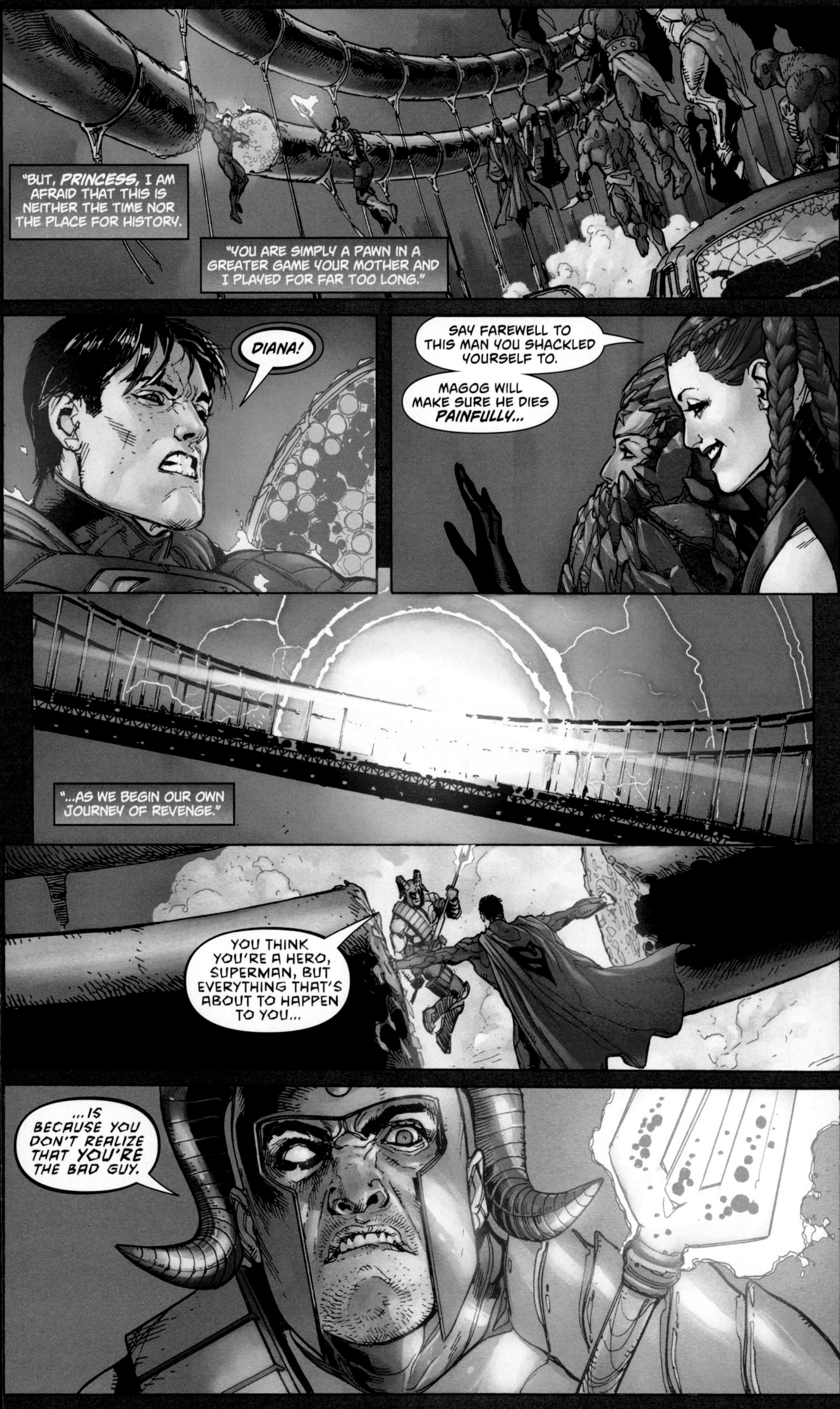
"BUT, PRINCESS, I AM AFRAID THAT THIS IS NEITHER THE TIME NOR THE PLACE FOR HISTORY.
"YOU ARE SIMPLY A PAWN IN A GREATER GAME YOUR MOTHER AND I PLAYED FOR FAR TOO LONG."
DIANA!
SAY FAREWELL TO THIS MAN YOU SHACKLED YOURSELF TO.
MAGOG WILL MAKE SURE HE DIES PAINFULLY...
"...AS WE BEGIN OUR OWN JOURNEY OF REVENGE."
YOU THINK YOU'RE A HERO, SUPERMAN, BUT EVERYTHING THAT'S ABOUT TO HAPPEN TO YOU...
...IS BECAUSE YOU DON'T REALIZE THAT YOU'RE THE BAD GUY.

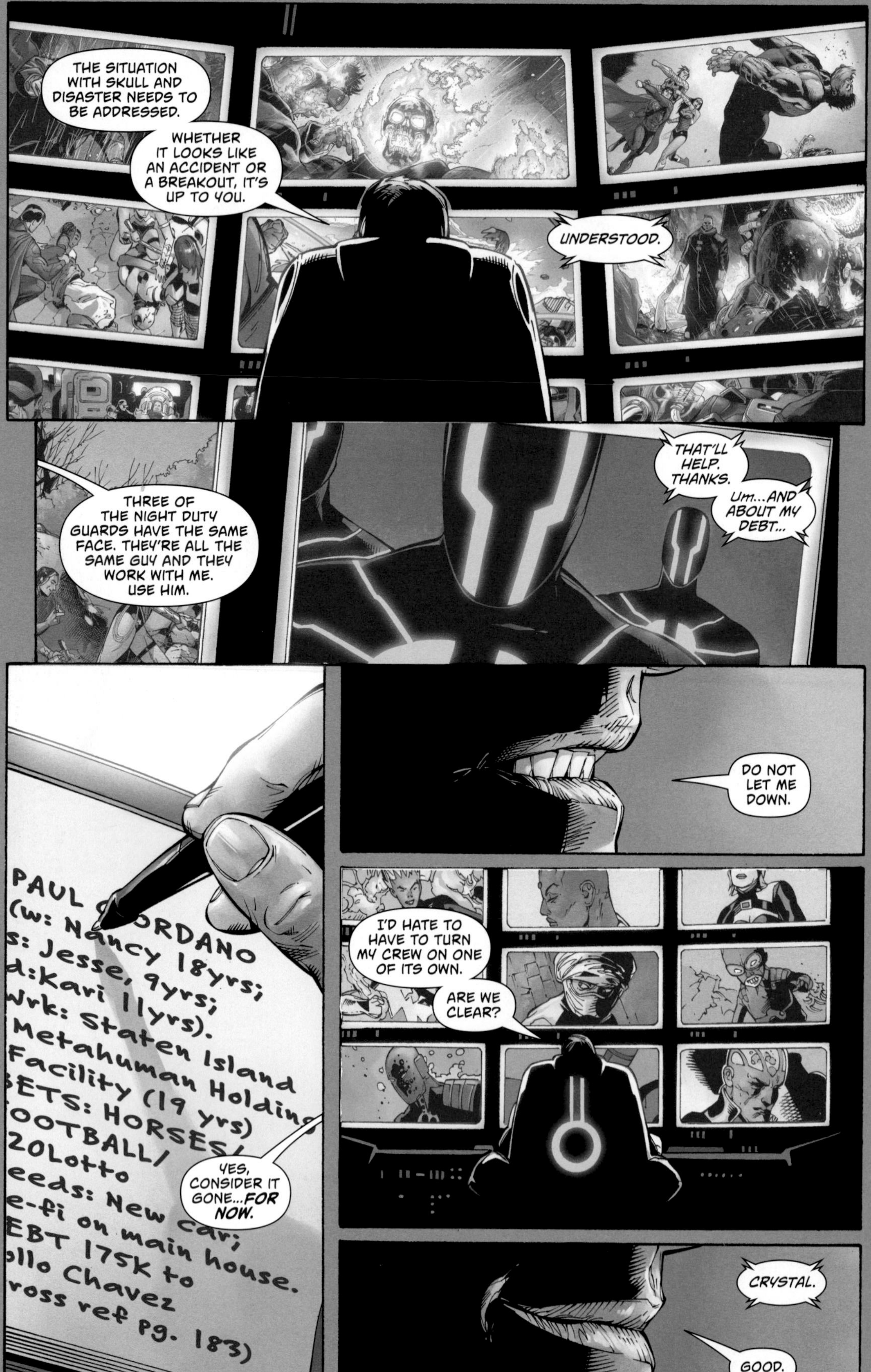
THE SITUATION WITH SKULL AND DISASTER NEEDS TO BE ADDRESSED.
WHETHER IT LOOKS LIKE AN ACCIDENT OR A BREAKOUT, IT'S UP TO YOU.
UNDERSTOOD.
THREE OF THE NIGHT DUTY GUARDS HAVE THE SAME FACE. THEY'RE ALL THE SAME GUY AND THEY WORK WITH ME. USE HIM.
THAT'LL HELP. THANKS.
Um...AND ABOUT MY DEBT...
DO NOT LET ME DOWN.
(w: Nancy 18yrs;
s: Jesse, 9yrs;
d:Kari 11yrs;
Wrk: Staten Island
Metahuman Holding
Facility (19 yrs)
OOTBALL/
20Lotto
eeds: New car;
e-fi on main house.
EBT 175K to
ollo Chavez
ross ref pg. 183)
YES, CONSIDER IT GONE...*FOR NOW.*
I'D HATE TO HAVE TO TURN MY CREW ON ONE OF ITS OWN.
ARE WE CLEAR?
CRYSTAL.
GOOD.

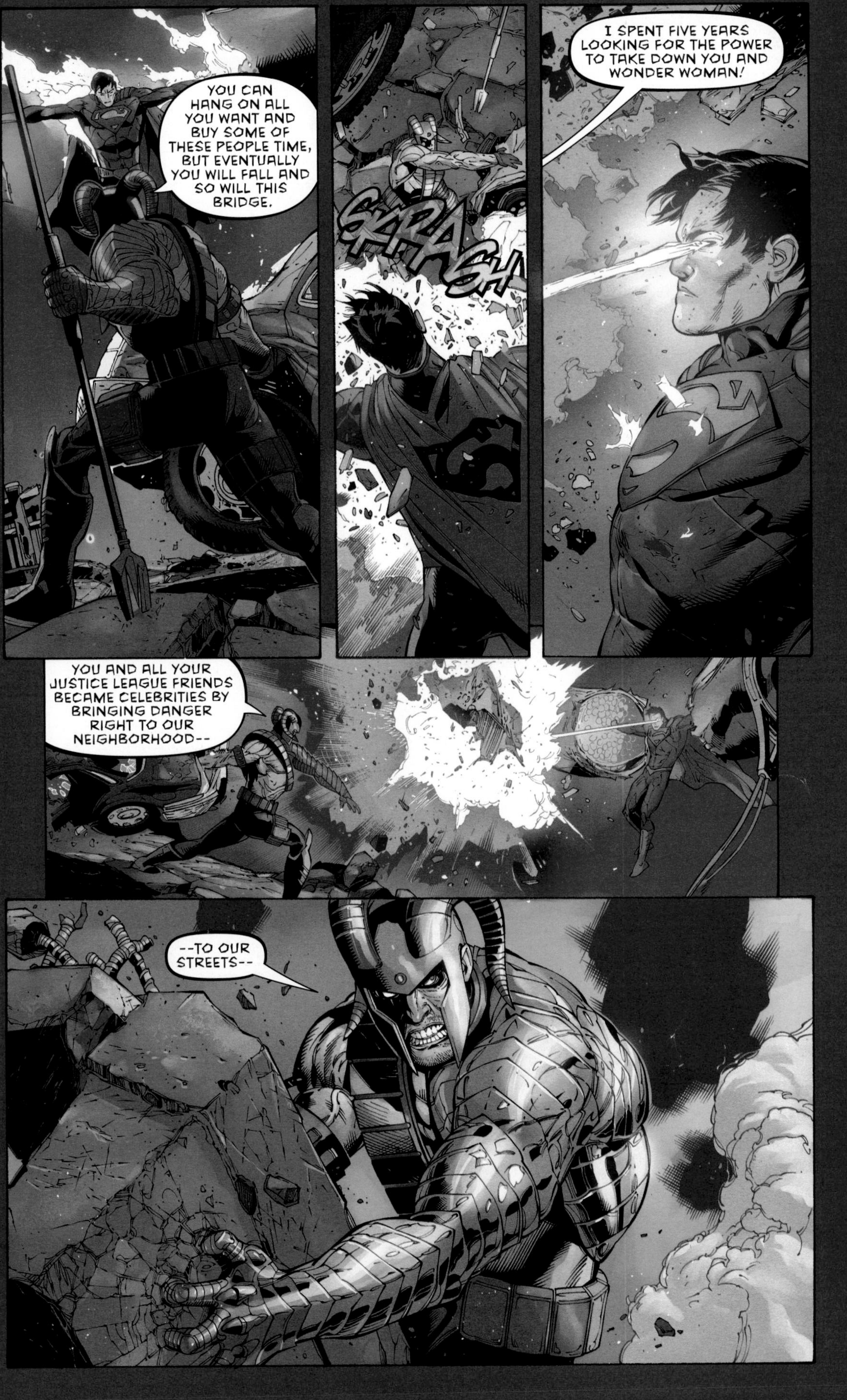
YOU CAN HANG ON ALL YOU WANT AND BUY SOME OF THESE PEOPLE TIME, BUT EVENTUALLY YOU WILL FALL AND SO WILL THIS BRIDGE.
SKRASH
I SPENT FIVE YEARS LOOKING FOR THE POWER TO TAKE DOWN YOU AND WONDER WOMAN!
YOU AND ALL YOUR JUSTICE LEAGUE FRIENDS BECAME CELEBRITIES BY BRINGING DANGER RIGHT TO OUR NEIGHBORHOOD--
--TO OUR STREETS--

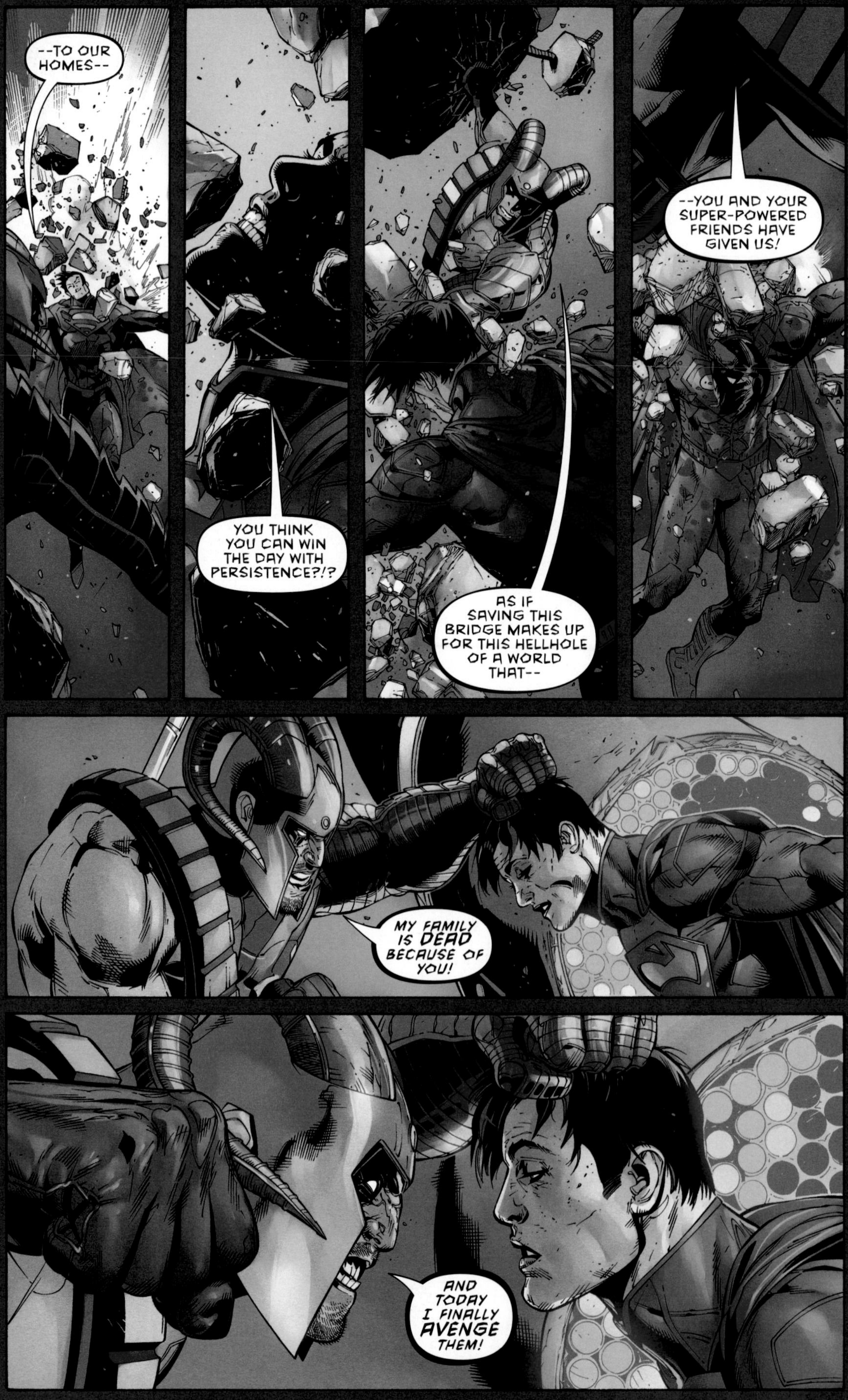
--TO OUR HOMES--
YOU THINK YOU CAN WIN THE DAY WITH PERSISTENCE?!?
AS IF SAVING THIS BRIDGE MAKES UP FOR THIS HELLHOLE OF A WORLD THAT--
--YOU AND YOUR SUPER-POWERED FRIENDS HAVE GIVEN US!
MY FAMILY IS DEAD BECAUSE OF YOU!
AND TODAY I FINALLY AVENGE THEM!

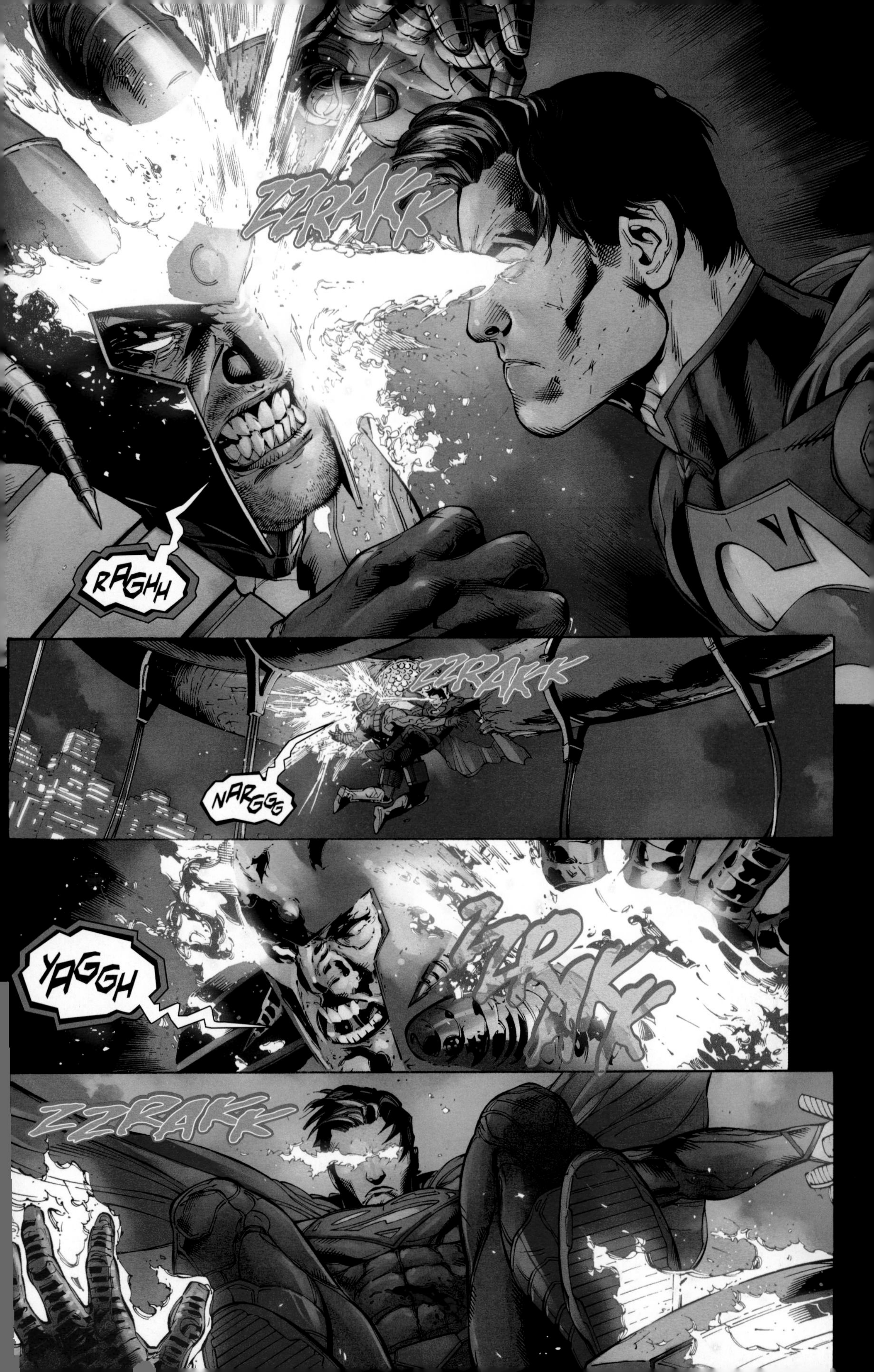
ZZRAKK
RAGHH
ZZRAKK
NARGGG
YAGGH
ZZRAKK

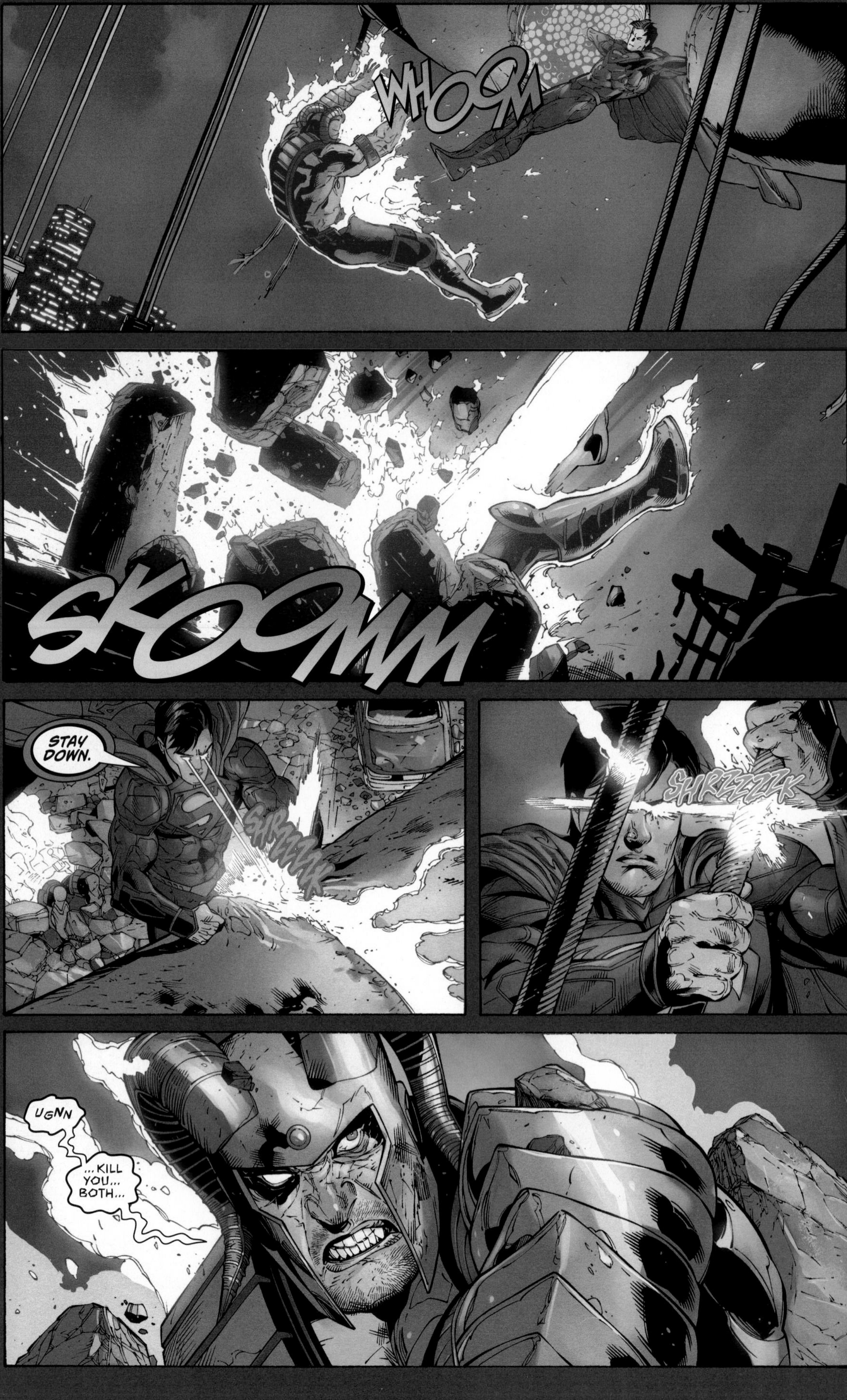
WHOOM
SKOOMM
STAY DOWN.
SHRZZZZK
SHRZZZZK
UGNN
...KILL YOU... BOTH...

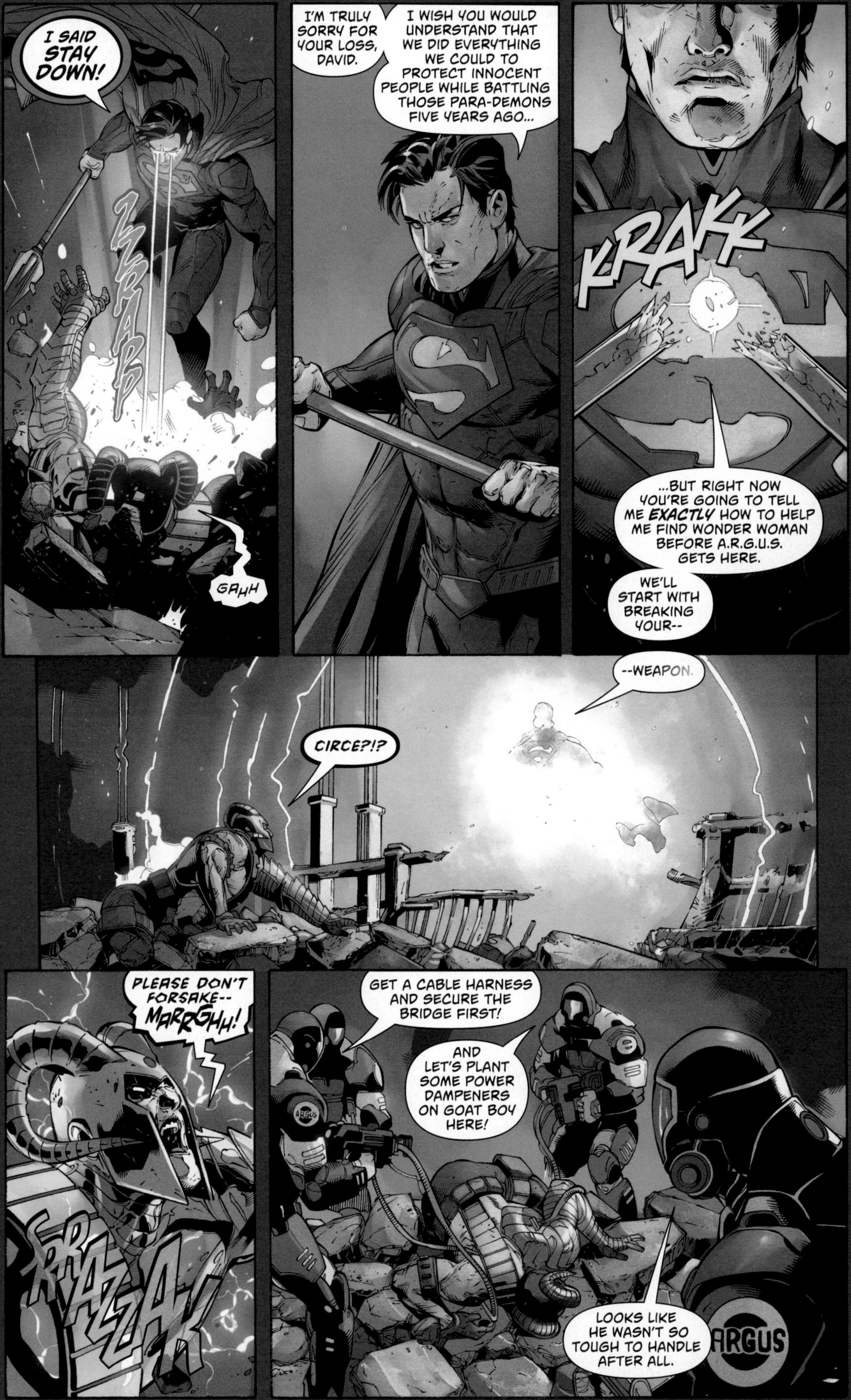
I SAID STAY DOWN!
ZZRAP
GAHH
I'M TRULY SORRY FOR YOUR LOSS, DAVID.
I WISH YOU WOULD UNDERSTAND THAT WE DID EVERYTHING WE COULD TO PROTECT INNOCENT PEOPLE WHILE BATTLING THOSE PARA-DEMONS FIVE YEARS AGO...
KRAKK
...BUT RIGHT NOW YOU'RE GOING TO TELL ME EXACTLY HOW TO HELP ME FIND WONDER WOMAN BEFORE A.R.G.U.S. GETS HERE.
WE'LL START WITH BREAKING YOUR--
--WEAPON.
CIRCE?!?
PLEASE DON'T FORSAKE-- MARRGHH!
KRAZZAK
GET A CABLE HARNESS AND SECURE THE BRIDGE FIRST!
AND LET'S PLANT SOME POWER DAMPENERS ON GOAT BOY HERE!
LOOKS LIKE HE WASN'T SO TOUGH TO HANDLE AFTER ALL.
ARGUS

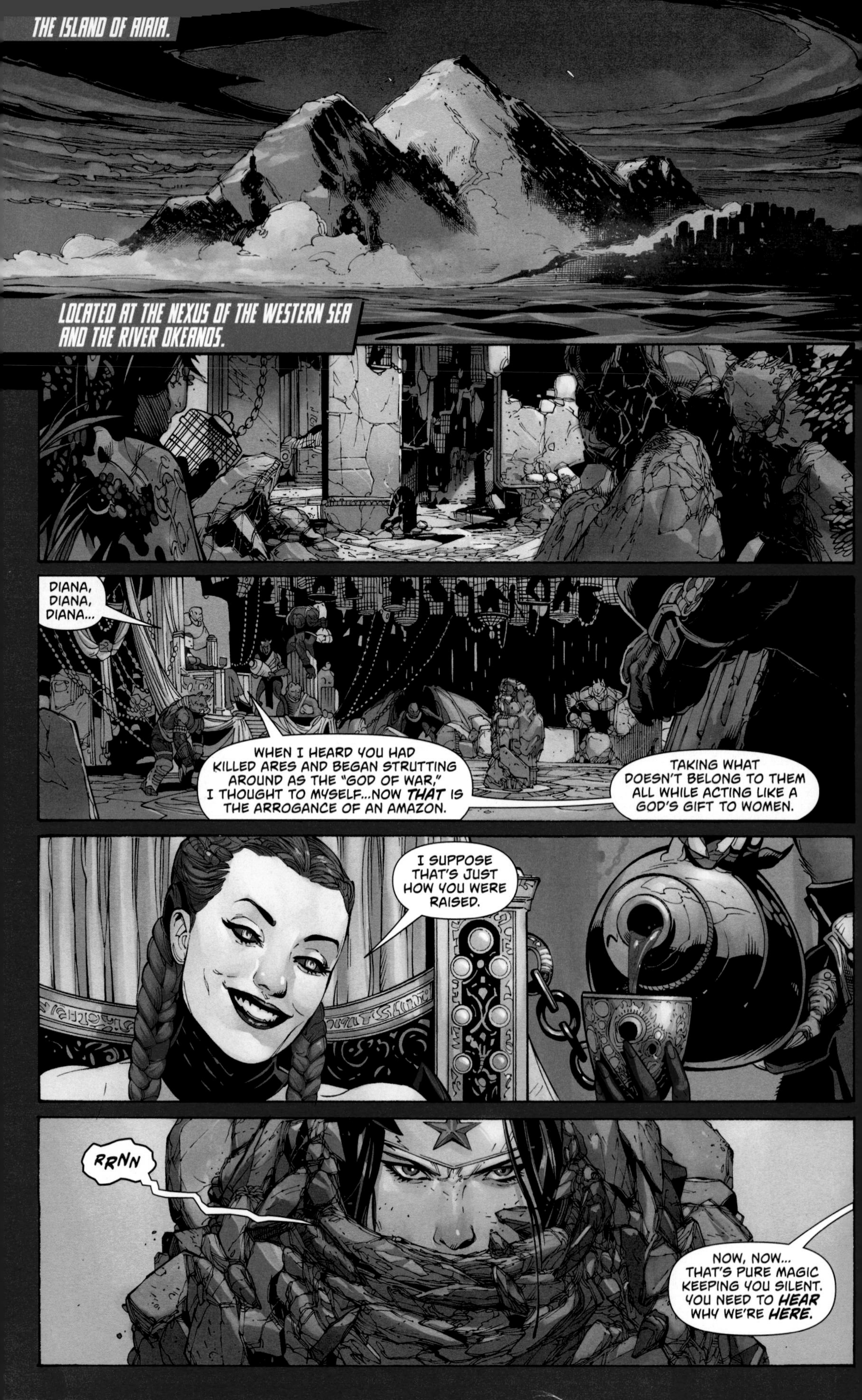
THE ISLAND OF AIAIA.
LOCATED AT THE NEXUS OF THE WESTERN SEA AND THE RIVER OKEANOS.
DIANA, DIANA, DIANA...
WHEN I HEARD YOU HAD KILLED ARES AND BEGAN STRUTTING AROUND AS THE "GOD OF WAR," I THOUGHT TO MYSELF...NOW THAT IS THE ARROGANCE OF AN AMAZON.
TAKING WHAT DOESN'T BELONG TO THEM ALL WHILE ACTING LIKE A GOD'S GIFT TO WOMEN.
I SUPPOSE THAT'S JUST HOW YOU WERE RAISED.
RRNN
NOW, NOW... THAT'S PURE MAGIC KEEPING YOU SILENT. YOU NEED TO HEAR WHY WE'RE HERE.

I WANT YOU TO KNOW EVERY HUMILIATION YOUR MOTHER RAINED UPON ME.

FROM WHAT I UNDERSTAND, WE HAVE *THAT* IN COMMON.

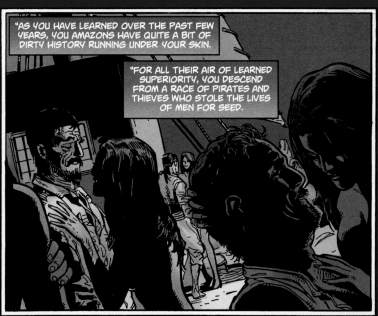

"AS YOU HAVE LEARNED OVER THE PAST FEW YEARS, YOU AMAZONS HAVE QUITE A BIT OF DIRTY HISTORY RUNNING UNDER YOUR SKIN.

"FOR ALL THEIR AIR OF LEARNED SUPERIORITY, YOU DESCEND FROM A RACE OF PIRATES AND THIEVES WHO STOLE THE LIVES OF MEN FOR SEED.

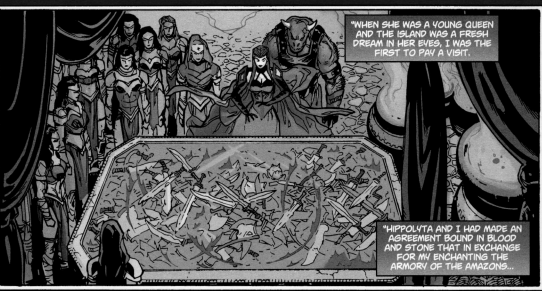

"WHEN SHE WAS A YOUNG QUEEN AND THE ISLAND WAS A FRESH DREAM IN HER EYES, I WAS THE FIRST TO PAY A VISIT.

"HIPPOLYTA AND I HAD MADE AN AGREEMENT BOUND IN BLOOD AND STONE THAT IN EXCHANGE FOR MY ENCHANTING THE ARMORY OF THE AMAZONS...

"...SHE WOULD DELIVER TO ME *ALL* THE SURVIVING MALES OF HER ILL-MOTIVATED EFFORTS. YOUNG BOYS AND OLD MEN.

"THERE WERE NO LIMITATIONS ON THE TREASURE SHE PROMISED.

"I WOULD THEN HAVE THE HUMAN FODDER I NEEDED TO CREATE MY ARMY OF ANI-MEN...

"...AND AN OPPORTUNITY TO BREAK FREE OF MY OWN CHAINS...JUST AS THE AMAZONS HAD DONE.

THAT *WAS* THE DEAL WE MADE. BUT WHEN THE TIME CAME I DISCOVERED THAT HIPPOLYTA HAD *LIED.*

NAÏVE OF ME TO THINK SHE WOULD DO ANYTHING ELSE CONSIDERING SHE HAD WHORED HERSELF TO ZEUS JUST TO MAKE HERSELF A DAUGHTER WHO WOULD CHOOSE TO LIVE WITH HUMANS RATHER THAN HER OWN MOTHER.

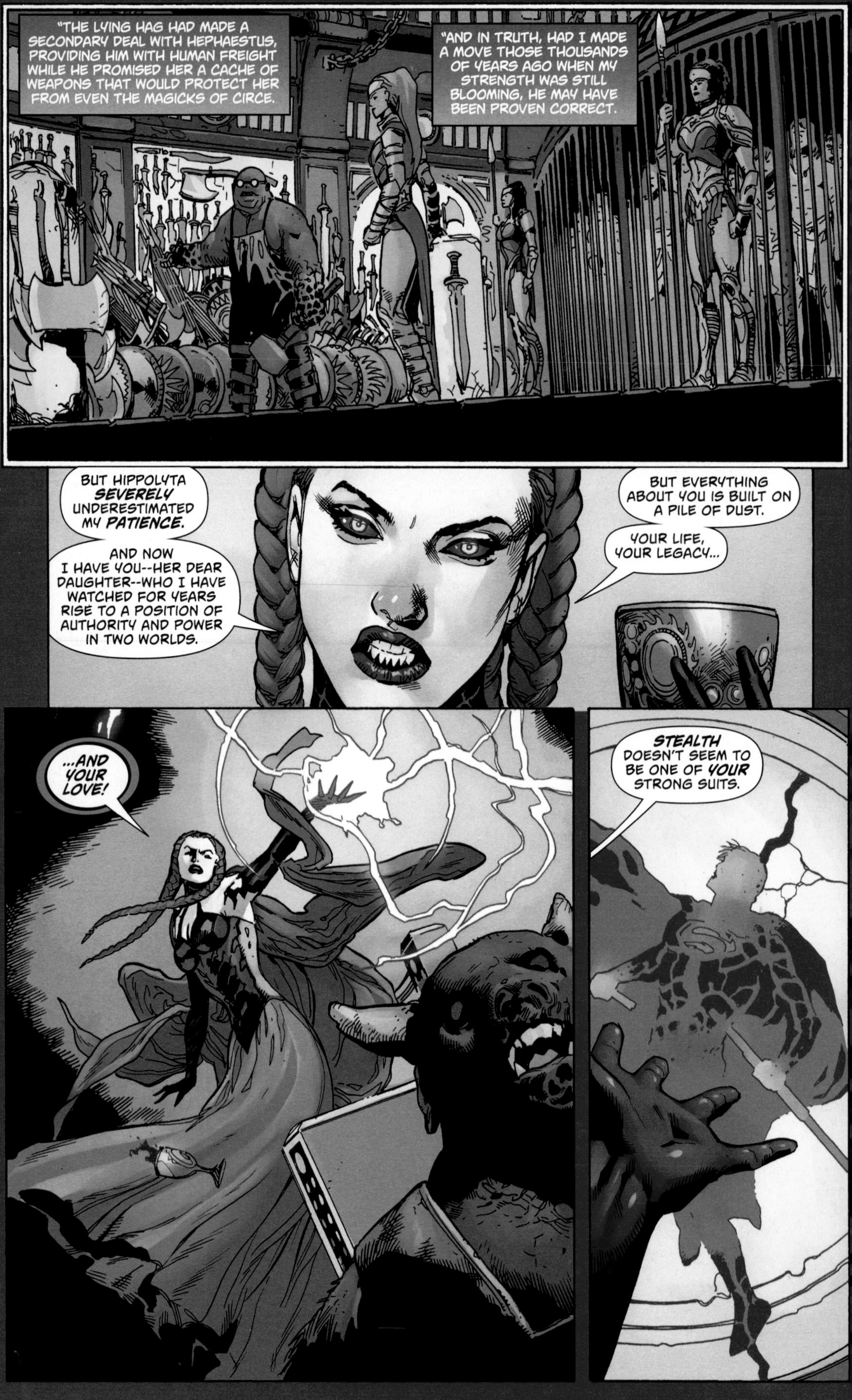
"THE LYING HAG HAD MADE A SECONDARY DEAL WITH HEPHAESTUS, PROVIDING HIM WITH HUMAN FREIGHT WHILE HE PROMISED HER A CACHE OF WEAPONS THAT WOULD PROTECT HER FROM EVEN THE MAGICKS OF CIRCE.
"AND IN TRUTH, HAD I MADE A MOVE THOSE THOUSANDS OF YEARS AGO WHEN MY STRENGTH WAS STILL BLOOMING, HE MAY HAVE BEEN PROVEN CORRECT.
BUT HIPPOLYTA SEVERELY UNDERESTIMATED MY PATIENCE.
AND NOW I HAVE YOU--HER DEAR DAUGHTER--WHO I HAVE WATCHED FOR YEARS RISE TO A POSITION OF AUTHORITY AND POWER IN TWO WORLDS.
BUT EVERYTHING ABOUT YOU IS BUILT ON A PILE OF DUST.
YOUR LIFE, YOUR LEGACY...
...AND YOUR LOVE!
STEALTH DOESN'T SEEM TO BE ONE OF YOUR STRONG SUITS.

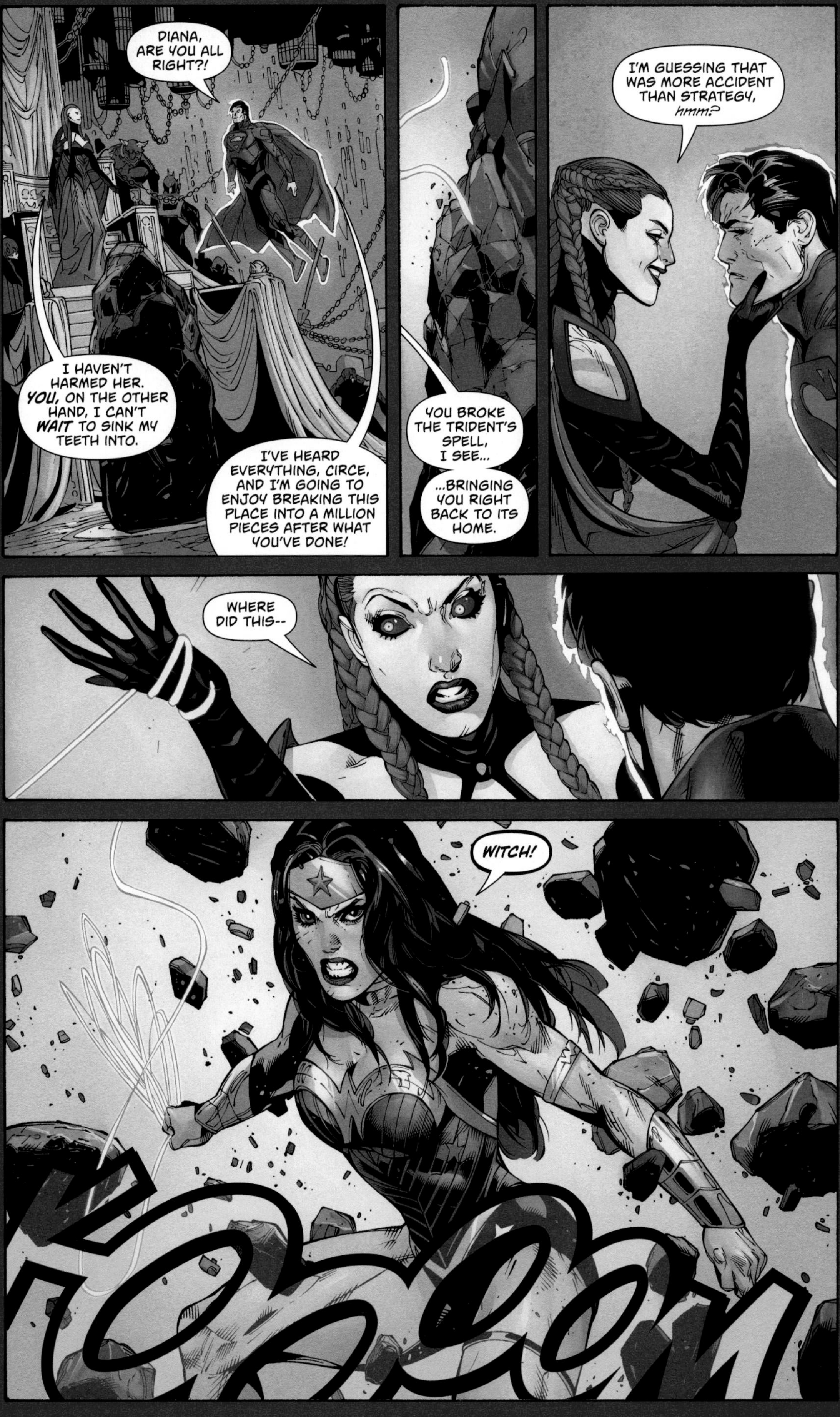
DIANA, ARE YOU ALL RIGHT?!
I HAVEN'T HARMED HER. YOU, ON THE OTHER HAND, I CAN'T WAIT TO SINK MY TEETH INTO.
I'VE HEARD EVERYTHING, CIRCE, AND I'M GOING TO ENJOY BREAKING THIS PLACE INTO A MILLION PIECES AFTER WHAT YOU'VE DONE!
YOU BROKE THE TRIDENT'S SPELL, I SEE...
...BRINGING YOU RIGHT BACK TO ITS HOME.
I'M GUESSING THAT WAS MORE ACCIDENT THAN STRATEGY, hmm?
WHERE DID THIS--
WITCH!
KRAKOOM

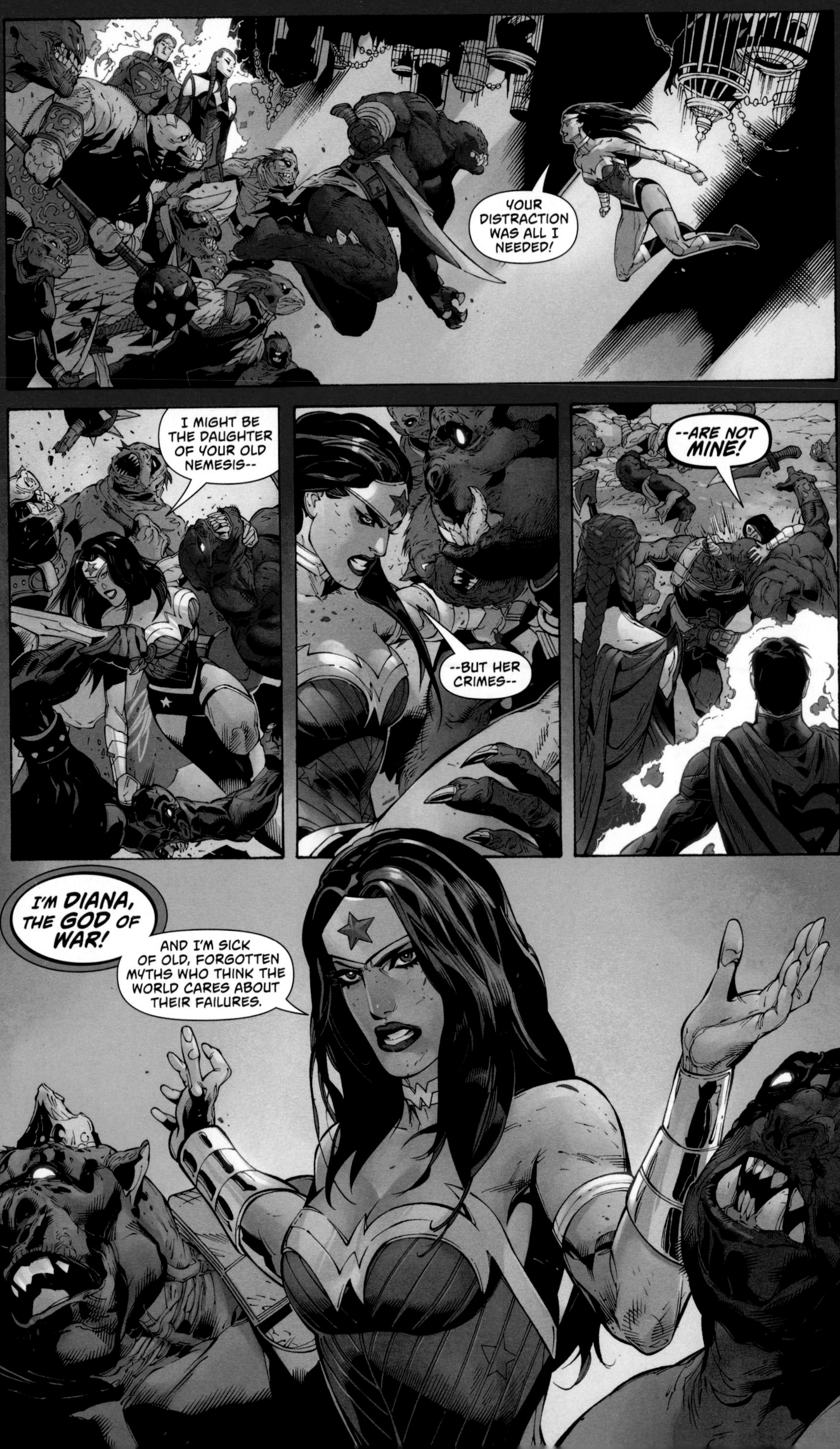

YOUR DISTRACTION WAS ALL I NEEDED!
I MIGHT BE THE DAUGHTER OF YOUR OLD NEMESIS--
--BUT HER CRIMES--
--ARE NOT MINE!
I'M DIANA, THE GOD OF WAR!
AND I'M SICK OF OLD, FORGOTTEN MYTHS WHO THINK THE WORLD CARES ABOUT THEIR FAILURES.

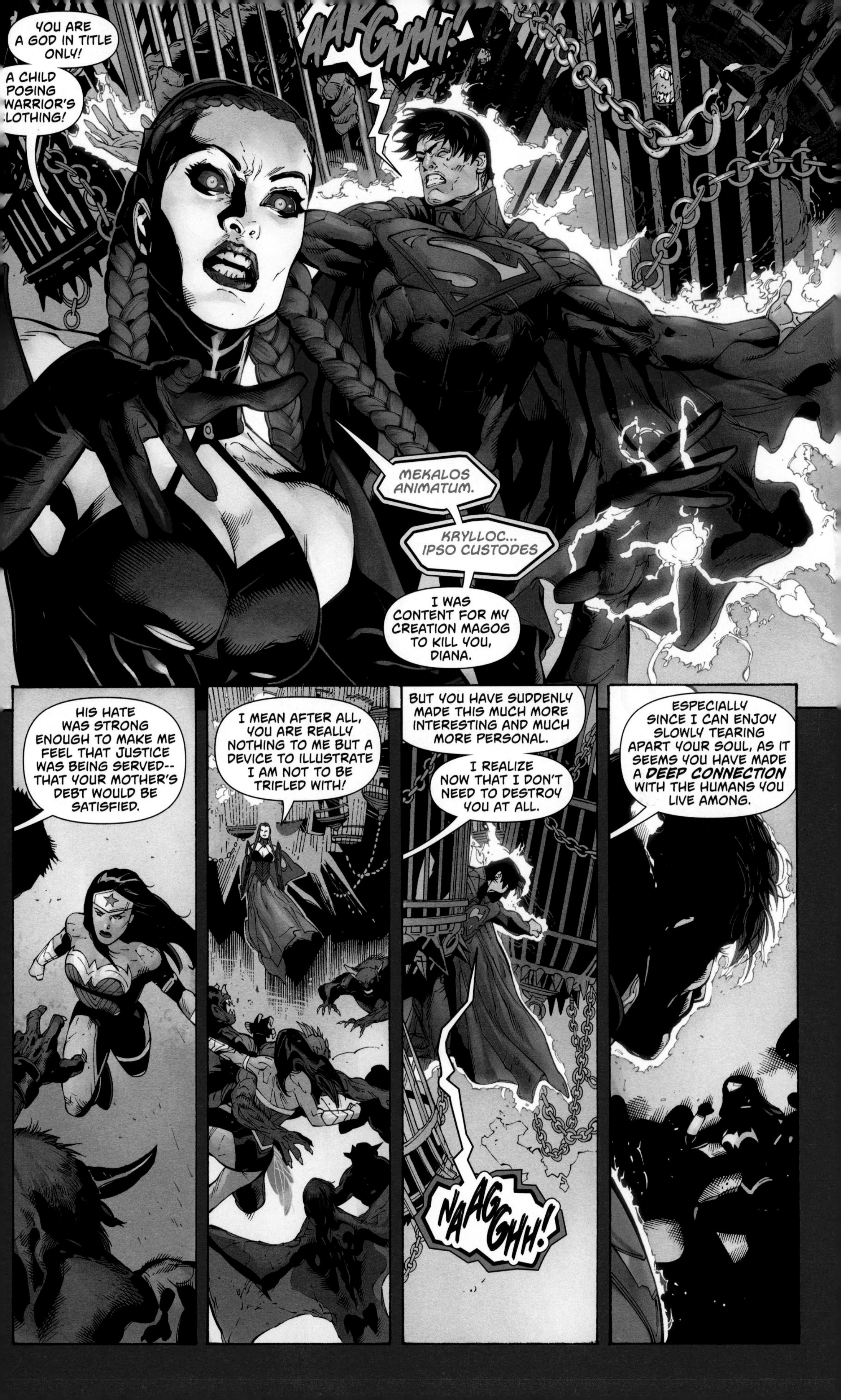

YOU ARE A GOD IN TITLE ONLY!
A CHILD POSING WARRIOR'S CLOTHING!
AAKGHHH!
MEKALOS ANIMATUM.
KRYLLOC... IPSO CUSTODES
I WAS CONTENT FOR MY CREATION MAGOG TO KILL YOU, DIANA.
HIS HATE WAS STRONG ENOUGH TO MAKE ME FEEL THAT JUSTICE WAS BEING SERVED-- THAT YOUR MOTHER'S DEBT WOULD BE SATISFIED.
I MEAN AFTER ALL, YOU ARE REALLY NOTHING TO ME BUT A DEVICE TO ILLUSTRATE I AM NOT TO BE TRIFLED WITH!
BUT YOU HAVE SUDDENLY MADE THIS MUCH MORE INTERESTING AND MUCH MORE PERSONAL.
I REALIZE NOW THAT I DON'T NEED TO DESTROY YOU AT ALL.
NAAGGHH!
ESPECIALLY SINCE I CAN ENJOY SLOWLY TEARING APART YOUR SOUL, AS IT SEEMS YOU HAVE MADE A *DEEP CONNECTION* WITH THE HUMANS YOU LIVE AMONG.

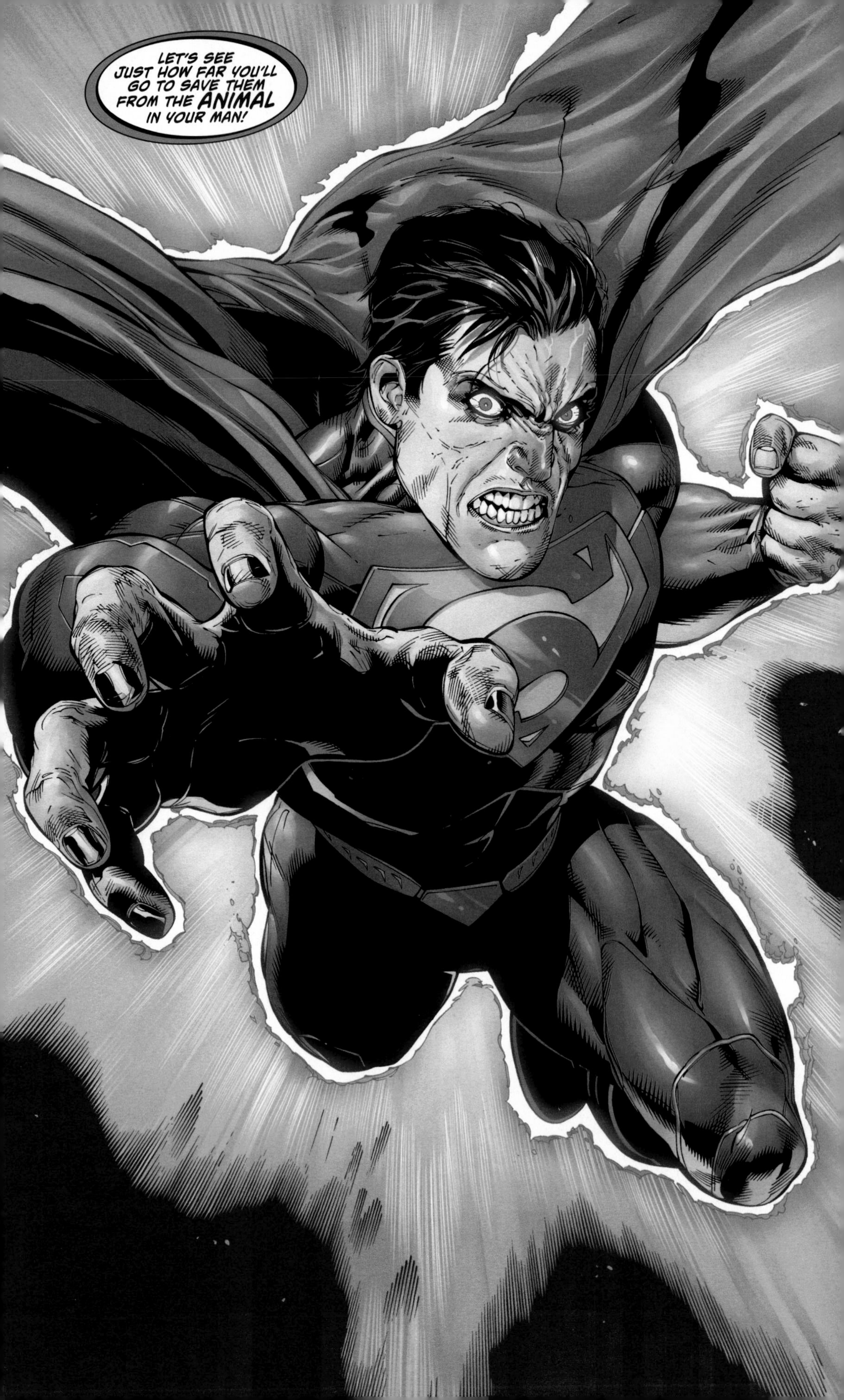
LET'S SEE JUST HOW FAR YOU'LL GO TO SAVE THEM FROM THE ANIMAL IN YOUR MAN!

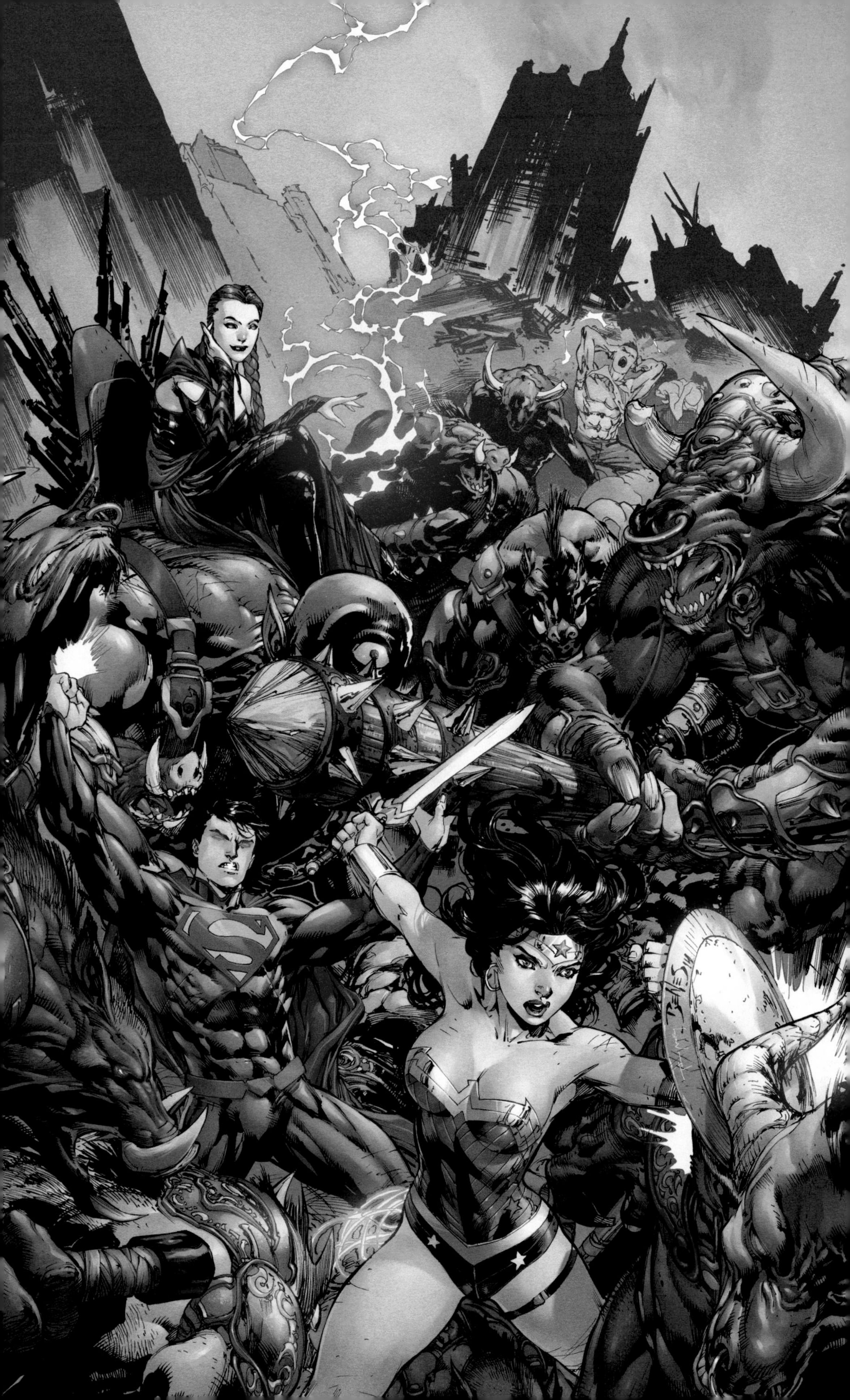

CASUALTIES OF WAR

PETER J. TOMASI writer **DOUG MAHNKE ED BENES** pencillers **JAIME MENDOZA KEITH CHAMPAGNE MARK IRWIN ED BENES** inkers **WIL QUINTANA** colorist
ROB LEIGH letterer cover by **BENES & MOREY**

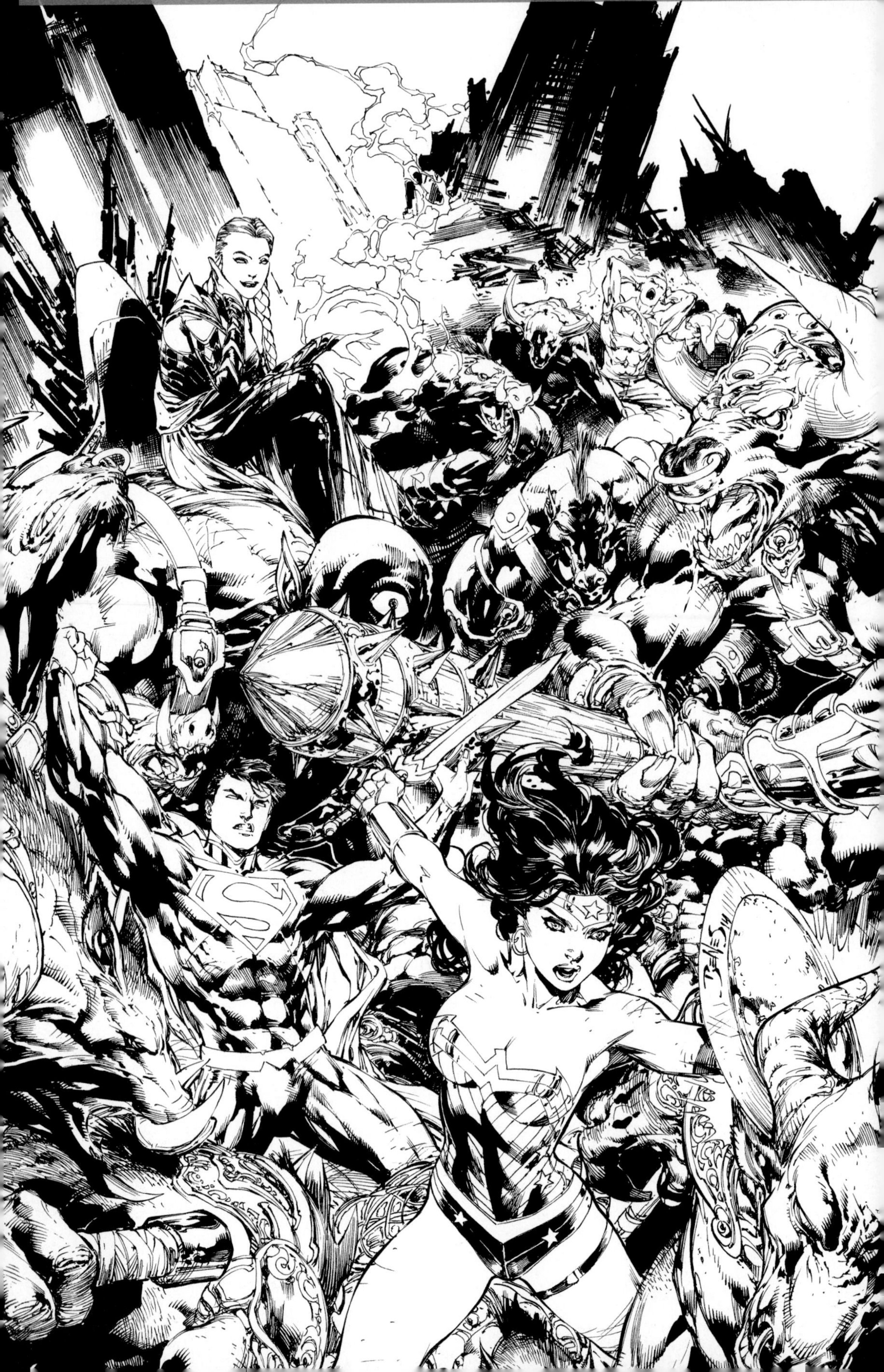

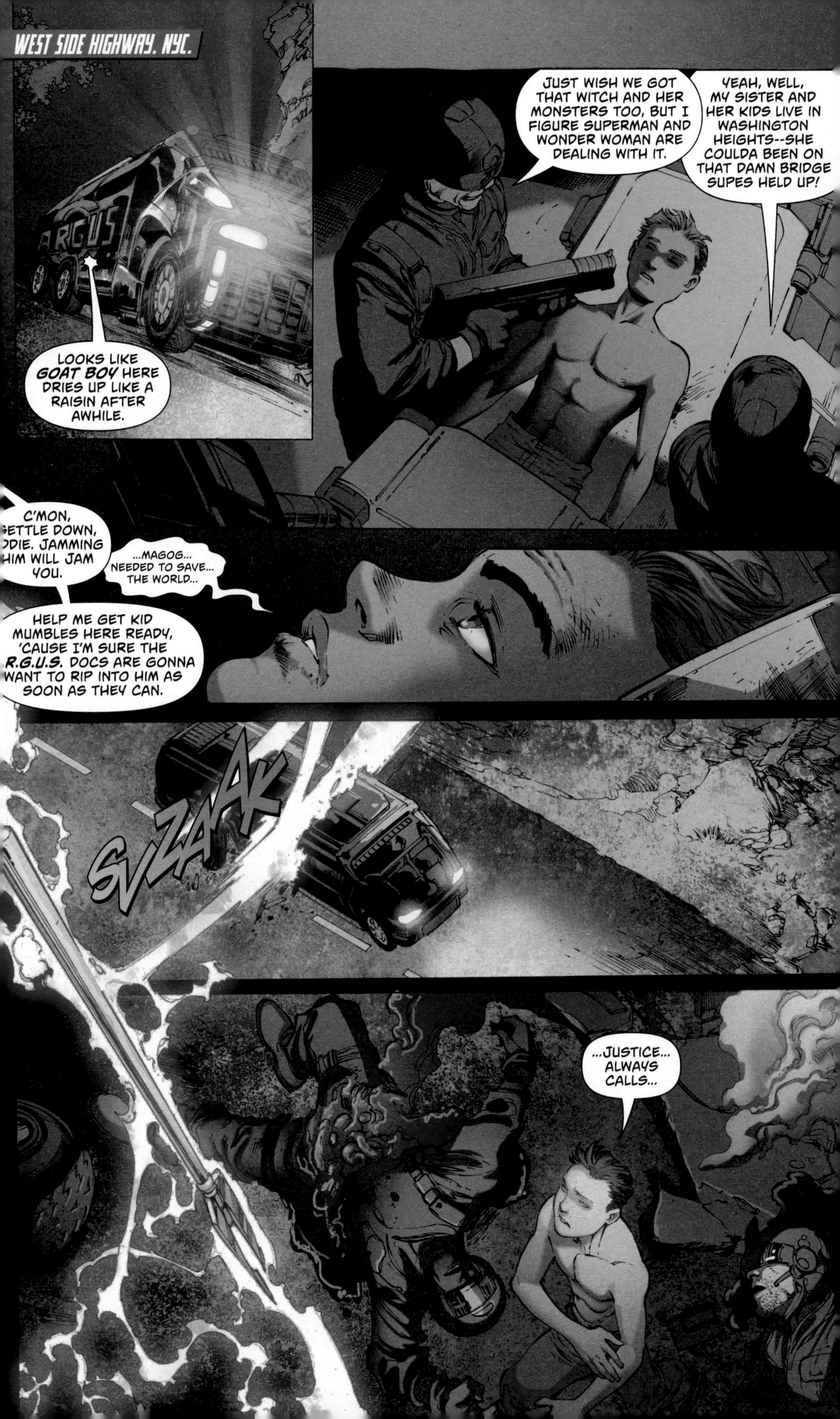
WEST SIDE HIGHWAY. NYC.
LOOKS LIKE GOAT BOY HERE DRIES UP LIKE A RAISIN AFTER AWHILE.
JUST WISH WE GOT THAT WITCH AND HER MONSTERS TOO, BUT I FIGURE SUPERMAN AND WONDER WOMAN ARE DEALING WITH IT.
YEAH, WELL, MY SISTER AND HER KIDS LIVE IN WASHINGTON HEIGHTS--SHE COULDA BEEN ON THAT DAMN BRIDGE SUPES HELD UP!
C'MON, SETTLE DOWN, DDIE. JAMMING HIM WILL JAM YOU.
HELP ME GET KID MUMBLES HERE READY, 'CAUSE I'M SURE THE R.G.U.S. DOCS ARE GONNA WANT TO RIP INTO HIM AS SOON AS THEY CAN.
...MAGOG... NEEDED TO SAVE... THE WORLD...
SVZAAK
...JUSTICE... ALWAYS CALLS...

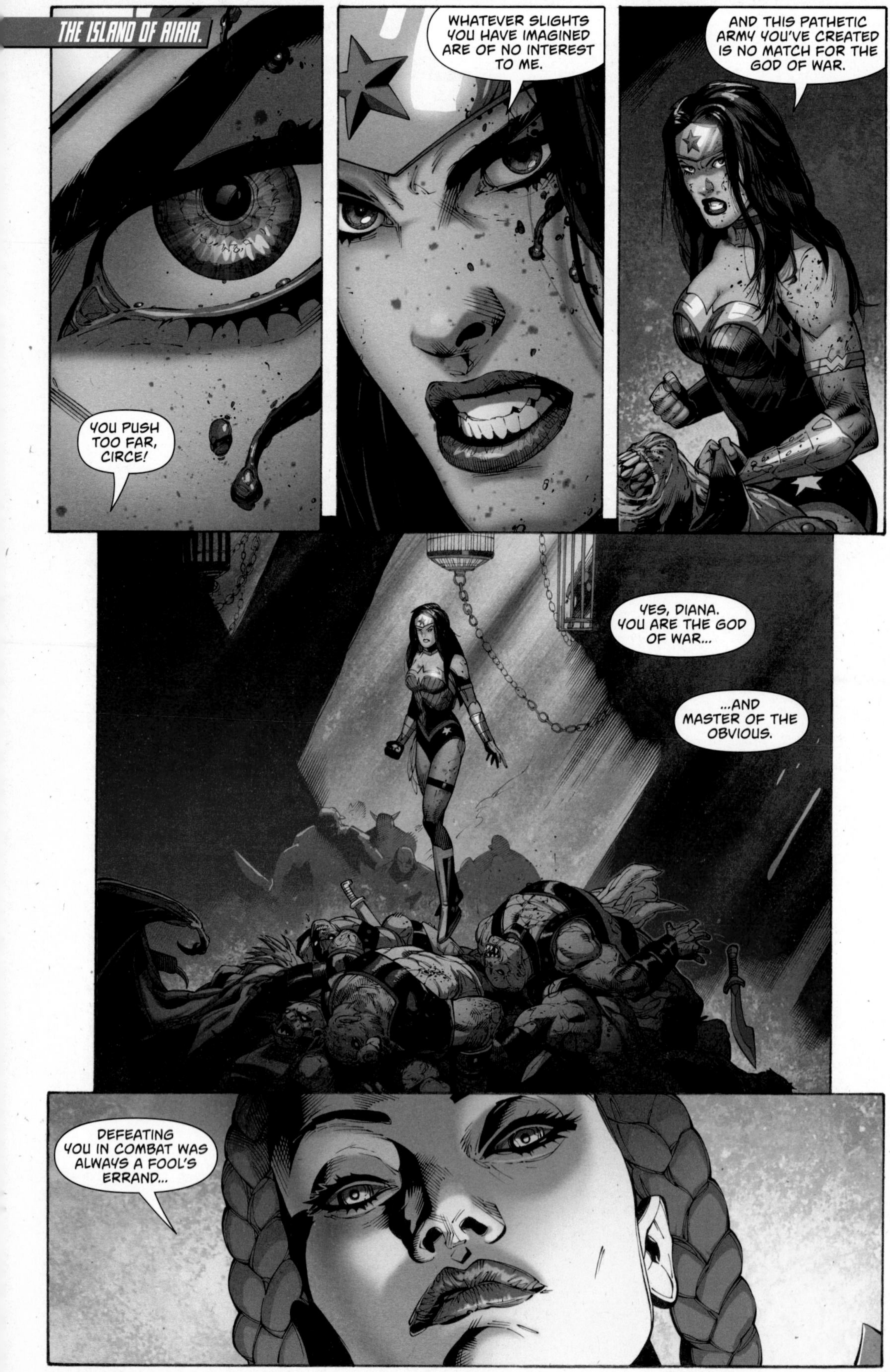
THE ISLAND OF AIAIA.
YOU PUSH TOO FAR, CIRCE!
WHATEVER SLIGHTS YOU HAVE IMAGINED ARE OF NO INTEREST TO ME.
AND THIS PATHETIC ARMY YOU'VE CREATED IS NO MATCH FOR THE GOD OF WAR.
YES, DIANA. YOU ARE THE GOD OF WAR...
...AND MASTER OF THE OBVIOUS.
DEFEATING YOU IN COMBAT WAS ALWAYS A FOOL'S ERRAND...

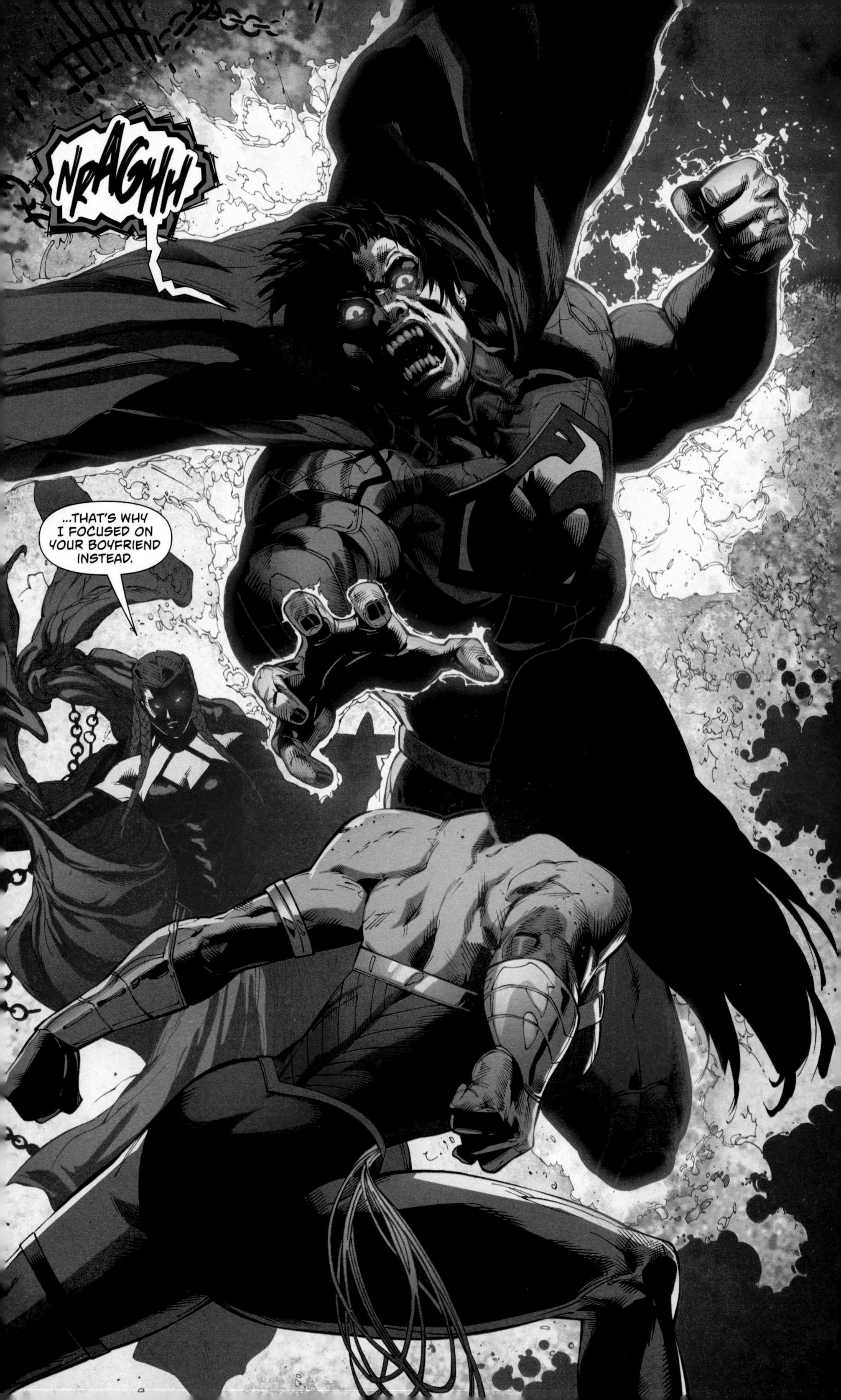
NRAGHH
...THAT'S WHY I FOCUSED ON YOUR BOYFRIEND INSTEAD.

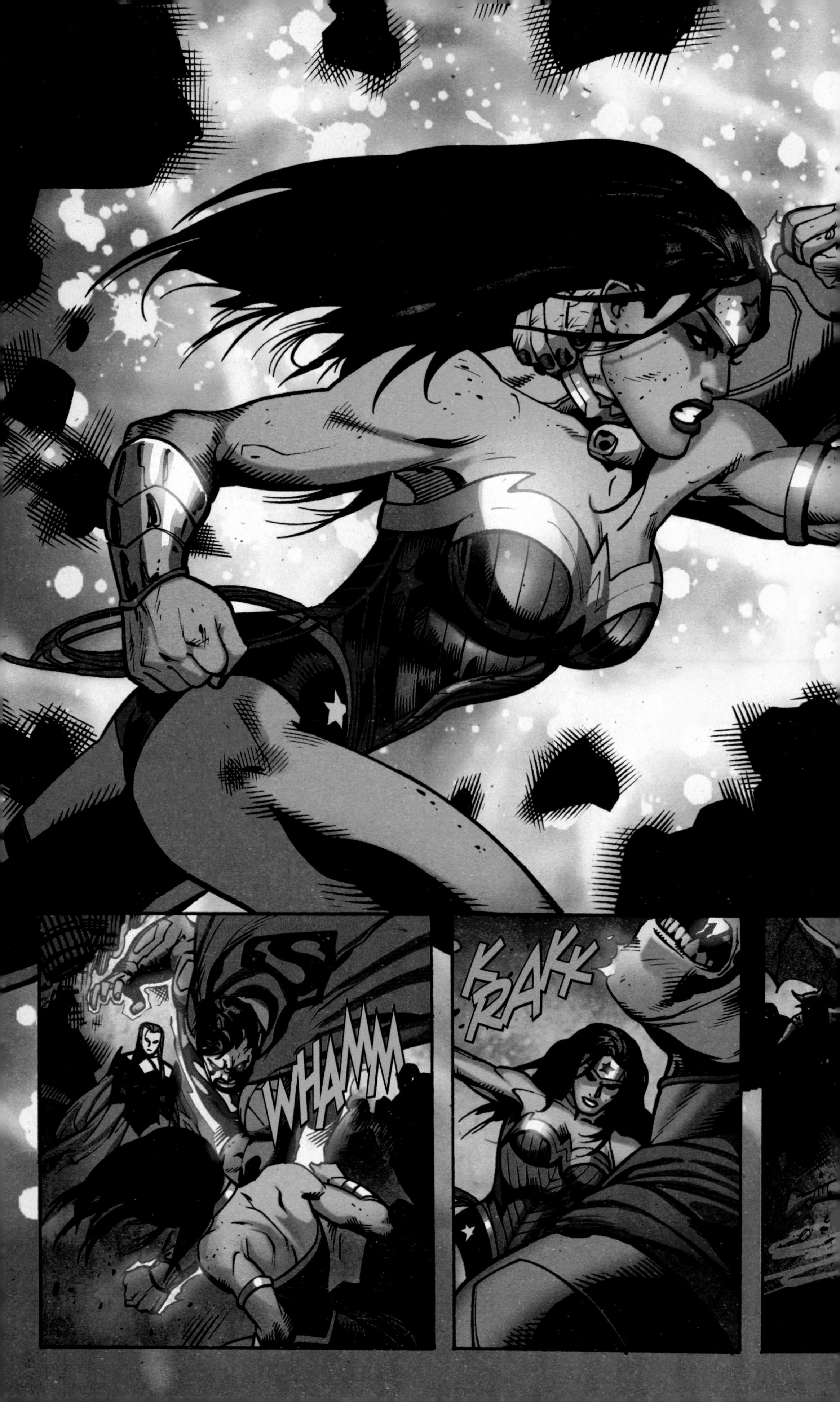
WHAMM
KRAKK

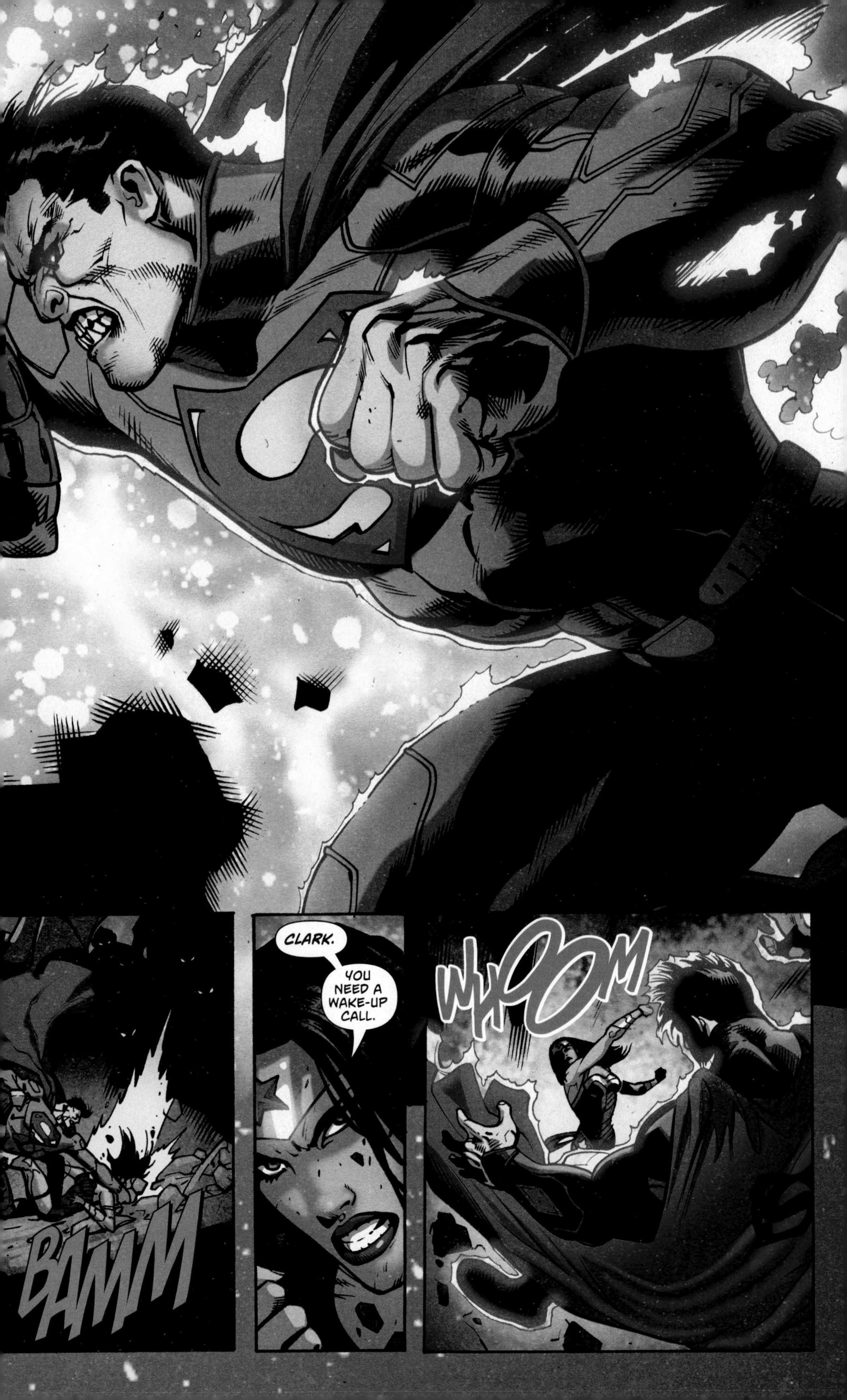
BAMM
CLARK.
YOU NEED A WAKE-UP CALL.
WHOOM

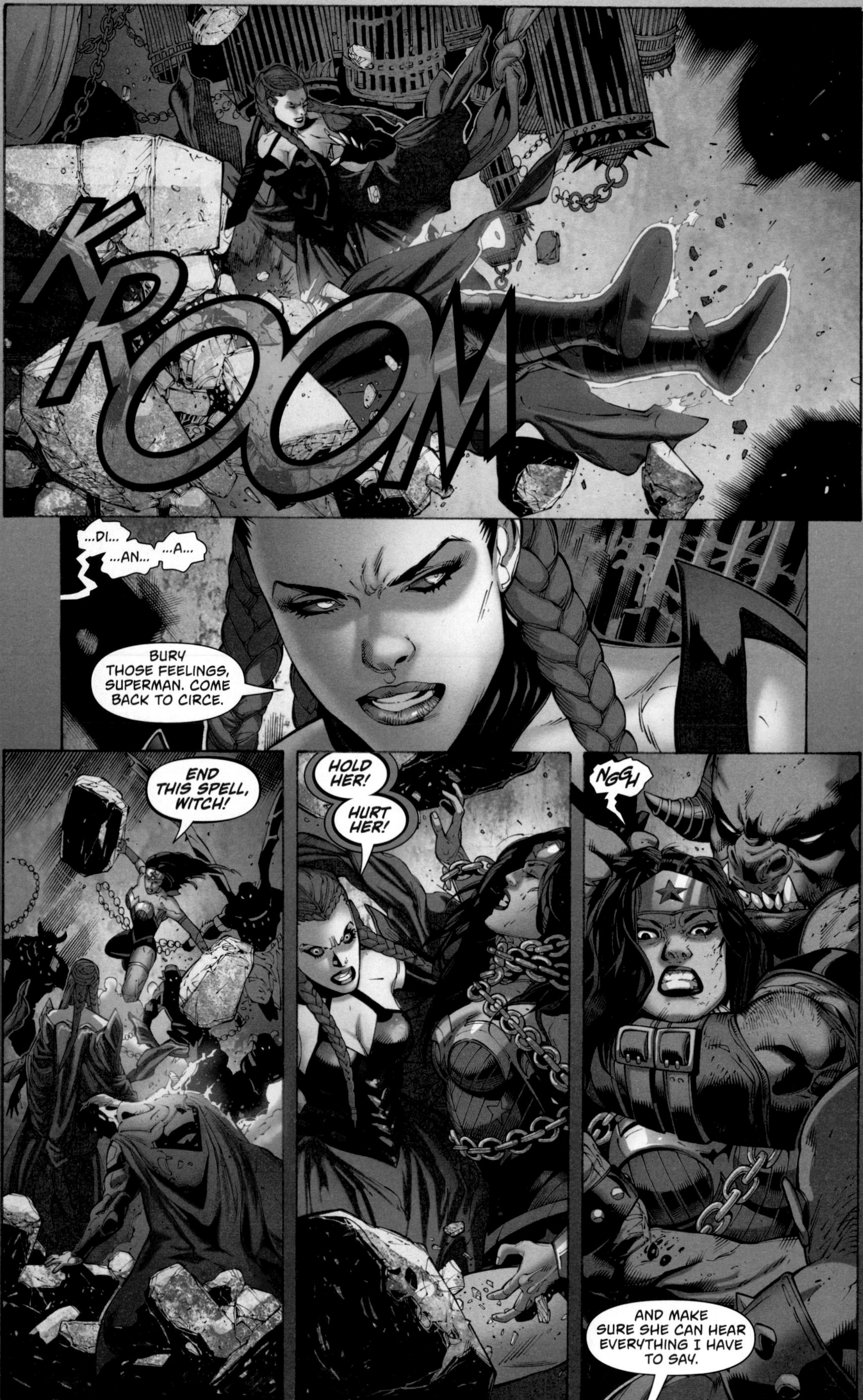
KROOM
...DI...
...AN...
...A...
BURY THOSE FEELINGS, SUPERMAN. COME BACK TO CIRCE.
END THIS SPELL, WITCH!
HOLD HER!
HURT HER!
NGGH
AND MAKE SURE SHE CAN HEAR EVERYTHING I HAVE TO SAY.

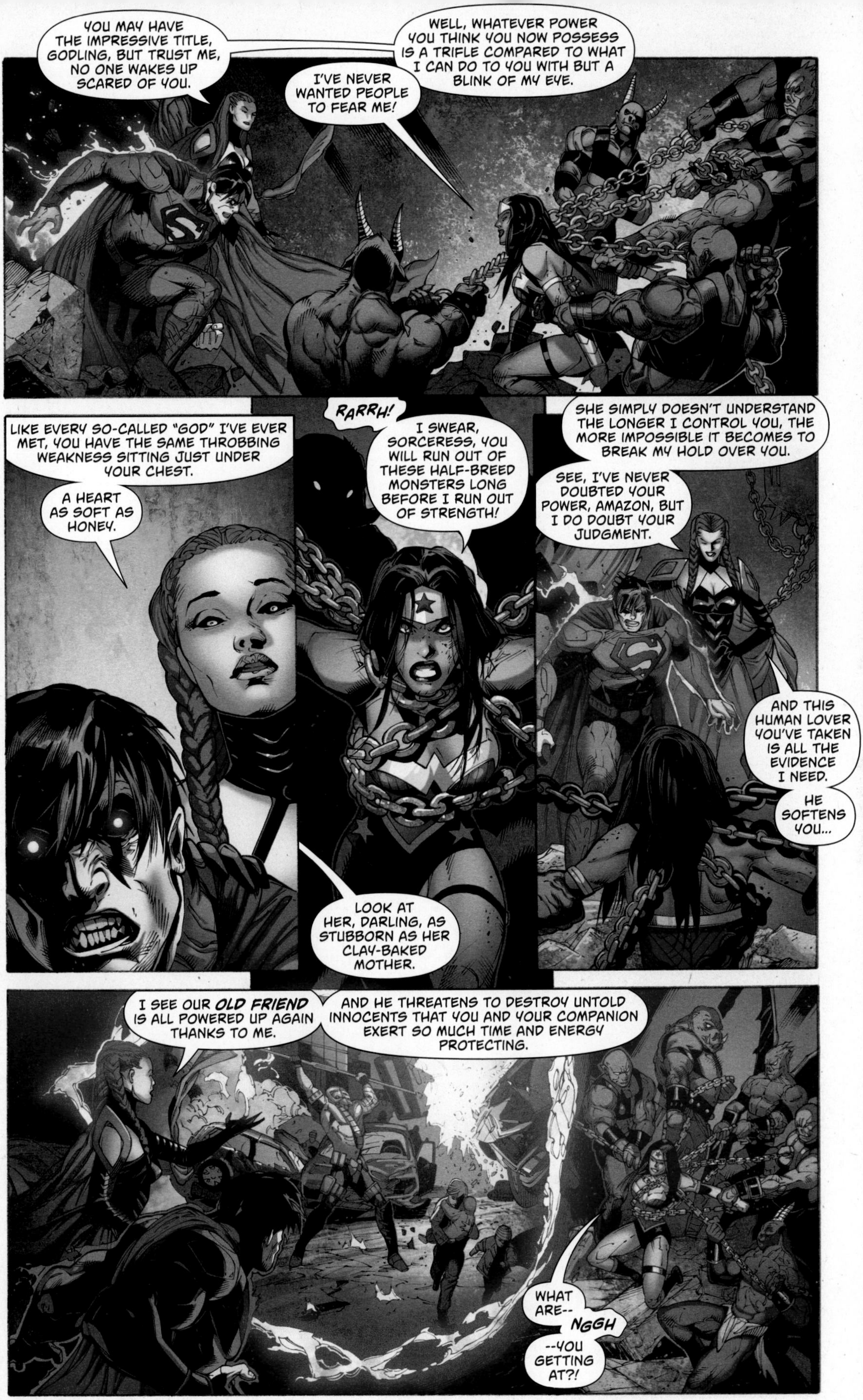

YOU MAY HAVE THE IMPRESSIVE TITLE, GODLING, BUT TRUST ME, NO ONE WAKES UP SCARED OF YOU.
I'VE NEVER WANTED PEOPLE TO FEAR ME!
WELL, WHATEVER POWER YOU THINK YOU NOW POSSESS IS A TRIFLE COMPARED TO WHAT I CAN DO TO YOU WITH BUT A BLINK OF MY EYE.
LIKE EVERY SO-CALLED "GOD" I'VE EVER MET, YOU HAVE THE SAME THROBBING WEAKNESS SITTING JUST UNDER YOUR CHEST.
A HEART AS SOFT AS HONEY.
RARRH!
I SWEAR, SORCERESS, YOU WILL RUN OUT OF THESE HALF-BREED MONSTERS LONG BEFORE I RUN OUT OF STRENGTH!
LOOK AT HER, DARLING, AS STUBBORN AS HER CLAY-BAKED MOTHER.
SHE SIMPLY DOESN'T UNDERSTAND THE LONGER I CONTROL YOU, THE MORE IMPOSSIBLE IT BECOMES TO BREAK MY HOLD OVER YOU.
SEE, I'VE NEVER DOUBTED YOUR POWER, AMAZON, BUT I DO DOUBT YOUR JUDGMENT.
AND THIS HUMAN LOVER YOU'VE TAKEN IS ALL THE EVIDENCE I NEED.
HE SOFTENS YOU...
I SEE OUR OLD FRIEND IS ALL POWERED UP AGAIN THANKS TO ME.
AND HE THREATENS TO DESTROY UNTOLD INNOCENTS THAT YOU AND YOUR COMPANION EXERT SO MUCH TIME AND ENERGY PROTECTING.
WHAT ARE--
NGGH
--YOU GETTING AT?!

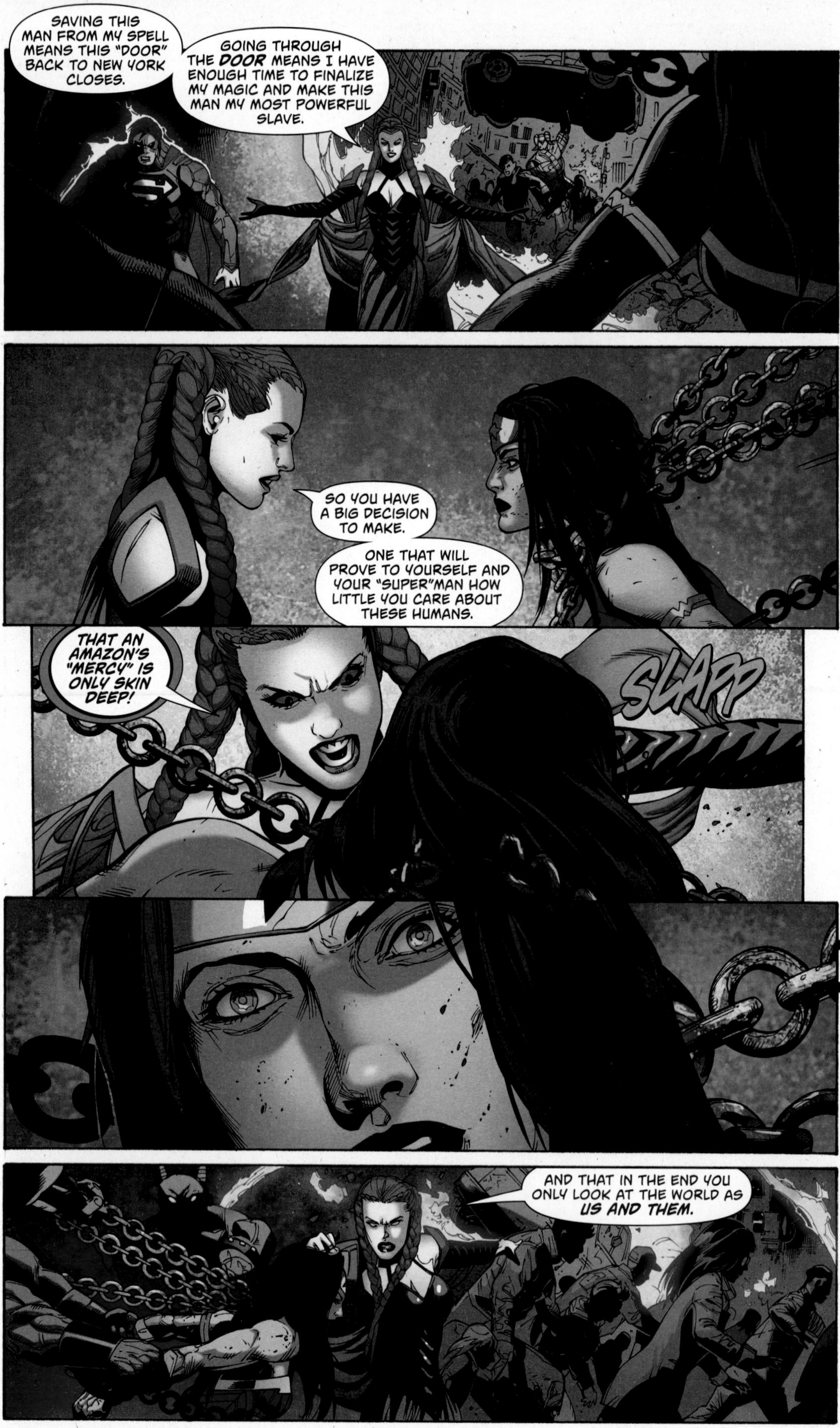
SAVING THIS MAN FROM MY SPELL MEANS THIS "DOOR" BACK TO NEW YORK CLOSES.
GOING THROUGH THE **DOOR** MEANS I HAVE ENOUGH TIME TO FINALIZE MY MAGIC AND MAKE THIS MAN MY MOST POWERFUL SLAVE.
SO YOU HAVE A BIG DECISION TO MAKE.
ONE THAT WILL PROVE TO YOURSELF AND YOUR "SUPER"MAN HOW LITTLE YOU CARE ABOUT THESE HUMANS.
THAT AN AMAZON'S "MERCY" IS ONLY SKIN DEEP!
SLAPP
AND THAT IN THE END YOU ONLY LOOK AT THE WORLD AS **US AND THEM.**

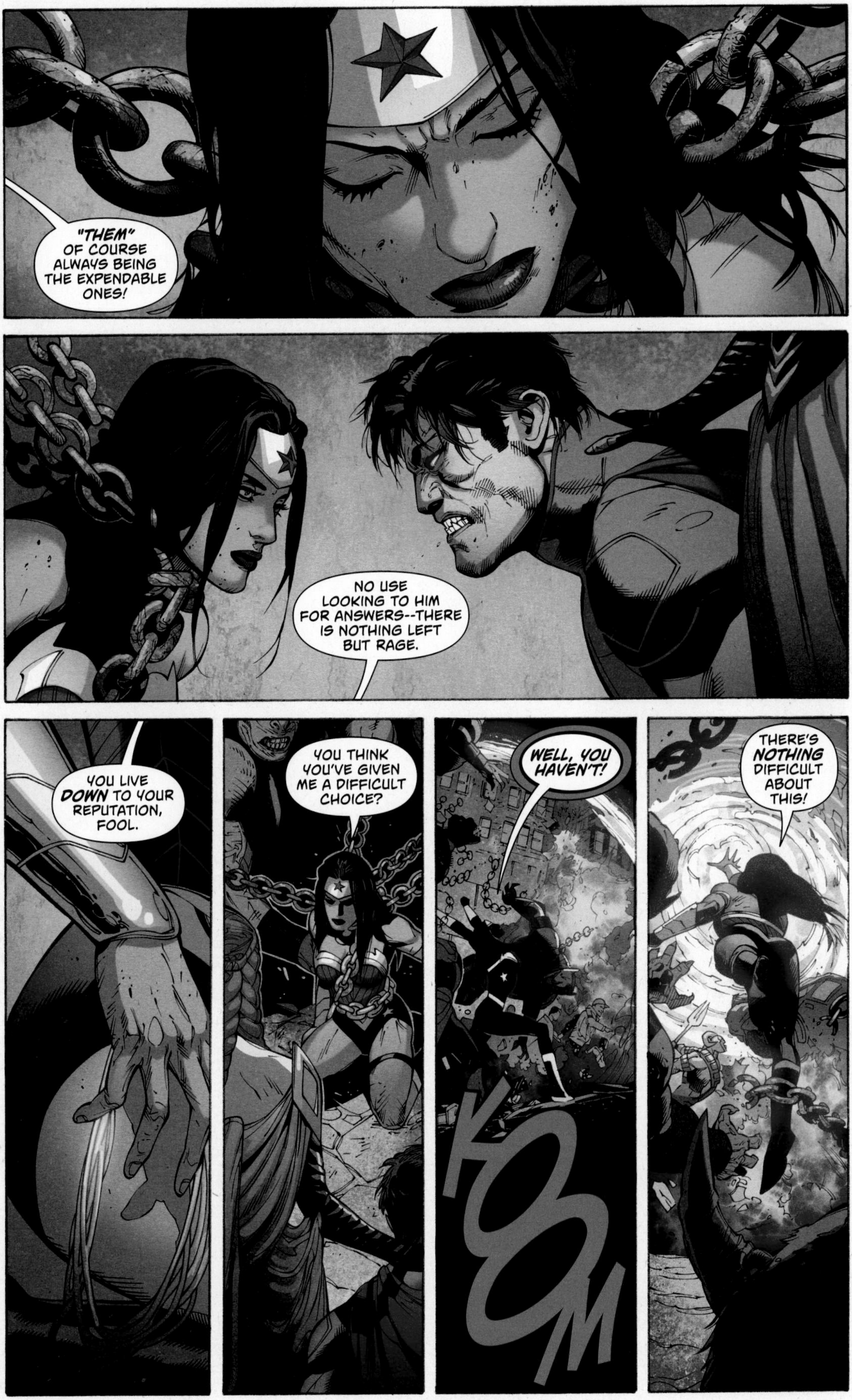
"THEM" OF COURSE ALWAYS BEING THE EXPENDABLE ONES!
NO USE LOOKING TO HIM FOR ANSWERS--THERE IS NOTHING LEFT BUT RAGE.
YOU LIVE DOWN TO YOUR REPUTATION, FOOL.
YOU THINK YOU'VE GIVEN ME A DIFFICULT CHOICE?
WELL, YOU HAVEN'T!
KOOM
THERE'S NOTHING DIFFICULT ABOUT THIS!

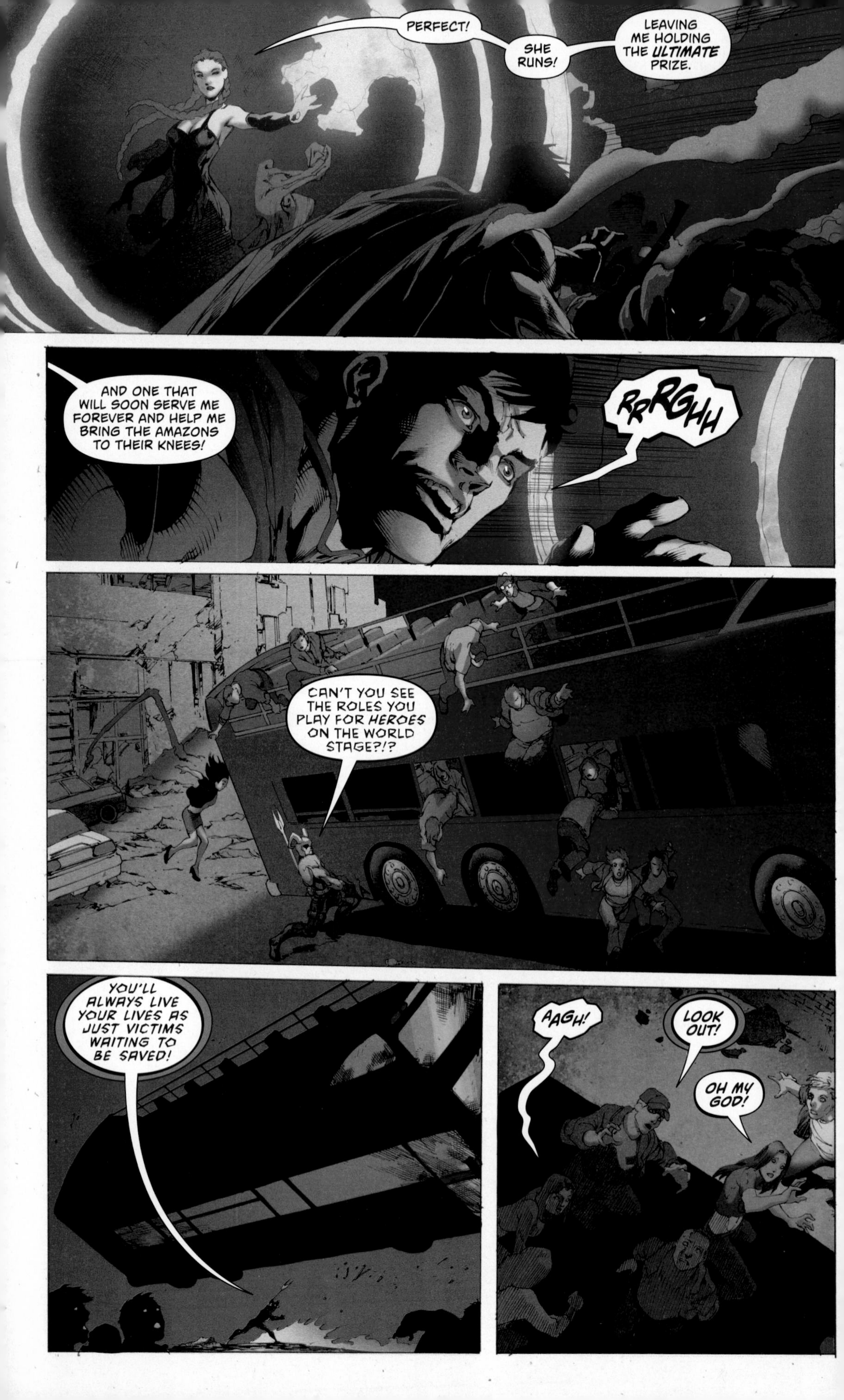
PERFECT!
SHE RUNS!
LEAVING ME HOLDING THE ULTIMATE PRIZE.
AND ONE THAT WILL SOON SERVE ME FOREVER AND HELP ME BRING THE AMAZONS TO THEIR KNEES!
RRRGHH
CAN'T YOU SEE THE ROLES YOU PLAY FOR HEROES ON THE WORLD STAGE?!?
YOU'LL ALWAYS LIVE YOUR LIVES AS JUST VICTIMS WAITING TO BE SAVED!
AAGH!
LOOK OUT!
OH MY GOD!

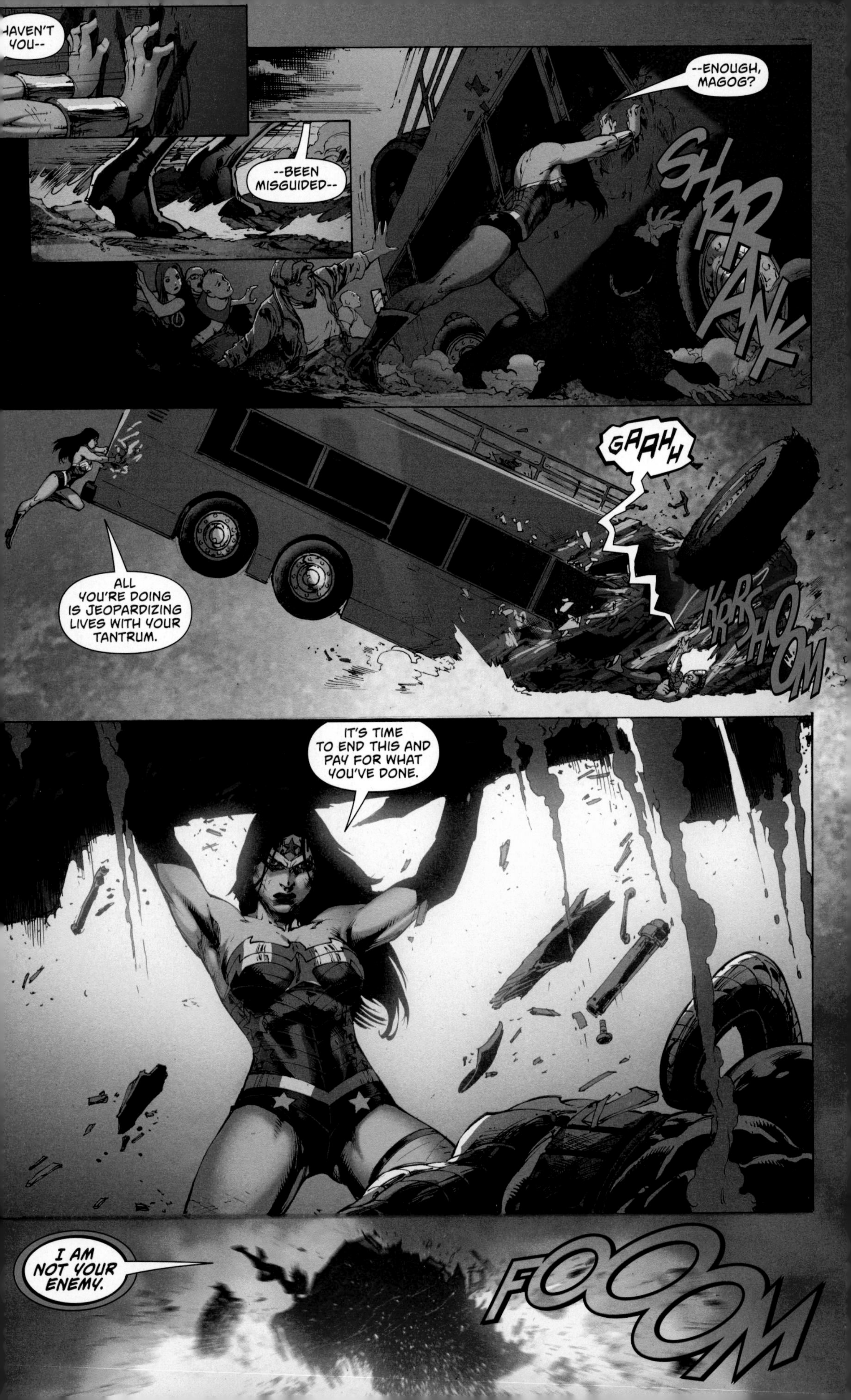
HAVEN'T YOU--
--BEEN MISGUIDED--
--ENOUGH, MAGOG?
SHRRRANK
ALL YOU'RE DOING IS JEOPARDIZING LIVES WITH YOUR TANTRUM.
GAAHH
KRRSHOOM
IT'S TIME TO END THIS AND PAY FOR WHAT YOU'VE DONE.
I AM NOT YOUR ENEMY.
FOOOOM

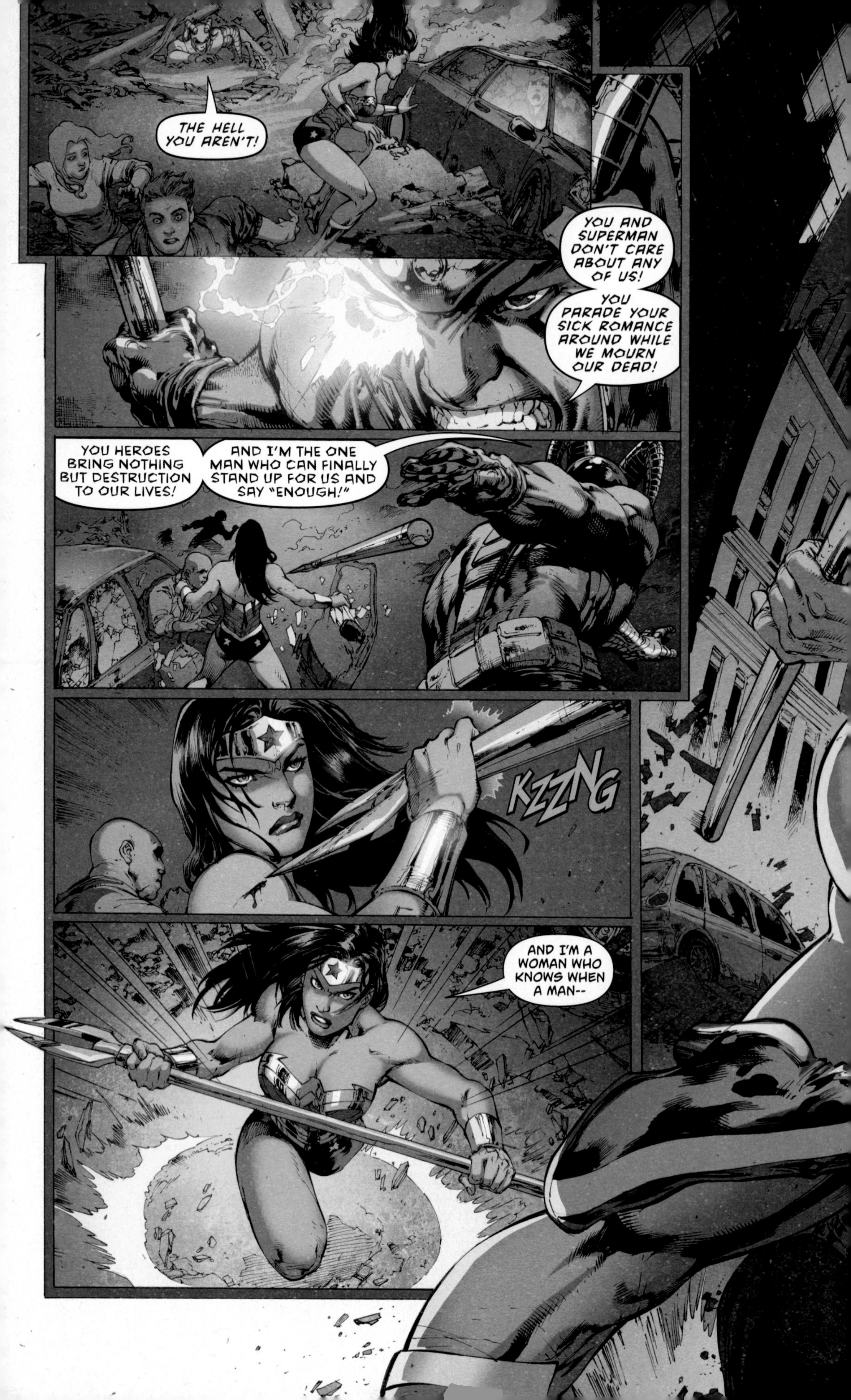
THE HELL YOU AREN'T!
YOU AND SUPERMAN DON'T CARE ABOUT ANY OF US!
YOU PARADE YOUR SICK ROMANCE AROUND WHILE WE MOURN OUR DEAD!
YOU HEROES BRING NOTHING BUT DESTRUCTION TO OUR LIVES!
AND I'M THE ONE MAN WHO CAN FINALLY STAND UP FOR US AND SAY "ENOUGH!"
KZZNG
AND I'M A WOMAN WHO KNOWS WHEN A MAN--

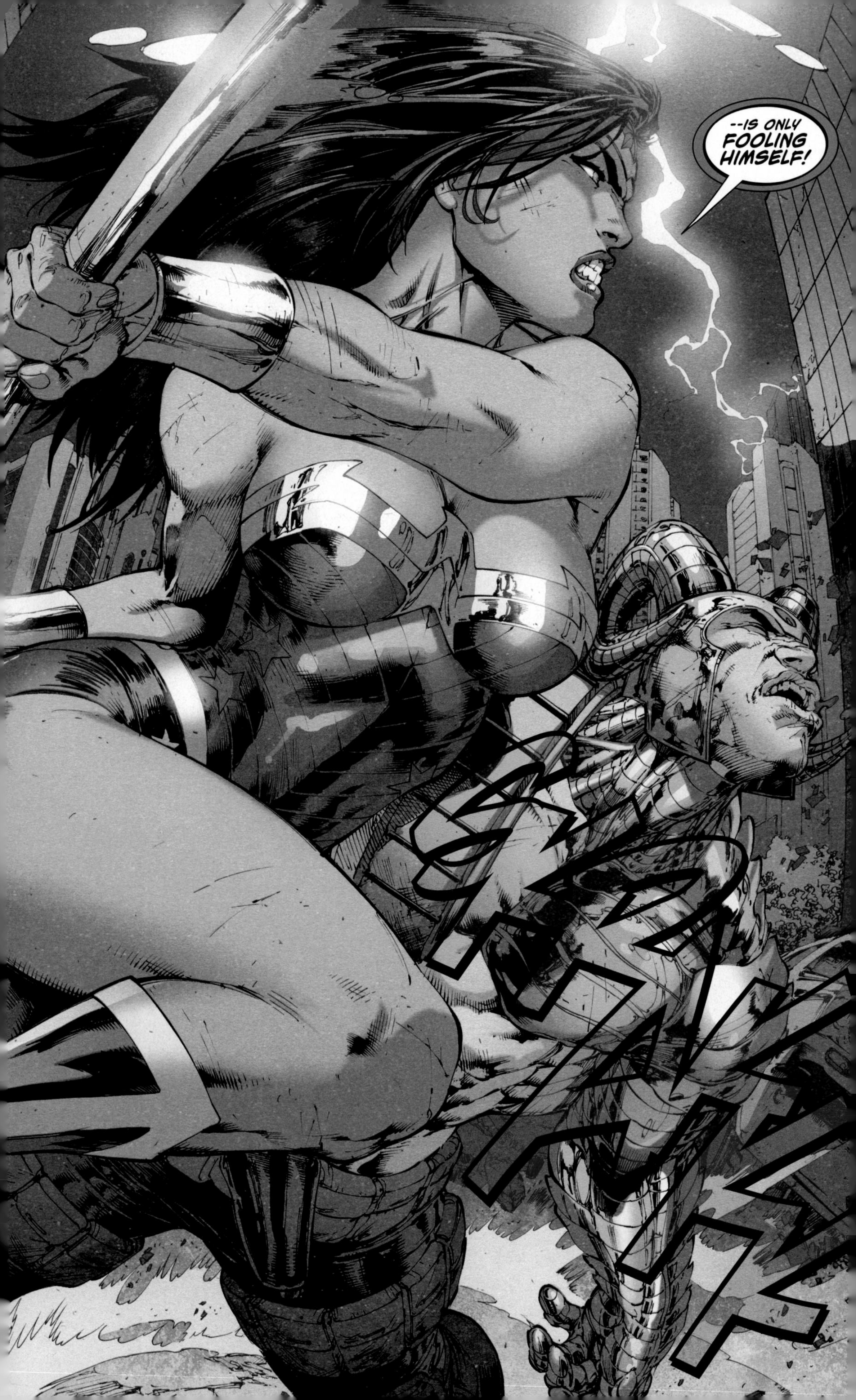
--IS ONLY FOOLING HIMSELF!

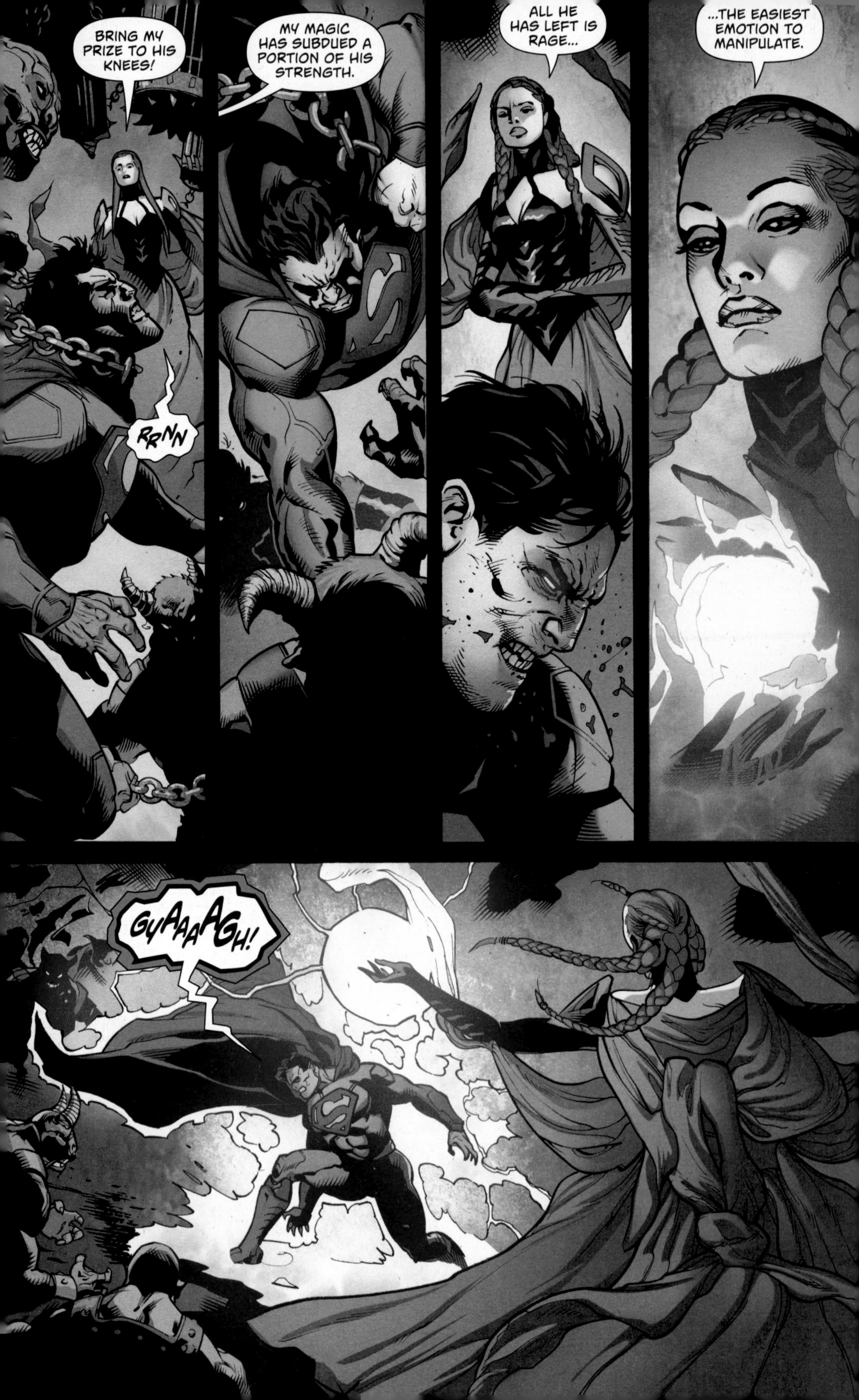
BRING MY PRIZE TO HIS KNEES!
RRNN
MY MAGIC HAS SUBDUED A PORTION OF HIS STRENGTH.
ALL HE HAS LEFT IS RAGE...
...THE EASIEST EMOTION TO MANIPULATE.
GYAAAAAGH!

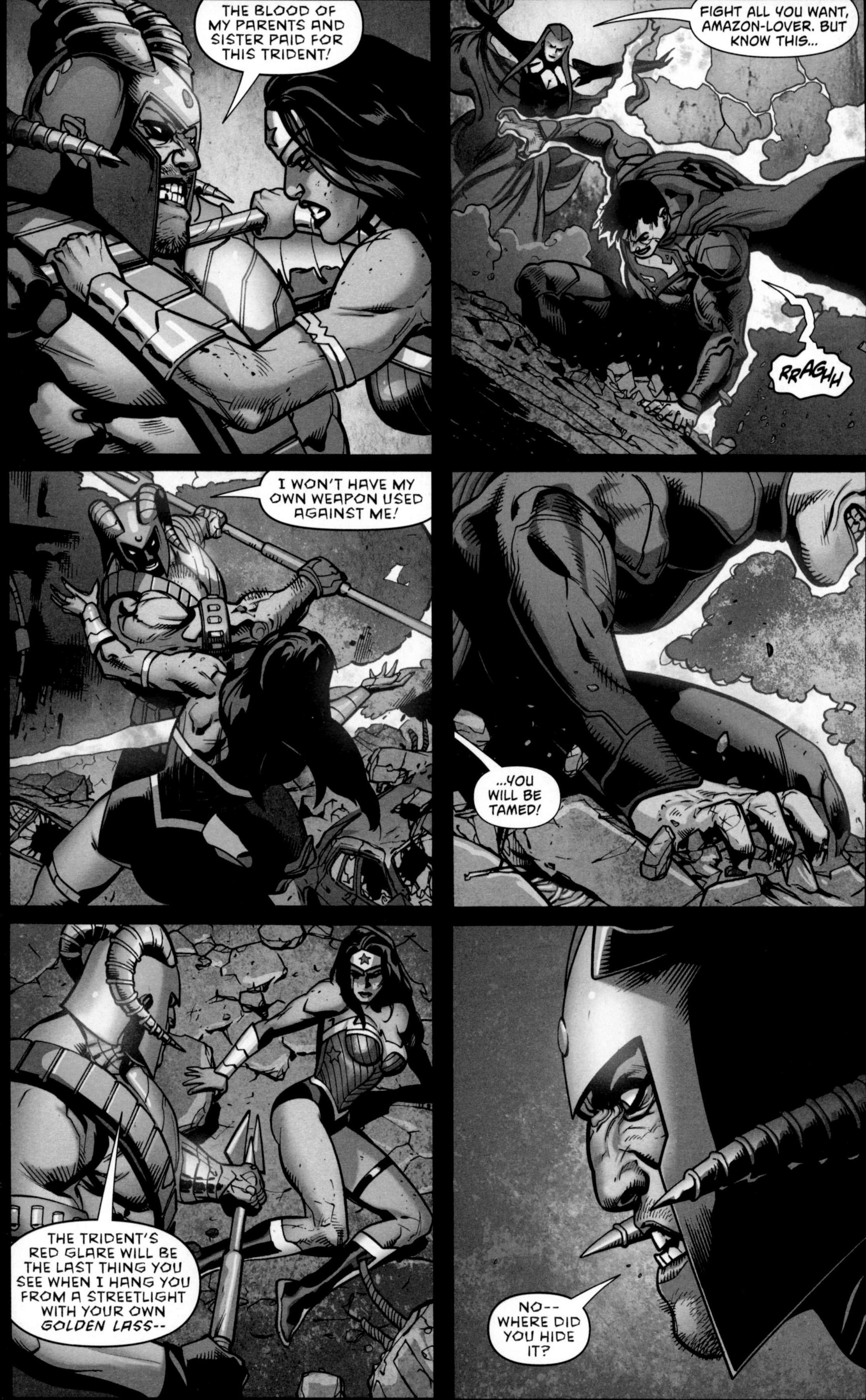
THE BLOOD OF MY PARENTS AND SISTER PAID FOR THIS TRIDENT!
FIGHT ALL YOU WANT, AMAZON-LOVER. BUT KNOW THIS...
RRAGHH
I WON'T HAVE MY OWN WEAPON USED AGAINST ME!
...YOU WILL BE TAMED!
THE TRIDENT'S RED GLARE WILL BE THE LAST THING YOU SEE WHEN I HANG YOU FROM A STREETLIGHT WITH YOUR OWN GOLDEN LASS--
NO-- WHERE DID YOU HIDE IT?

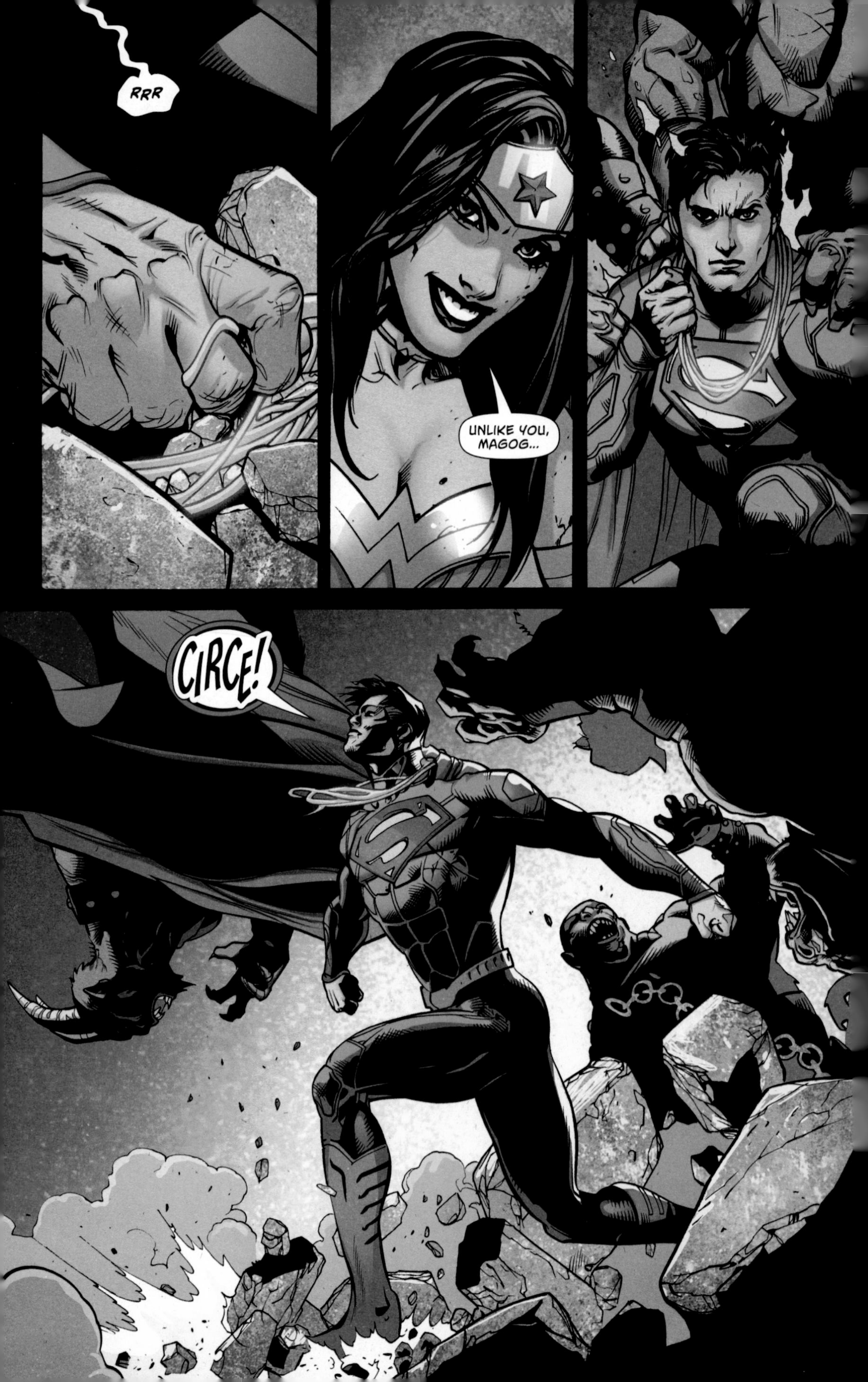
RRR
UNLIKE YOU, MAGOG...
CIRCE!

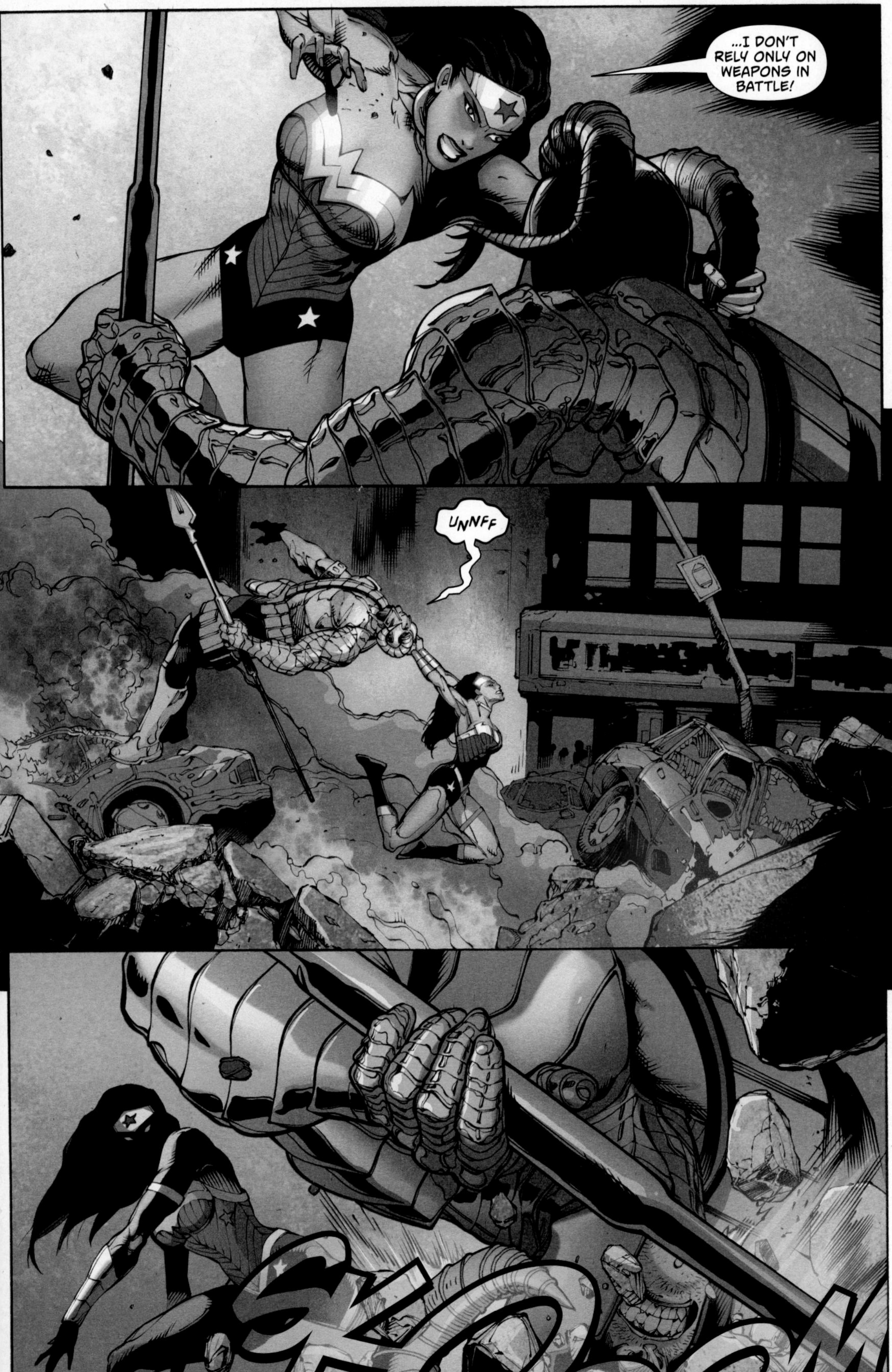
...I DON'T RELY ONLY ON WEAPONS IN BATTLE!
UNNFF
SKOOOM

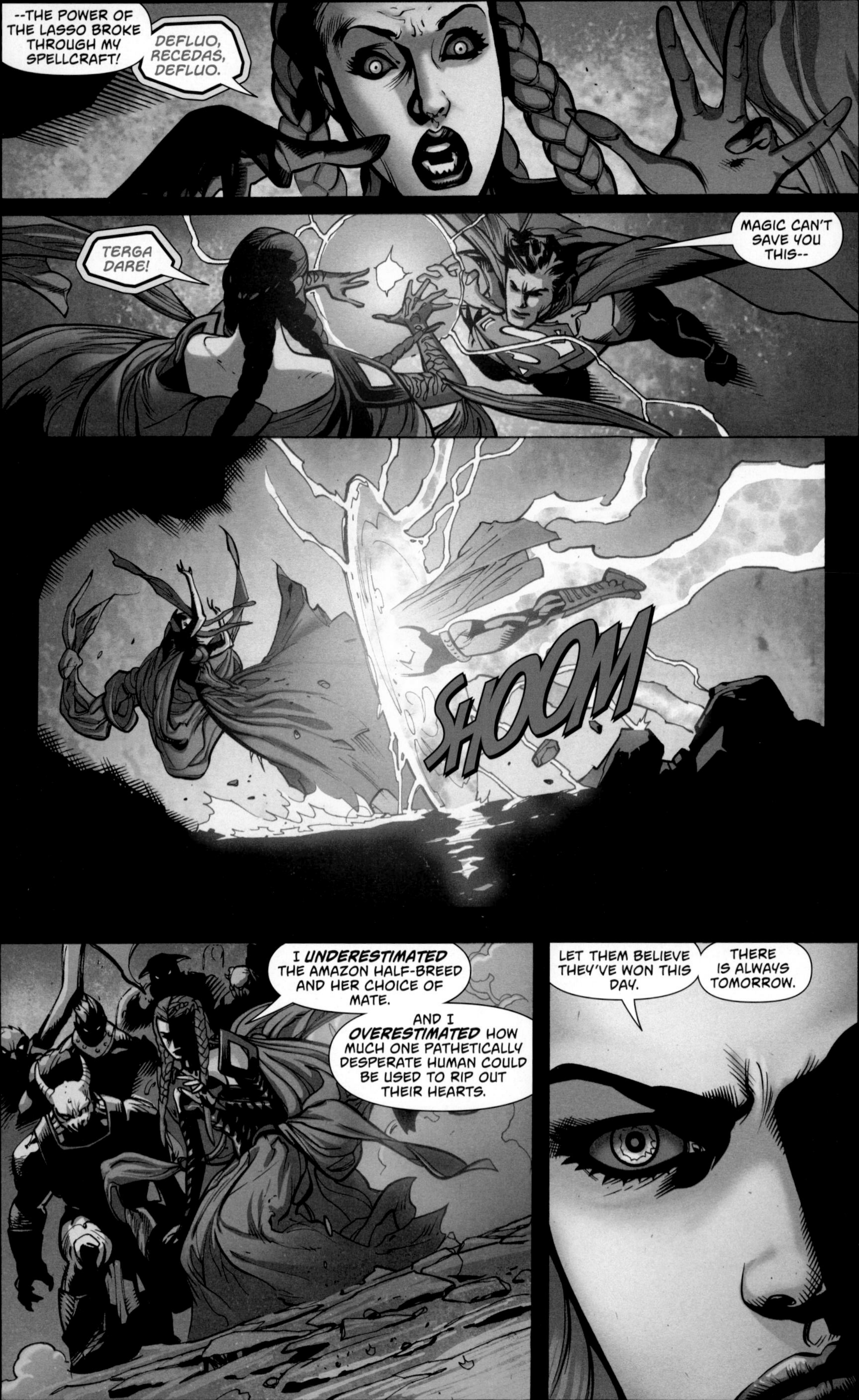
--THE POWER OF THE LASSO BROKE THROUGH MY SPELLCRAFT!
DEFLUO, RECEDAS, DEFLUO.
TERGA DARE!
MAGIC CAN'T SAVE YOU THIS--
SHOOM
I UNDERESTIMATED THE AMAZON HALF-BREED AND HER CHOICE OF MATE.
AND I OVERESTIMATED HOW MUCH ONE PATHETICALLY DESPERATE HUMAN COULD BE USED TO RIP OUT THEIR HEARTS.
LET THEM BELIEVE THEY'VE WON THIS DAY.
THERE IS ALWAYS TOMORROW.

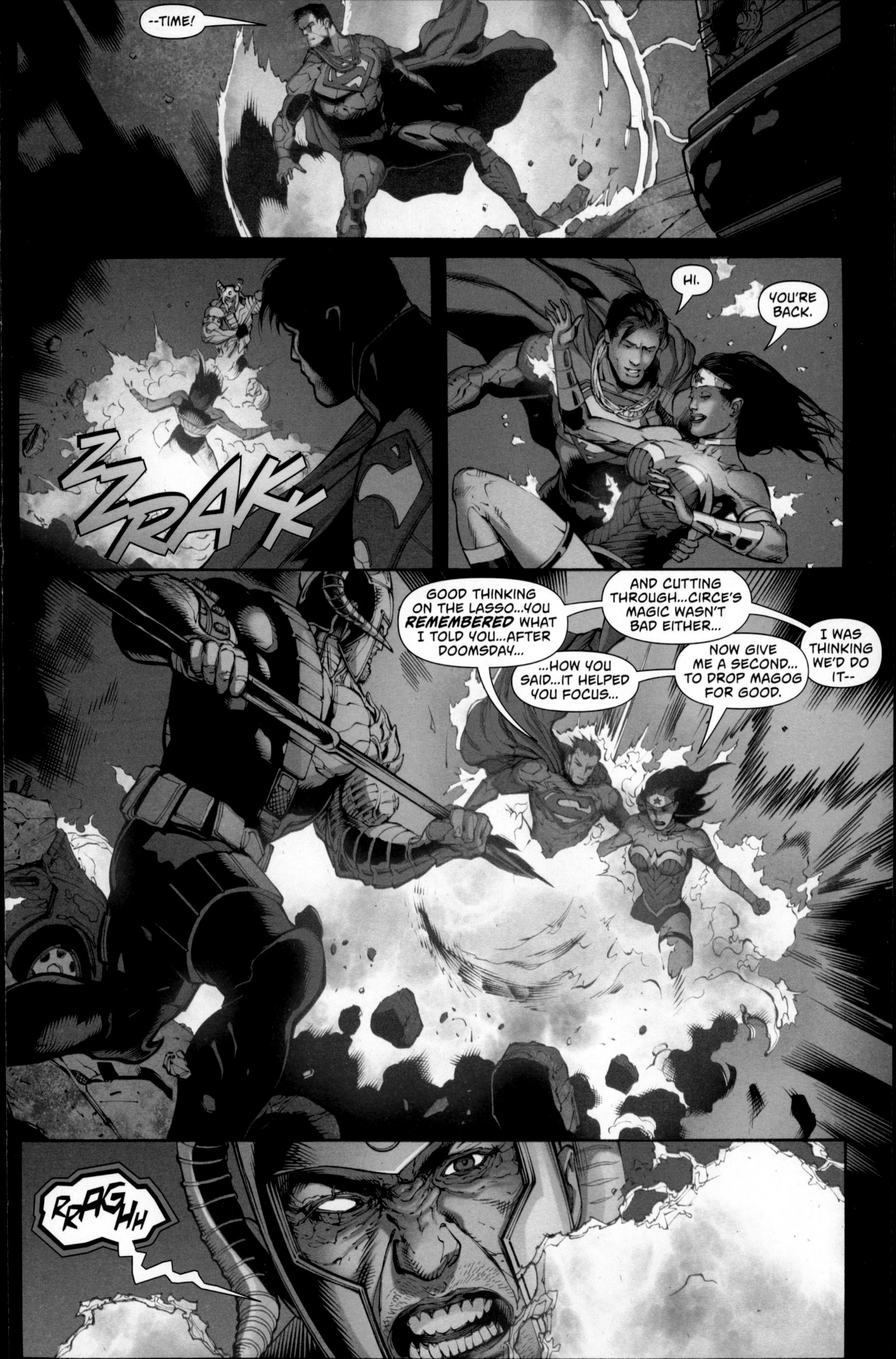
--TIME!
ZZRAKK
HI.
YOU'RE BACK.
GOOD THINKING ON THE LASSO...YOU REMEMBERED WHAT I TOLD YOU...AFTER DOOMSDAY...
...HOW YOU SAID...IT HELPED YOU FOCUS...
AND CUTTING THROUGH...CIRCE'S MAGIC WASN'T BAD EITHER...
NOW GIVE ME A SECOND... TO DROP MAGOG FOR GOOD.
I WAS THINKING WE'D DO IT--
RRAGHH

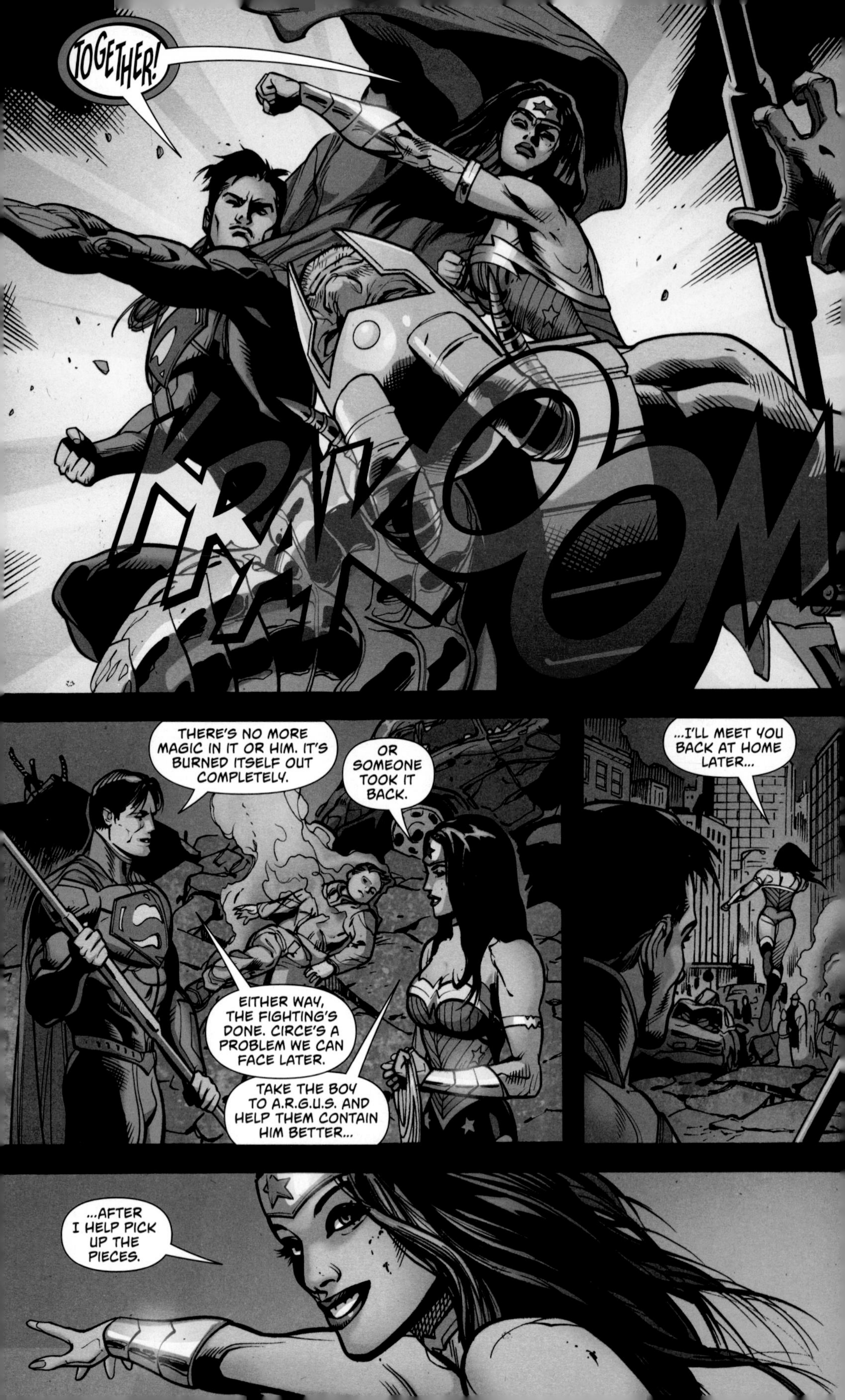
TOGETHER!
KRAKOOM
THERE'S NO MORE MAGIC IN IT OR HIM. IT'S BURNED ITSELF OUT COMPLETELY.
OR SOMEONE TOOK IT BACK.
EITHER WAY, THE FIGHTING'S DONE. CIRCE'S A PROBLEM WE CAN FACE LATER.
TAKE THE BOY TO A.R.G.U.S. AND HELP THEM CONTAIN HIM BETTER...
...I'LL MEET YOU BACK AT HOME LATER...
...AFTER I HELP PICK UP THE PIECES.

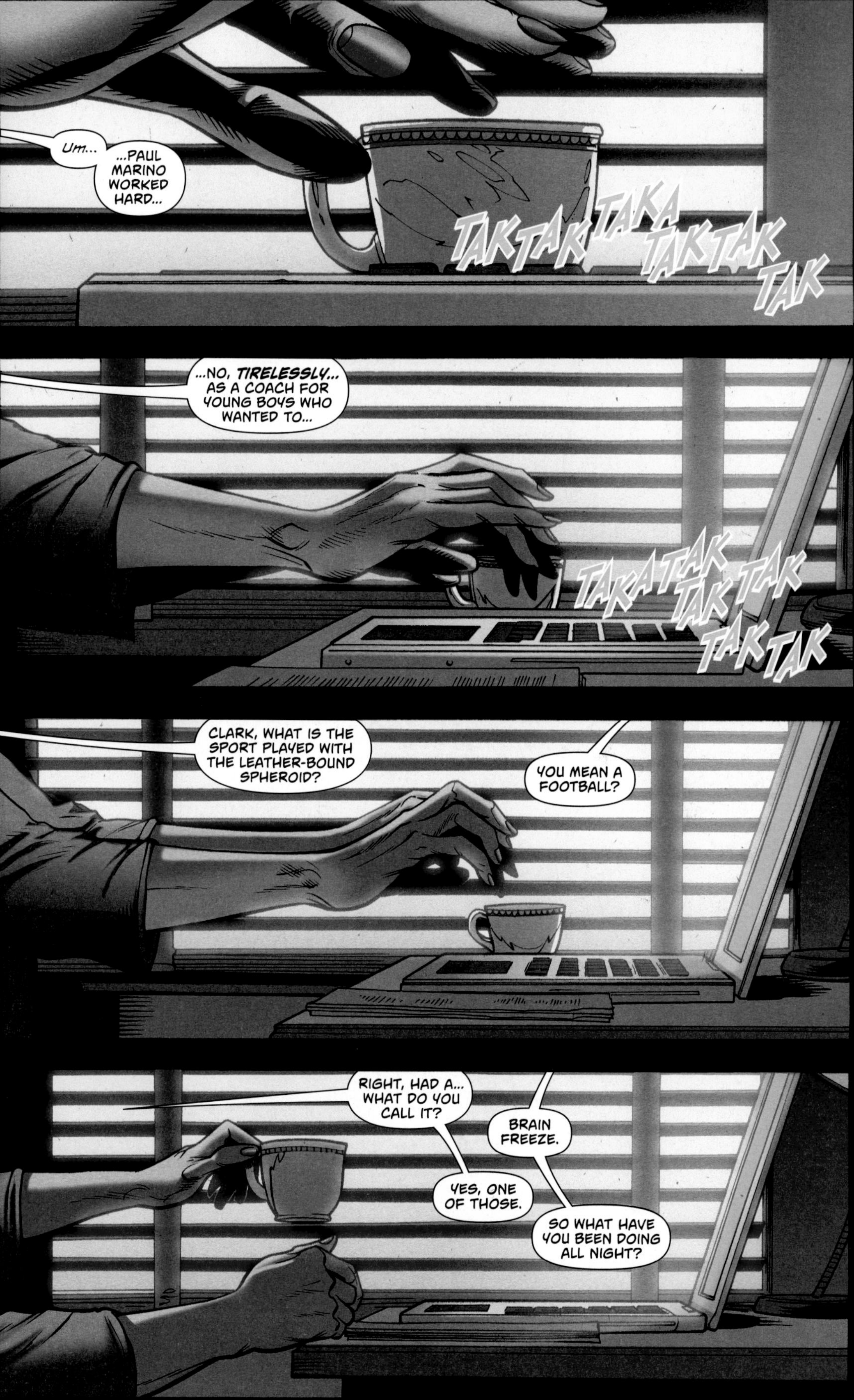
Um...
...PAUL MARINO WORKED HARD...
TAKTAKTAKA TAKTAK TAK
...NO, TIRELESSLY... AS A COACH FOR YOUNG BOYS WHO WANTED TO...
TAKATAK TAKTAK TAKTAK
CLARK, WHAT IS THE SPORT PLAYED WITH THE LEATHER-BOUND SPHEROID?
YOU MEAN A FOOTBALL?
RIGHT, HAD A... WHAT DO YOU CALL IT?
BRAIN FREEZE.
YES, ONE OF THOSE.
SO WHAT HAVE YOU BEEN DOING ALL NIGHT?

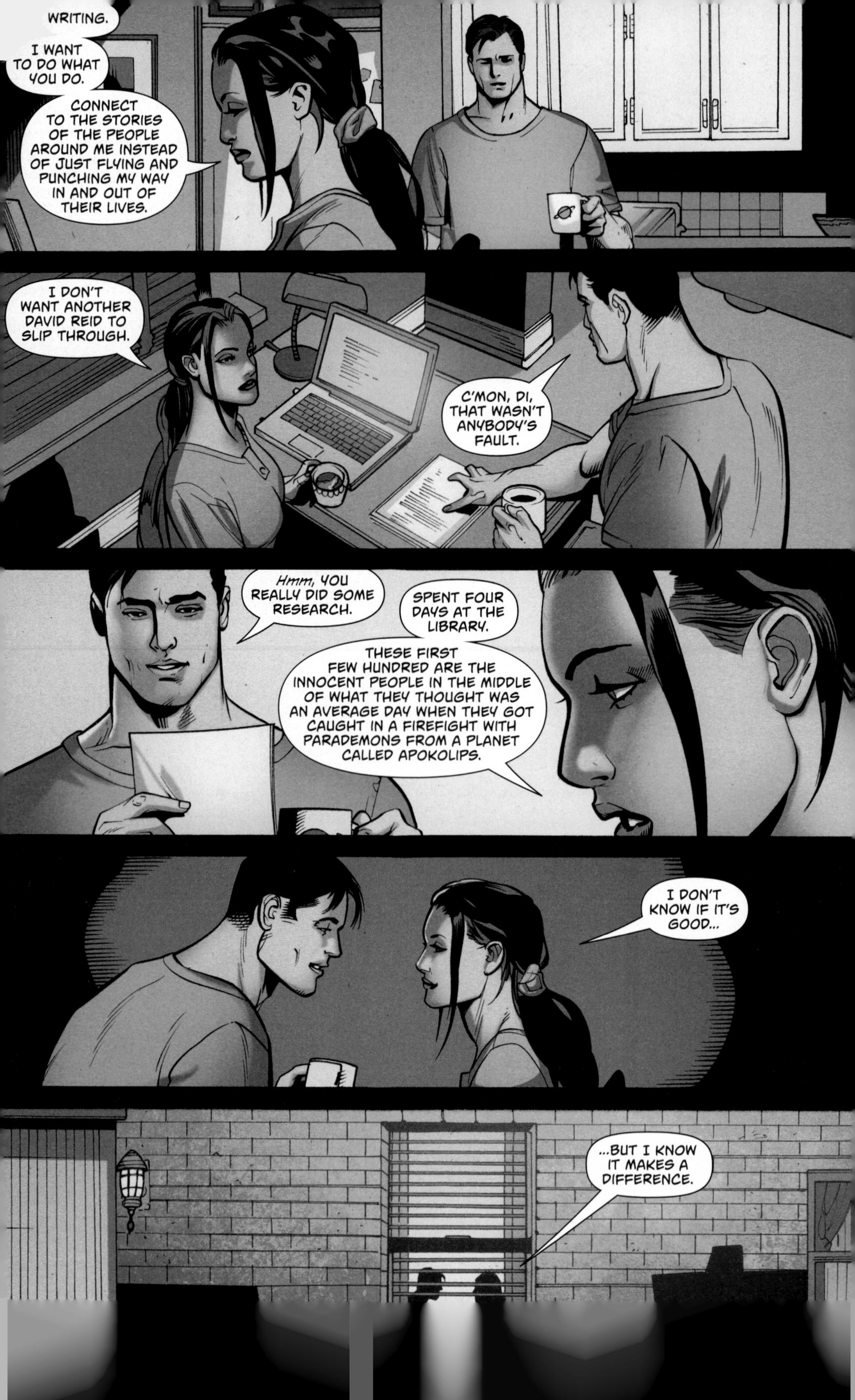
WRITING.
I WANT TO DO WHAT YOU DO.
CONNECT TO THE STORIES OF THE PEOPLE AROUND ME INSTEAD OF JUST FLYING AND PUNCHING MY WAY IN AND OUT OF THEIR LIVES.
I DON'T WANT ANOTHER DAVID REID TO SLIP THROUGH.
C'MON, DI, THAT WASN'T ANYBODY'S FAULT.
Hmm, YOU REALLY DID SOME RESEARCH.
SPENT FOUR DAYS AT THE LIBRARY.
THESE FIRST FEW HUNDRED ARE THE INNOCENT PEOPLE IN THE MIDDLE OF WHAT THEY THOUGHT WAS AN AVERAGE DAY WHEN THEY GOT CAUGHT IN A FIREFIGHT WITH PARADEMONS FROM A PLANET CALLED APOKOLIPS.
I DON'T KNOW IF IT'S GOOD...
...BUT I KNOW IT MAKES A DIFFERENCE.

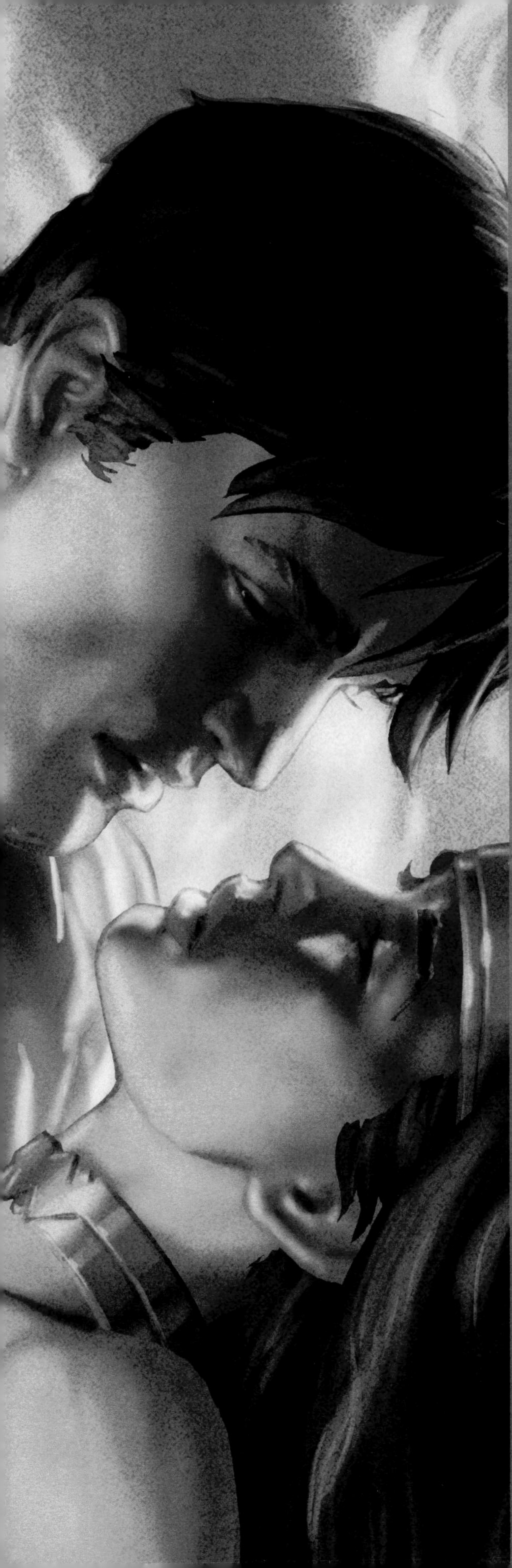

VARIANT COVER GALLERY

SUPERMAN/ WONDER WOMAN #13
LEGO VARIANT COVER

SUPERMAN/ WONDER WOMAN #15
FLASH 75TH ANNIVERSARY COVER BY IVAN REIS

SUPERMAN/ WONDER WOMAN #14
VARIANT COVER BY DARWYN COOKE

SUPERMAN/ WONDER WOMAN #16
HARLEY QUINN VARIANT COVER BY FRANCIS MANAPUL

SUPERMAN/ WONDER WOMAN #17
MOVIE VARIANT COVER BY GENE HA

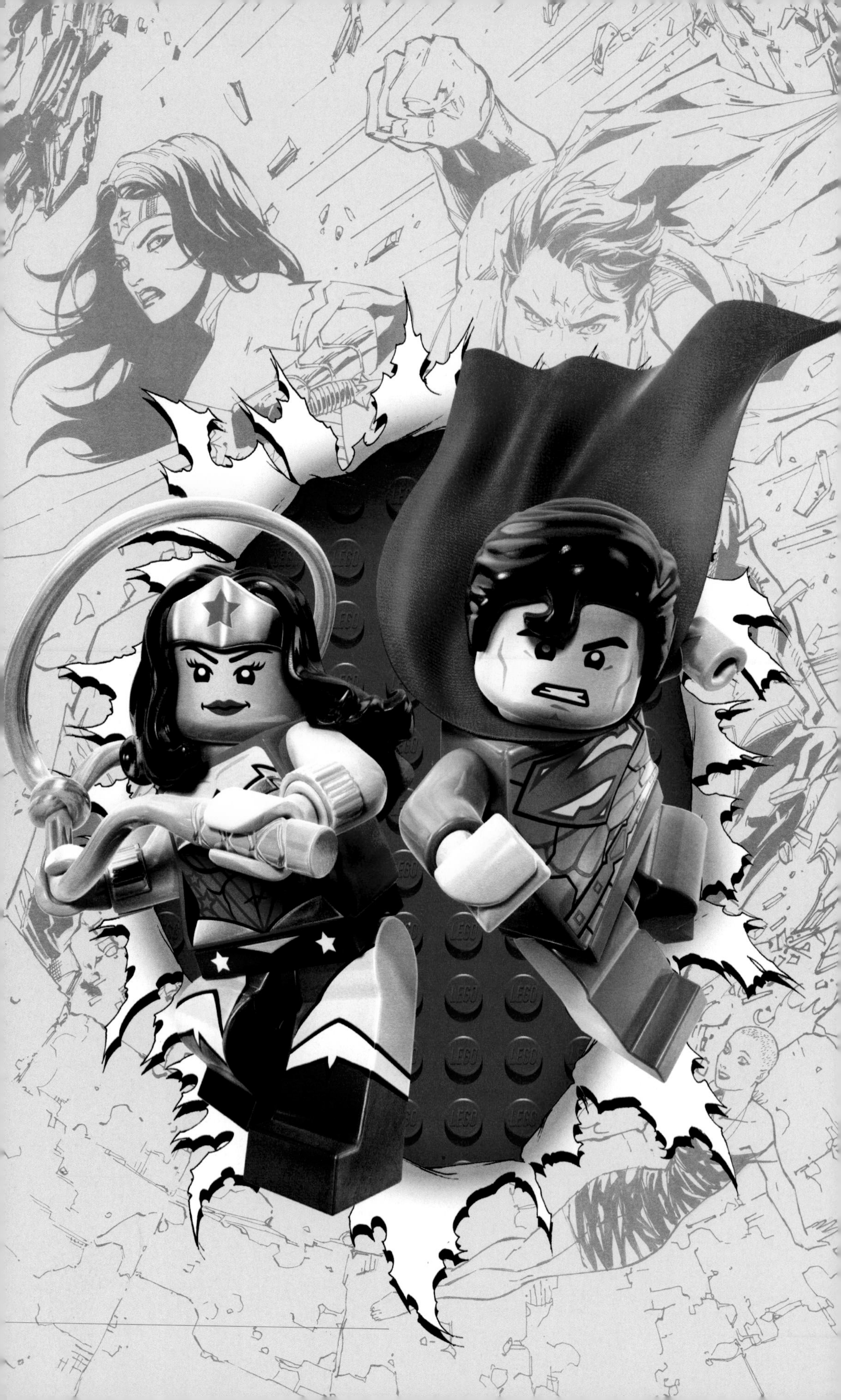

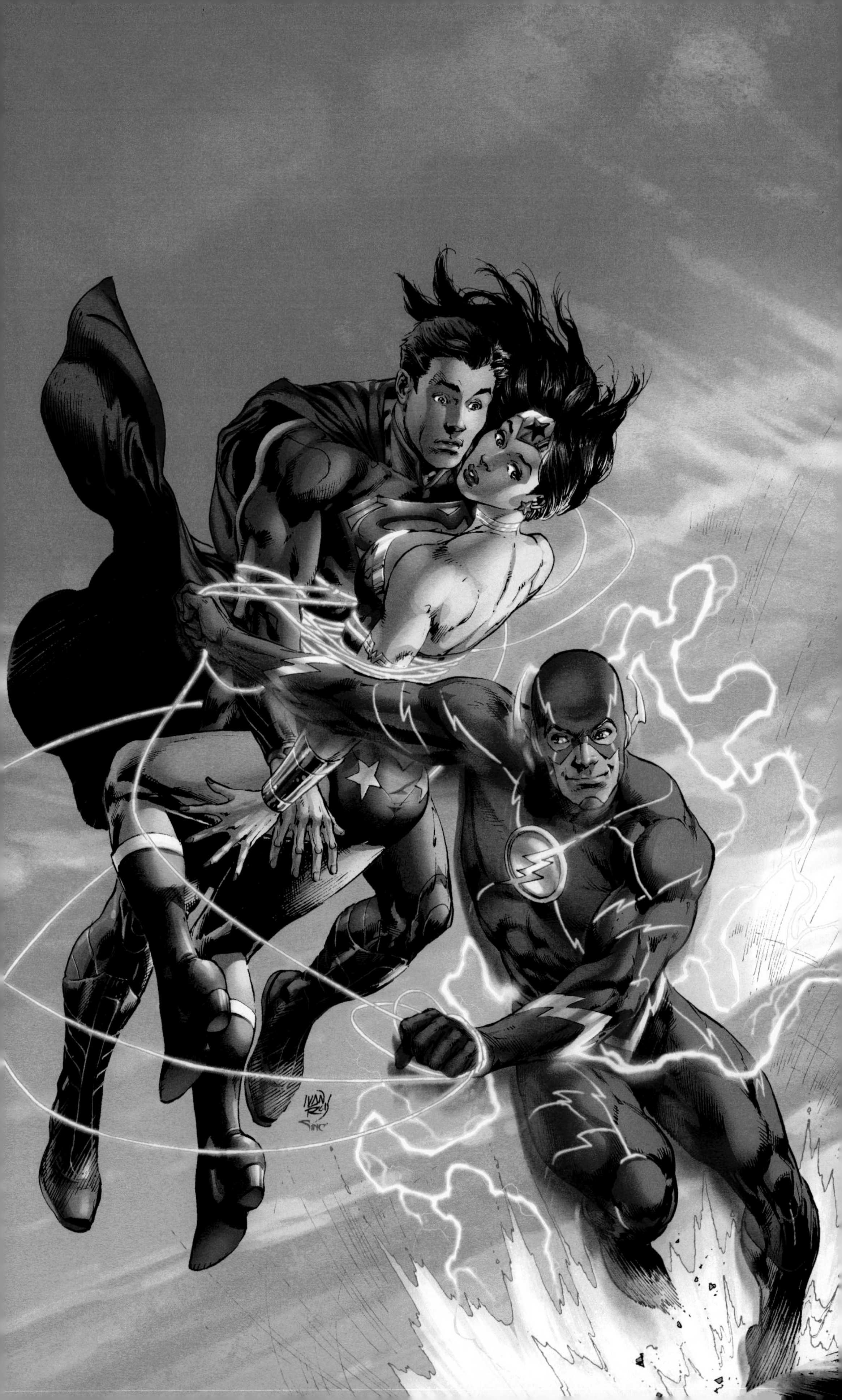

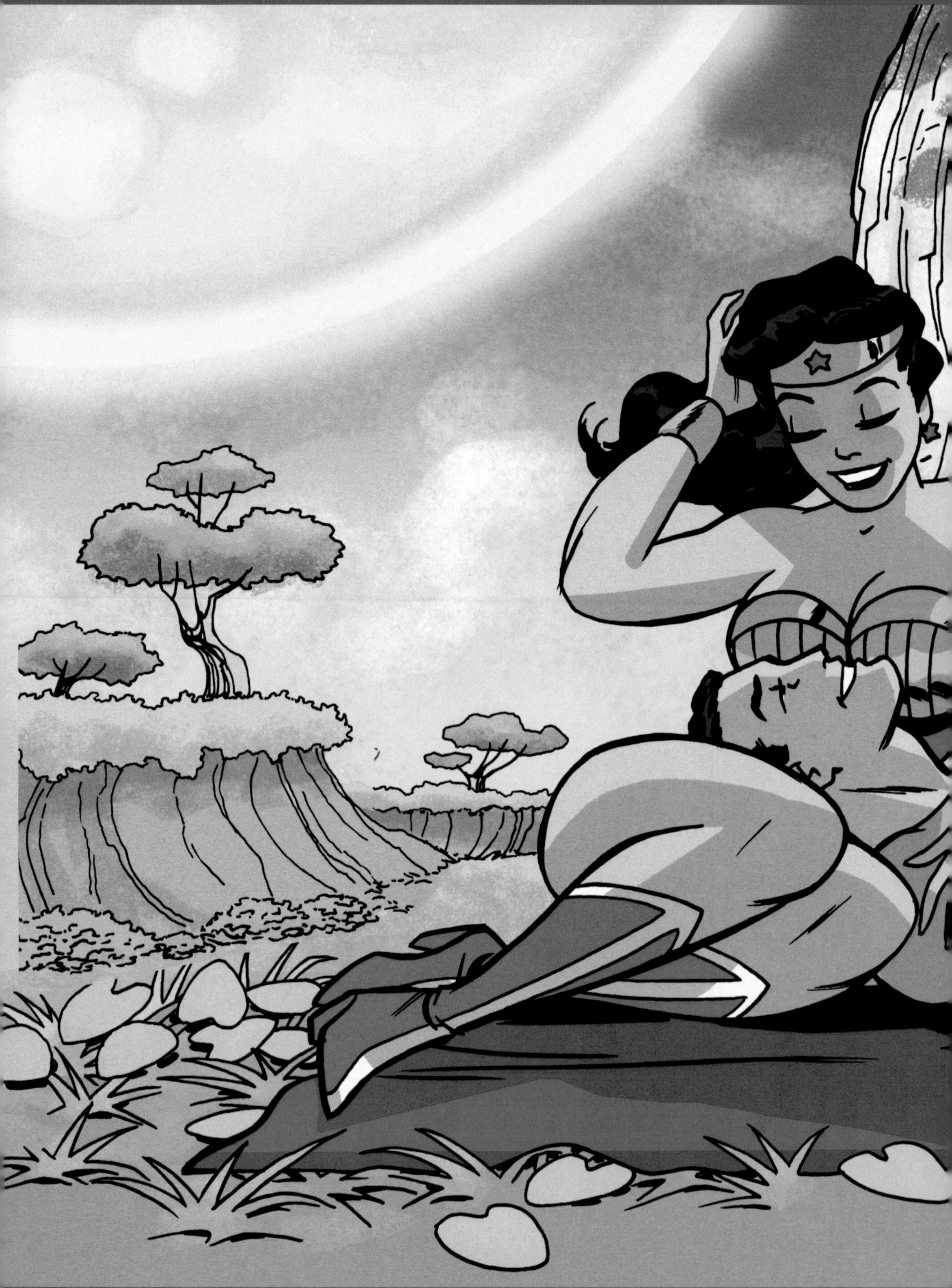

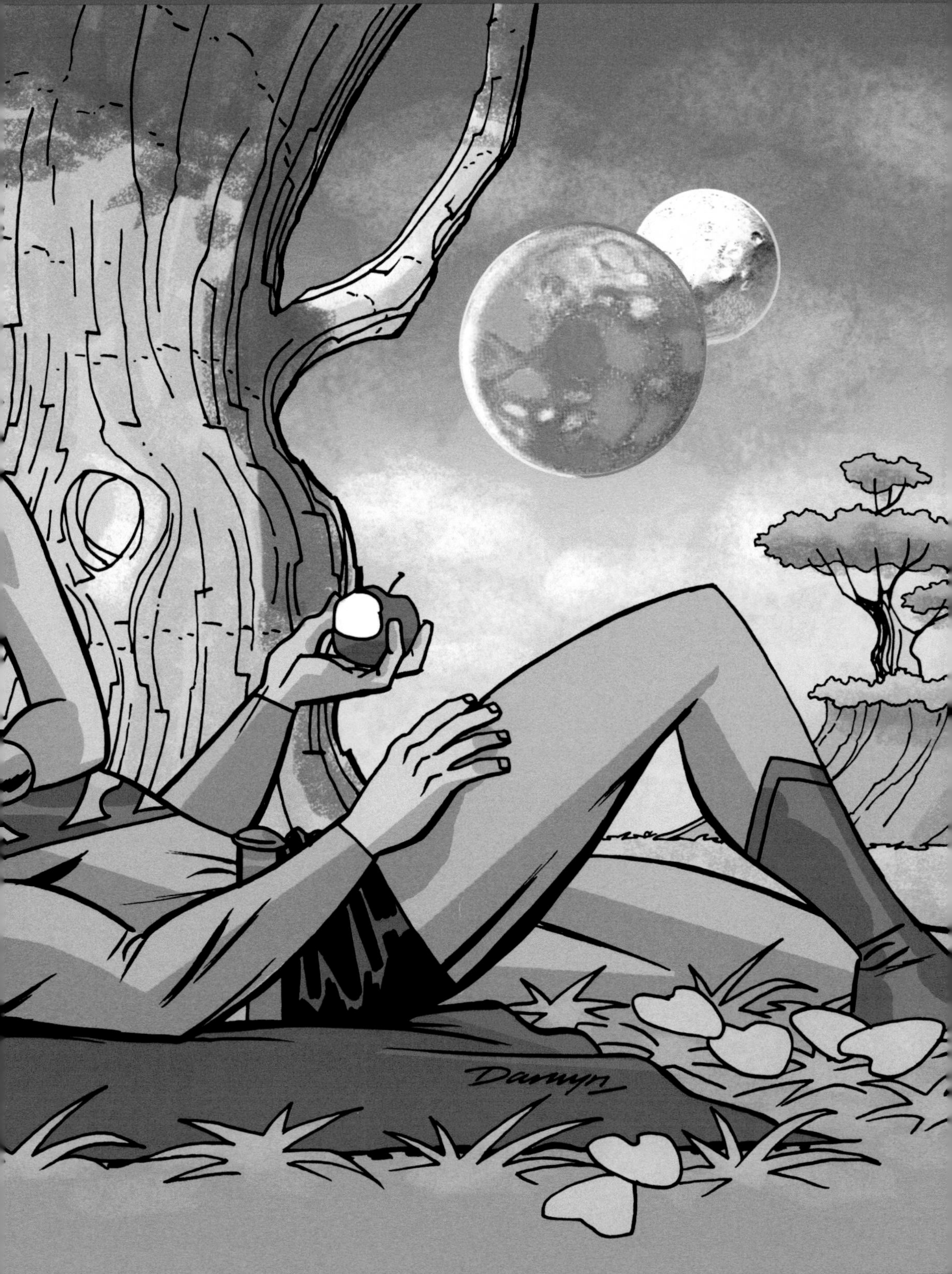
Darwyn

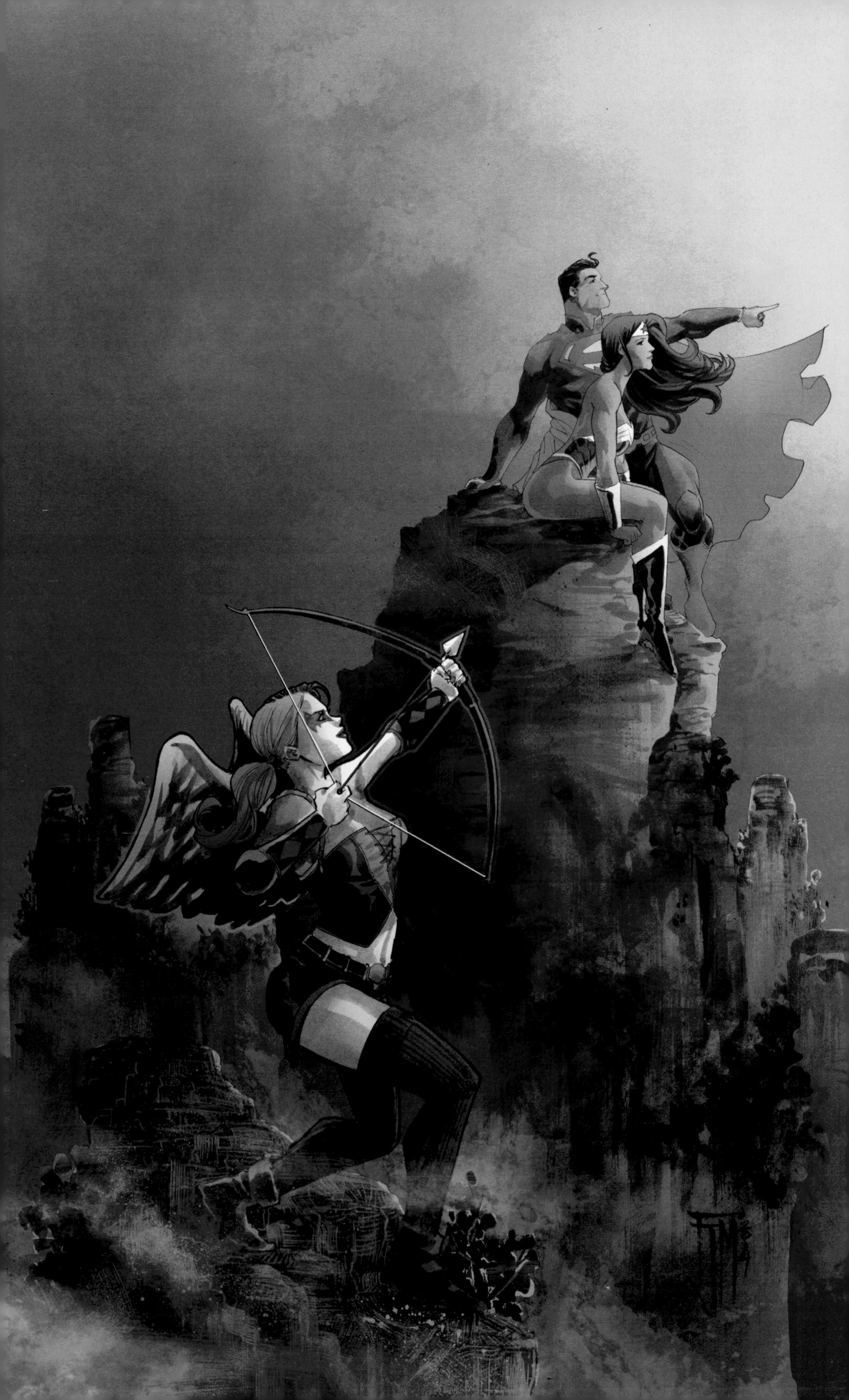

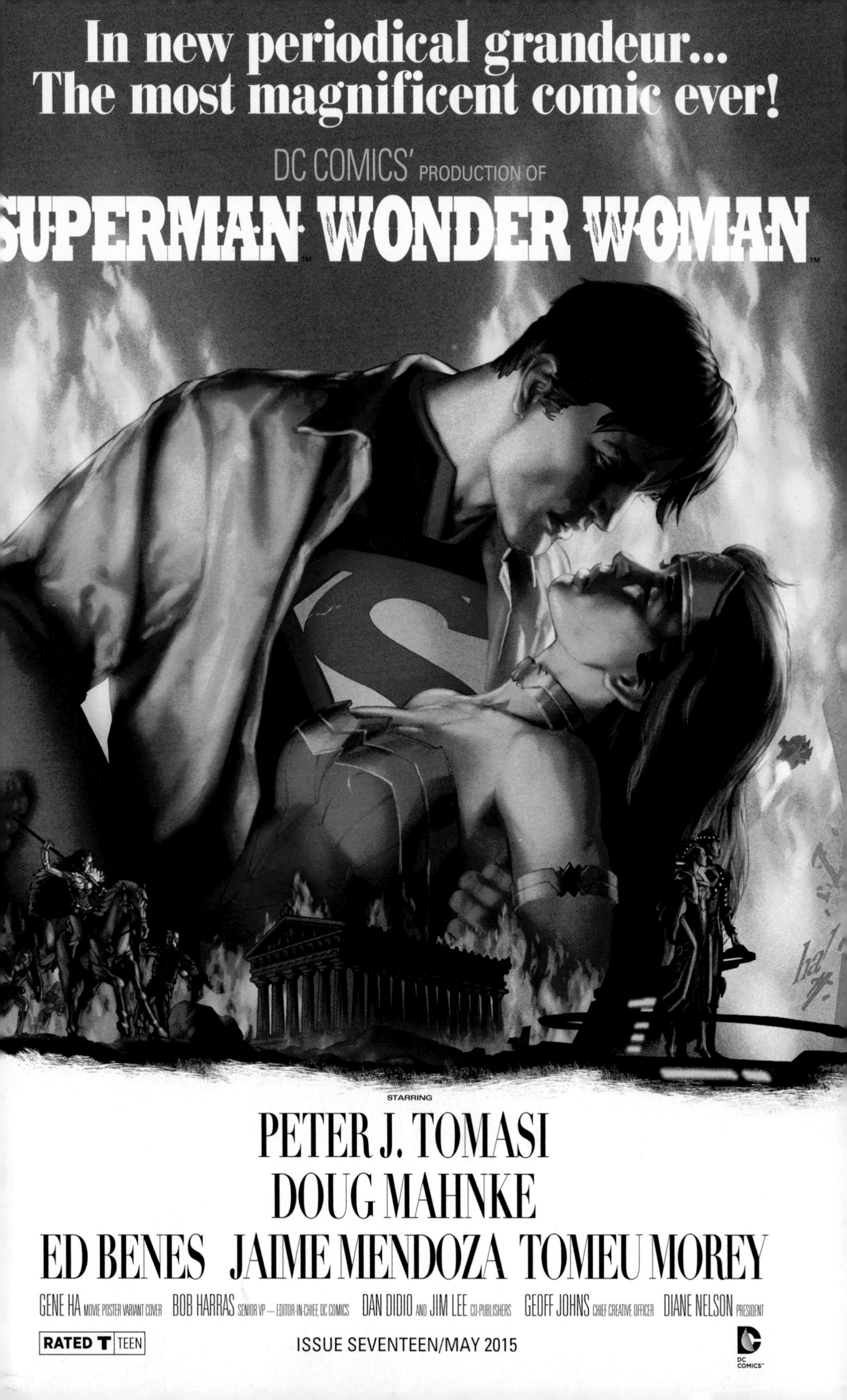
In new periodical grandeur...
The most magnificent comic ever!
DC COMICS' PRODUCTION OF
SUPERMAN™ WONDER WOMAN™
STARRING
PETER J. TOMASI
DOUG MAHNKE
ED BENES JAIME MENDOZA TOMEU MOREY
GENE HA MOVIE POSTER VARIANT COVER BOB HARRAS SENIOR VP — EDITOR-IN-CHIEF, DC COMICS DAN DIDIO AND JIM LEE CO-PUBLISHERS GEOFF JOHNS CHIEF CREATIVE OFFICER DIANE NELSON PRESIDENT
RATED T TEEN
ISSUE SEVENTEEN/MAY 2015
DC COMICS™

SUPERMAN/WONDER WOMAN #13 BEHIND-THE-SCENES
SCRIPT BY PETER J. TOMASI PENCILS BY DOUG MAHNKE

PAGE 1

Alright, Doug, and away we go, our first real chunk of stuff since Black Adam! Gonna do my best to keep this issue visually open for ya, not too many panels when I can help it. Also, in this first sequence, remember it's their first meet, so they are experiencing each other for the first time. We're playing with Geoff and Jim's JUSTICE LEAGUE #1 pages 14-15 from a different angle (get ref from Eddie)

Angle straight on at Wonder Woman with her sword drawn as she slices and dices her way through a bunch of Parademons.

And it's important that we can see behind her that Superman's also punching out Parademons.

Doug, give this whole sequence a sense of immediacy and urgency in everyone's body language and talking. Also, as the flashback sequence progresses, have the battle slowly winding down. There's still Parademons but their numbers are dwindling and the Justice League has almost got it under control. Call me to discuss if ya want.

BANNER CAP: Metropolis.

BANNER CAP: Five Years Ago. (or whatever it would be now, Eddie)

WONDER WOMAN: Back to Hades!

TITLE AND CREDITS ACROSS BOTTOM

STILL WORKING ON TITLE
Peter J. Tomasi - story and words
Doug Mahnke - penciller
Jaime Mendoza and Don Ho - inkers
Tomeu Morey - colorist
Carlos M. Mangual - letterer
Eddie Berganza - editor

SUPERMAN created by Jerry Siegel and Joe Shuster
By special arrangement with the Jerry Siegel family

WONDER WOMAN created by William Moulton Marston

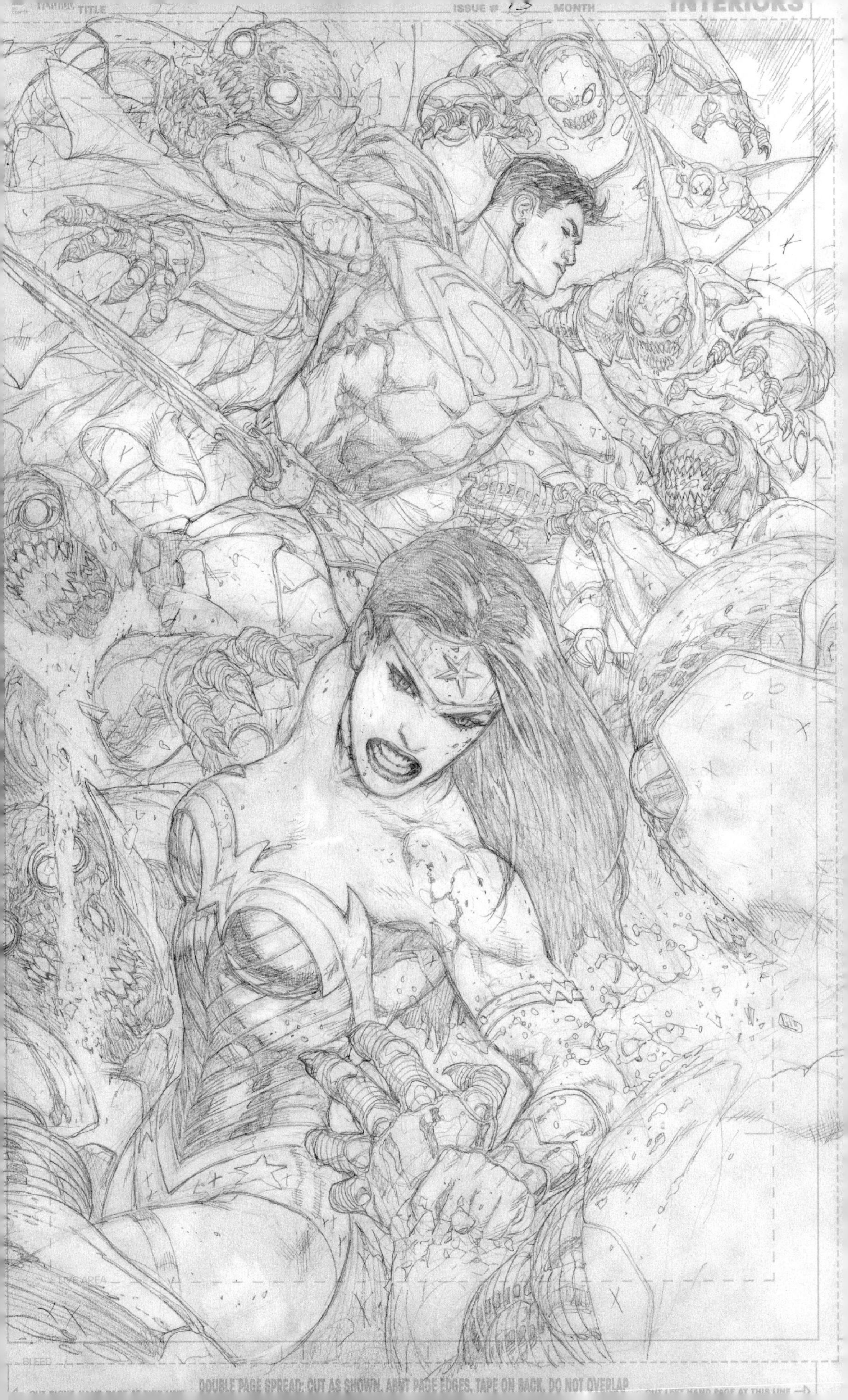
TITLE
ISSUE #
MONTH
INTERIORS
BLEED
DOUBLE PAGE SPREAD: CUT AS SHOWN. ABUT PAGE EDGES. TAPE ON BACK. DO NOT OVERLAP

PAGE 2

panel 1

Big and wide. Another moment from JUSTICE LEAGUE #1. This time page 16, as Superman and Wonder Woman fight alongside one another. Also great if you can pop in FLASH and GREEN LANTERN in the background.

SUPERMAN: You're strong.

WONDER WOMAN: I know.

SUPERMAN: And obviously modest.

panel 2

Angle on Superman purposefully grabbing/throwing debris as he starts building a wall to protect innocent cowering civilians as Wonder Woman continues fighting the Parademons.

At this point, Doug, the feeling I'm going for here is that adults and kids are scared ███less about the sudden appearance of these super-powered beings battling flying death demons. Superman is ready to help them. WW at the moment is focused only on the battle and enemy at hand.

SUPERMAN: Help me build a buffer wall so we can protect these people from shrapnel and buy them some time to escape.

WONDER WOMAN: No.

panel 3

Angle on Superman as he continues working.

SUPERMAN: No?

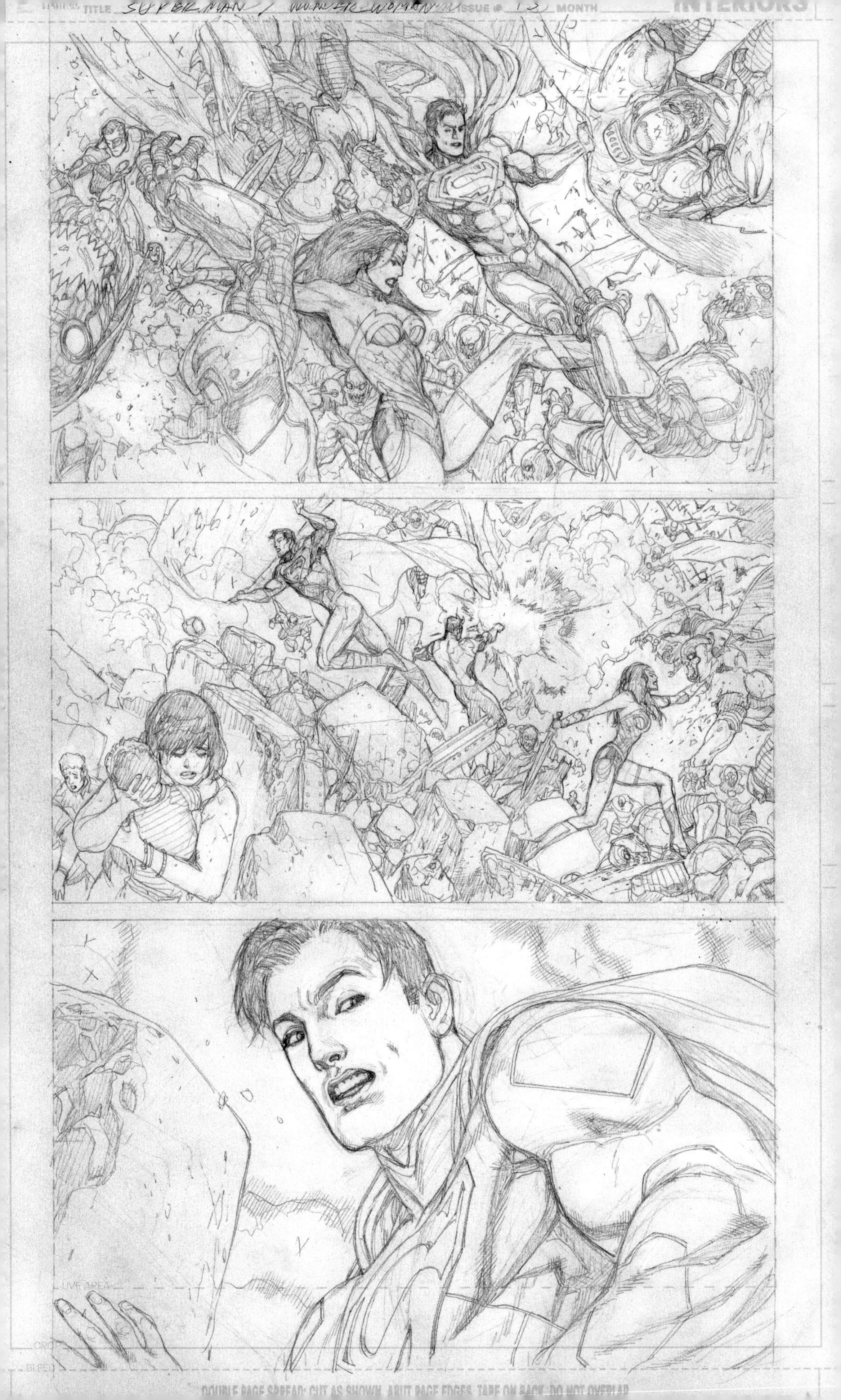
TITLE SUPERMAN / WONDER WOMAN ISSUE # 13 MONTH
INTERIORS
DOUBLE PAGE SPREAD: CUT AS SHOWN. ABUT PAGE EDGES. TAPE ON BACK. DO NOT OVERLAP

PAGE 3

panel 1
Angle on WW thrusting her sword all the way to the hilt into an unfortunate Parademon's abdomen. A CIVILIAN FAMILY in the background is horrified.

WONDER WOMAN: If you haven't noticed, these things can fly.

WONDER WOMAN: Your protective wall would be useless.

WONDER WOMAN: Time is better spent thinning out the ranks of these demons.

panel 2
Angle on Wonder Woman and Superman, she's still fighting and he's still building and maybe even punching a Parademon as he works. He's also slightly offended by her judgmental remarks.

SUPERMAN: I don't agree.

WONDER WOMAN: You fight with too much on your mind.

WONDER WOMAN: Who did you train under?

SUPERMAN: My dad.

panel 3
Angle on WW smashing her fist into the head of a Parademon. In the background we see the same Civilian Family from panel 1, as the father is covering her son's eyes while his small daughter pumps her fist in the air.

WW: A male. (not sure we need this)

WW: Obviously.

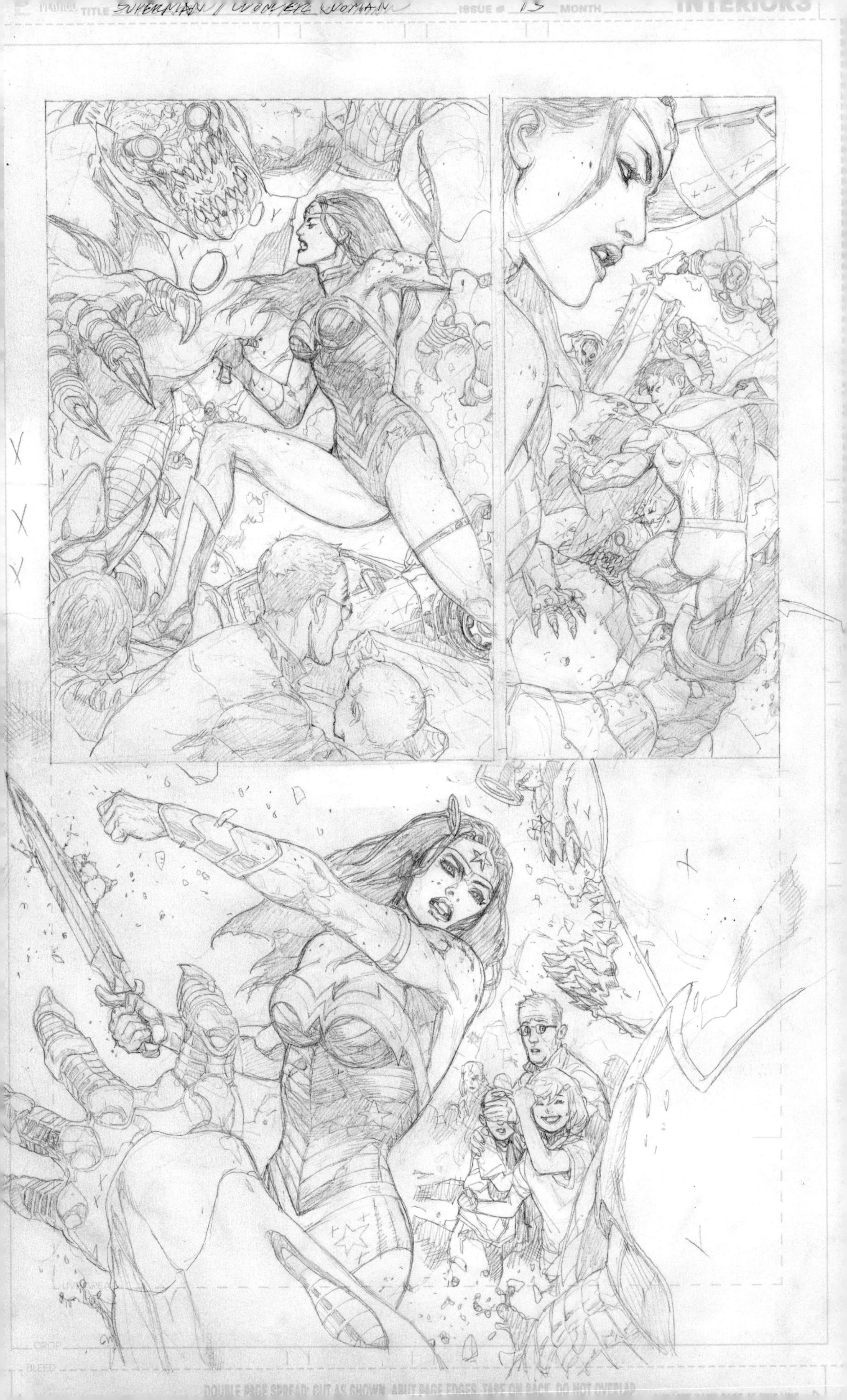
TITLE SUPERMAN / WONDER WOMAN
ISSUE # 13
MONTH
INTERIORS

SUPERMAN/WONDER WOMAN #13 BEHIND-THE-SCENES
SCRIPT BY PETER J. TOMASI PENCILS BY DOUG MAHNKE

PAGE 4

panel 1
Angle on Superman as he smashes/punches a piece of debris heading right for some more civilians as Wonder Woman swings her sword and cuts a Parademon in two down the middle.

SUPERMAN: Well you fight with too little on your mind.

WONDER WOMAN: The biggest threat gets all my attention.

panel 2
Angle on Superman lifting some big ass rubble off some people who are hurt pretty badly. Maybe he even gives a hand to one as he does it. Also, in the background, Doug, we can see Flash/GL/Batman all fighting off Parademons.

SUPERMAN: At least help me get these people clear. We've already lost too many today.

SUPERMAN: Protecting them is our first priority.

SUPERMAN: Watch your step everyone. I can handle the load, but I don't know how well balanced it is.

panel 3
Angle on Wonder Woman looking down at a nearly unconscious middle aged guy hurt in the rubble.

WONDER WOMAN: This world is so odd.

WONDER WOMAN: It has some so many wonders...so many beautiful things worth fighting for...

INJURED GUY(weak): – nnn –

WONDER WOMAN: ...but you are all so weak and fragile....

panel 4
WW looking back at Superman who blasts Parademons with his heat vision as they encroach on the civilians behind him.

WONDER WOMAN: ...well, most of you...

panel 5
On WW kneeling beside the guy as she's taken his hand. He's scared and amazed all at the same time.

INJURED GUY (weak): ...hhh...help...need to find my son...

WONDER WOMAN: In my culture, this fragility would be your downfall. Here it's practically a virtue.

WONDER WOMAN: I've been doing my best to help some of you since my arrival, but how will you ever grow stronger if you need us every waking moment.

panel 6
Similar shot as previous panel, but now only Superman's boots/legs have entered the foreground and Wonder Woman is looking up at him as she releases wounded guys hand.

SUPERMAN: Don't worry, we'll manage.

SUPERMAN: Now get out of the way.

WONDER WOMAN: "We'll."

WONDER WOMAN: You're most definitely not one of them.

PAGE 5

panel 1
Angle on Superman as he gently lifts the injured guy while staring hard at Wonder Woman, as 2 PARAMEDICS carrying a stretcher step up. Supes ain't happy.

SUPERMAN: This man has internal bleeding and needs immediate help. You should have done something instead of talking to him.

panel 2
Angle on Superman as he gently lowers the injured guy onto the stretcher as Wonder Woman watches.

MED 1: We got him now.

MED 2: Hospital's mostly intact and around the corner. You two get back to fighting these freakin' monsters. We need you out there.

panel 3
Angle on Wonder Woman as she approaches Superman proudly, a smile on her face, but he is pissed.

WONDER WOMAN: My name is —

SUPERMAN: We don't just let people die!

panel 4
Wonder Woman gets right back in his face, but not angry. She's in control of her emotions and doesn't rise to quick anger the way we/he does.

WONDER WOMAN: I wasn't going to let him die.

panel 5
Angle on Wonder Woman as she takes off towards the rest of the League who are mopping up in the background as Superman is left looking up at her go, the way he often leaves people.

SILENT

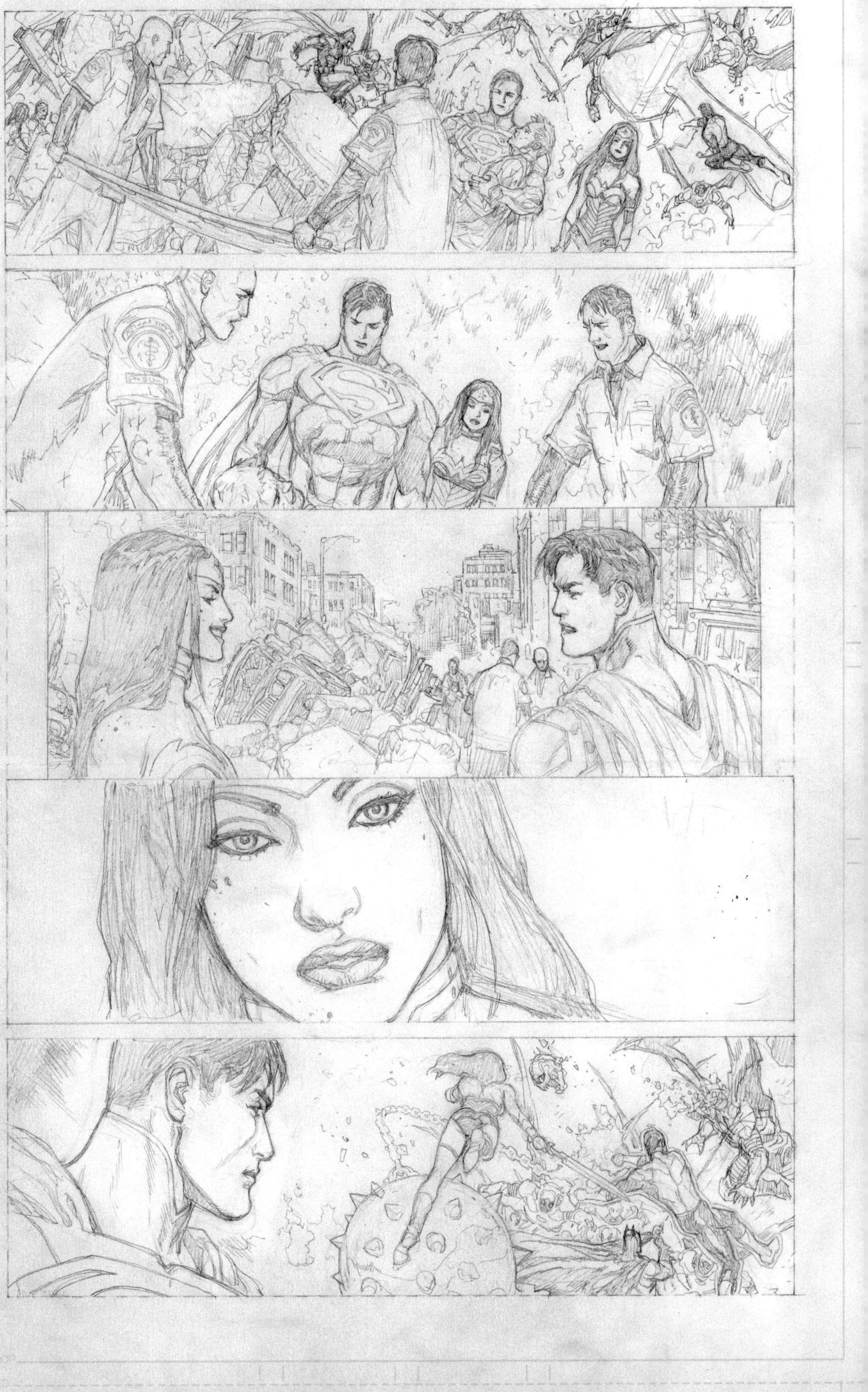

CROP

BLEED

DOUBLE PAGE SPREAD: CUT AS SHOWN, ABUT PAGE EDGES, TAPE ON BACK, DO NOT OVERLAP

SUPERMAN/WONDER WOMAN #13
COVER SKETCH BY **DOUG MAHNKE**

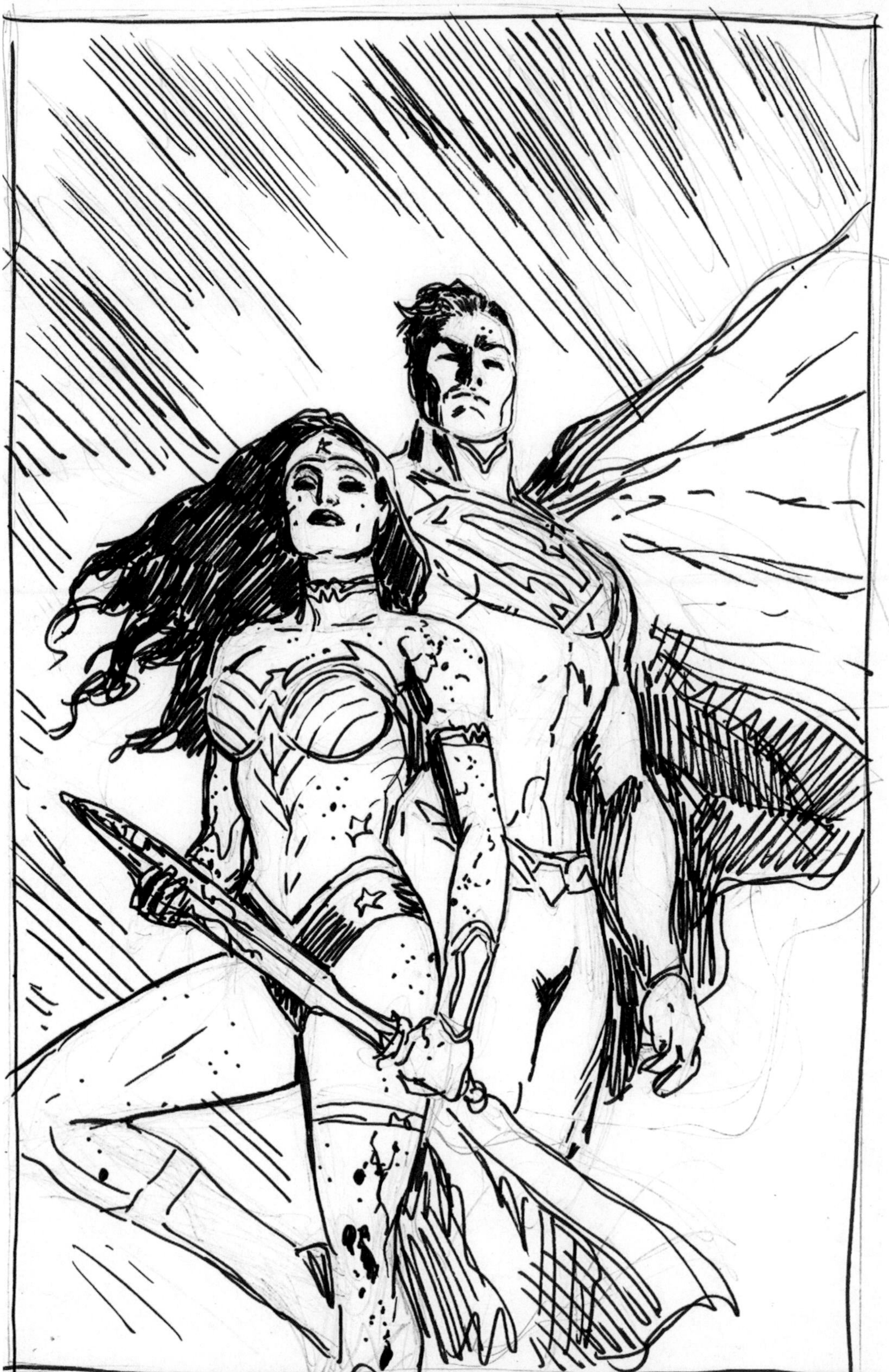

DC COMICS™

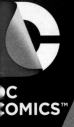

"Clear storytelling at its best. It's an intriguing concept and easy to grasp."—THE NEW YORK TIMES

"Azzarello is rebuilding the mythology of Wonder Woman." —CRAVE ONLINE

START AT THE BEGINNING!

WONDER WOMAN VOLUME 1: BLOOD

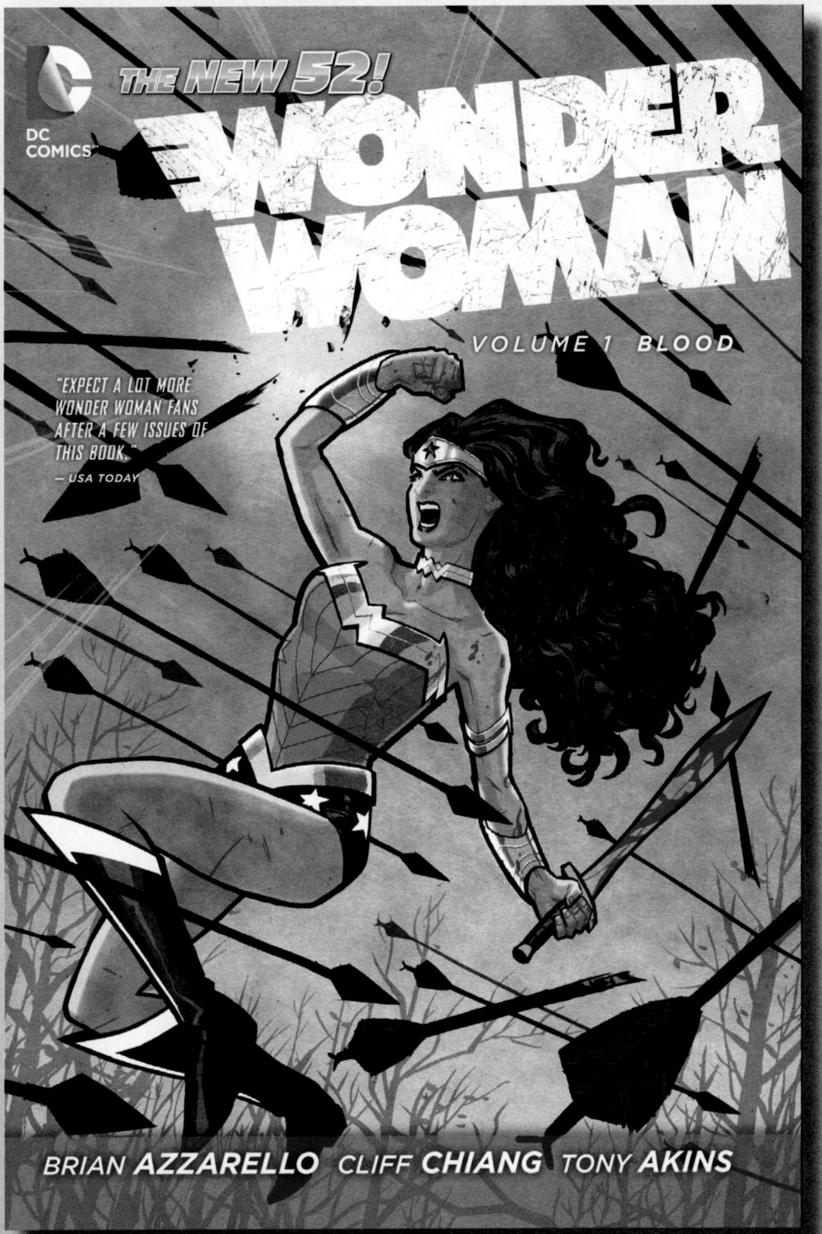
DC COMICS
THE NEW 52!
WONDER WOMAN
VOLUME 1 BLOOD
"EXPECT A LOT MORE WONDER WOMAN FANS AFTER A FEW ISSUES OF THIS BOOK." – USA TODAY
BRIAN AZZARELLO CLIFF CHIANG TONY AKINS

WONDER WOMAN VOL. 2: GUTS

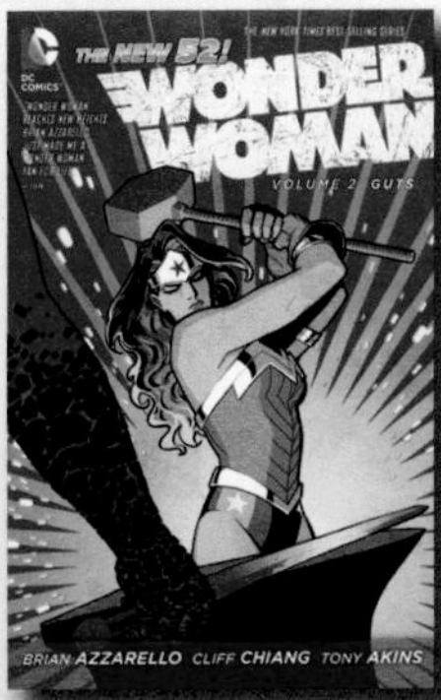
THE NEW 52!
WONDER WOMAN
VOLUME 2 GUTS
BRIAN AZZARELLO CLIFF CHIANG TONY AKINS

by BRIAN AZZARELLO and CLIFF CHIANG

WONDER WOMAN VOL. 3: IRON

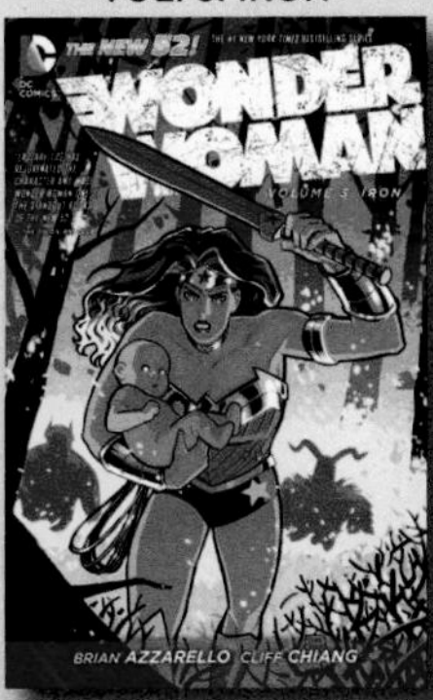
THE NEW 52!
WONDER WOMAN
BRIAN AZZARELLO CLIFF CHIANG

by BRIAN AZZARELLO and CLIFF CHIANG

SUPERGIRL VOL. 1: LAST DAUGHTER OF KRYPTON

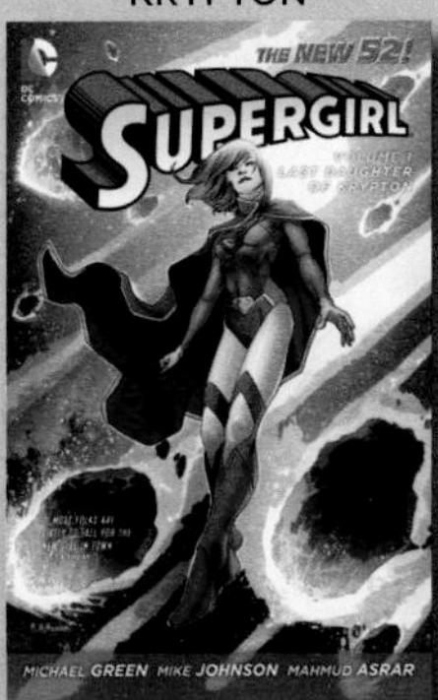
THE NEW 52!
SUPERGIRL
MICHAEL GREEN MIKE JOHNSON MAHMUD ASRAR